C000180867

Also available at all good book stores

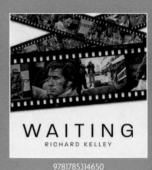

9781785314582

9781785315558

9781785314650

9781785313493

9781785313653

9781785314902

9781785314995

9781785314384

9781785315411

MEMORABLE
ISLE OF MAN
TT RACES

MEMORABLE
ISLE OF MAN
TT RACES

A Century of Battles on the
World's Toughest
Circuit

JAMES DRIVER-FISHER

FOREWORD BY MICHAEL RUTTER

First published by Pitch Publishing, 2019

Pitch Publishing
A2 Yeoman Gate
Yeoman Way
Worthing
Sussex
BN13 3QZ
www.pitchpublishing.co.uk
info@pitchpublishing.co.uk

A CIP catalogue record is available for this book
from the British Library.

ISBN 978 1 78531 549 7

Typesetting and origination by Pitch Publishing

Printed and bound by TJ International

CONTENTS

FOREWORD BY MICHAEL RUTTER

MY EARLIEST memories of the TT are being around my dad, Tony, when he was racing.

I've been going to the Isle of Man since I was born and I have not missed many years during my lifetime.

The first experiences I can recall are watching my dad, and the races that really stick in your mind are the ones he won.

I also remember the days when the weather turned and the races were almost rained off, leaving us sitting in the van with the windscreen wipers on, but in those days they would still go out and race in virtually any conditions.

Organisers started becoming a bit more safety-conscious later on and I probably raced for about three years before any sign of rain meant the race was pretty much delayed or cancelled every time.

We never tend to go out now unless the track is dry, which is a massive change, and it's a lot safer now than it used to be.

I probably realised I wanted to follow my dad and become a TT racer from the age of about ten or 11, but I suppose I was born with that drive and passion for the race.

From a very early age I had an interest in motorbikes, but it was when I reached that age that I really started pestering my family about going racing.

The TT has been two weeks of my life for as long as I remember and it was always a big family affair too, travelling with my mom and dad – even when mom didn't fancy it, I would usually pop along.

When you're travelling about for the races, the motorbike fraternity really becomes one big family. You travel all over Britain and abroad but you're always staying with, and chatting to, the same people.

The early days were really fun and I have fond memories of heading up to Scotland in a van that could barely make it, with my dad's bikes in the back. We'd all end up sleeping in the back or in tents during the race weekends.

Eventually we upgraded to a caravan but it was very basic and nothing like the motorhomes you see today.

When it eventually became time for me to go racing at the TT, I was quite lucky in a way because I didn't have to do the Manx GP. I couldn't afford to race for free at the time, which is what happened at the Manx because there was no prize money, and I was also lucky enough to start out with Robert Dunlop as my team-mate.

He was very, very good to me but unfortunately he had a really bad crash at the TT that year, in 1994, which nearly killed him and looked like it had ended his career.

His wheel basically collapsed. The same thing later happened to me but I was fortunate enough to have been going in a much slower section when I came off. After the race I was down to just two spokes left on the wheel.

I already knew full well how dangerous the TT was before all that happened and I suppose the worst situations for me have been when I've come across an incident, especially as a newcomer.

You see the wreckage and then the rider – and, for me, that's when it really hits home how dangerous a race it is.

But even still, after I started in 1994, which was a few years before the likes of Dave Jefferies, John McGuinness and Bruce Anstey all started racing there, I got so much help.

It was weird at first, having Robert Dunlop, Phil McCallen and Steve Hislop all showing me the ropes and showing me some great pointers and landmarks to look out for.

A few years later I started getting on the podium, standing next to them – and these were all heroes of mine.

The next thing, I'm passing them on the road, and then they're passing me back, it was such a surreal and fantastic feeling.

Straight away I started racing superbikes on the island. Looking back, I should probably have started on something like a 600cc, or maybe even smaller, because the Honda RC45 was also one of the hardest bikes to handle.

In my mind, just racing with the likes of Joey, McCallen and Hislop was such a strange feeling at first and when I finally started to get my head around it all I had a lot of years off because of my contract with HM Plant Honda in the British Superbikes (BSB), which meant I couldn't race in both the BSB and the TT at the same time.

It was seven years in total before I came back and by then the bikes had moved on so much and were so much faster than when I was first at the TT.

I was on an R1 Yamaha when I last hit the track but when I went out again for practice, for the first time in seven years, on a Kawasaki, it was just like a rocket ship.

It had 30 brake horsepower more power and it scared the life out of me.

The circuit itself hadn't changed but the track was now like a motorway. It had gone from being bumpy to being so smooth and that changed a lap so much.

Between 2000 and 2007, my hiatus, the track had become so much smoother and it took me years to get my head around that.

I couldn't race the track naturally and all my reference points had changed, so I had to readjust. It was just little things like the trees and bushes being slightly more overgrown in places.

It all changed my peripheral vision; even the tipping-in point at Bray Hill had changed, and the bumpy turn into Quarterbridge was different too. It took me three or four years to get used to it again.

The 600s were lapping as fast as the superbikes used to go – and now Michael Dunlop has pushed that up to 129mph.

So that was the main adjustment, getting used to the new speeds again and working out my new reference points. It all took time.

I'm still enjoying it now but it's very unrealistic I'll ever win a superbike race. It's very difficult, especially as you get older, to ride at 100 per cent around the TT course and get away with it, but now I feel some of the riders are pushing even harder than that.

I also think most of the bikes are very similar now and whether it's a factory Honda or not, for instance, it doesn't really make a great deal of difference.

It's very much an open field and even the superstock bikes are just as fast as the superbikes.

The TT Zero has also been another experience, which has taken a lot to get my head around. Those machines are pretty scary now because basically you're riding around on prototypes.

When it comes to the BMWs and Hondas, the manufacturers' test riders have done hundreds of thousands of miles on them, testing everything in minute detail, double checking everything before it's raced.

With the electric bikes, no one else has ever sat on the machine before you're on the start line – and these things are not slow any more.

A normal bike is around 170kg but these are 230kg, so they are very heavy machines. I've had all sorts of things happen when I've been riding them too, like handle bars snapping off and the rear axle breaking, but they are the future and that's why more and more manufacturers want to run them.

You're supposed to get three or four practice laps in before you set off for the race but we had problems with the Mugen in 2018 and, although I broke the lap record, it was a scary race.

I suppose my greatest memories would come on any bike I've ever won on but when you ride a Ducati around the island, and you can hear the exhaust echoing, that's always pretty special.

It was the same with the Paton, which I won the Lightweight TT on in 2017, because that bike has basically got no exhaust on it.

It's absolutely fantastic when you're travelling through the houses on one of those.

When you're leading a race there's no better feeling and sometimes you get time to think about things more, especially on the mountain mile.

You can have a look around, tuck yourself in a bit more, give your feet a shake on the foot pedals, listen out for things to see if anything sounds wrong – the Paton and Ducatis also sound fantastic when they're being ridden flat out too.

But I suppose my most special memory would have to be finishing second behind Joey in 2000 in the Formula One TT.

I remember seeing him in that race basically just clear off and no one could catch him. He had caught up with me and we ended up circling together for about four laps.

After the race he told me how much he had enjoyed it and even bought me a pint, which was really special and very rarely happened.

Of course he died a few weeks later in Estonia but to have the chance to race with someone like that – someone who had raced against my dad too, when he was a lot younger – someone as good as him is something I will remember and always treasure.

INTRODUCTION

AS MURRAY Walker once said, 'If motorcycle racing was not dangerous, I suspect they would not do it.'

It is the challenge of facing up to danger and overcoming it that attracts the racers to the Isle of Man.

They get some sort of spiritual satisfaction controlling powerful machines on the knife edge of safety and disaster.

It's a fine art because, if it goes wrong, they are going to get hurt. It looks insane for people looking in from the outside but when the top riders are on the bike, they feel in control, they know what they are doing and the thrill they get from road racing is unrivalled.

The furniture – the hedges, lamp posts and stone walls – cannot be removed. The riders have to block all that out and believe in their ability. Man versus machine in all its glory.

The fans are so close to the action, they feel a part of what's going on. The heat of the engine, the smell of the petrol, everything is just alive. Ask anyone who has been to the Isle of Man TT races and they will say that nothing, as spectator, comes remotely close to it.

It is amazing just to watch it, so fans can only imagine what it is like to be the rider actually sat on the bike. To see the videos online, just getting a glimpse at what it must be like doing those speeds through the country lanes, takes the breath away.

And yet most of us will never truly know what it is like to be a road racer, which is why every single TT racer, from first to last place, is a hero, a gladiator even, in the eyes of all fans.

Watching a road racer push themselves off the line, straight into the action, pushing their bikes to the absolute limits, is truly a mind-blowing experience.

From a standing start to nearly 200mph in the blink of an eye, and then it's close to flat out all the way – sometimes for another 226 miles.

Every single race that has ever taken place on the island since the first brave riders took it on back in 1907 could make the list of most memorable.

They all mean something different to each and every fan. And yet some of them have really stood out while standing the test of time while others are still fresh in the memory.

It would be impossible to include them all but this book tries to take in just a few while taking an historical and fond look back at where it all started and where it stands today.

From Stanley Woods, Freddie Frith, Geoff Duke and John Surtees, to Mike Hailwood, Giacomo Agostini, Mick Grant and Adrian Archibald, to current stars like Michael Dunlop, Ian Hutchinson, Dean Harrison and Peter Hickman – right down to the last-placed finisher in each TT race there has been. They are all superhuman and have all contributed to its unique history.

John McGuinness, Ian Lougher, Bruce Anstey, David Jefferies and David Molyneux – all are so much part and parcel of why the TT is the greatest sporting event on the planet.

And there's Joey Dunlop, whose 26 wins makes him the most successful TT rider ever.

Carl Fogarty – what a rider, who, despite all his success, and his close rivalry with another great racer, Steve Hislop, marks his TT wins, especially his first, as the best of his illustrious career.

His battles with Hislop ended in record-breaking clashes, which culminated in the 1992 Senior TT race. Speeds increased, race records fell and new memories were formed.

Then there was the Hailwood and Agostini rivalry. Could, or can, anyone ride a bike better than those two multiple work champions? Two of the greatest ever, going toe-to-toe during the 1960s. The style, the flair, the skill, they had it all.

Ireland's Woods was one of the earliest TT heroes, becoming the first man to win ten TT races. Only 'Mike the Bike' Hailwood was good enough to trouble his wins tally before going on to dominate with the likes of Ago.

However, there was still plenty of time for more TT heroes to make their mark in the years to come.

Duke, with his beautiful riding style, was the star of the show at the time but he was racing against Glaswegian Bob McIntyre. Duke may have been brilliant, but Bob Mac was the first to break the 100mph lap speed around the 37.73-mile course.

However, just when the world of motorsport thought the bar could not be raised any higher, Surtees would go on to win a world title in Formula One – becoming the only man to date to win a world championship on both two and four wheels – having claimed numerous TT titles too.

It would be ridiculous not to mention Phil Read, one of the greatest who, before temporarily boycotting the TT, had to make way for Charlie Williams, who himself went on to claim eight TT wins.

And then there is the sidecar heroes. David Molyneux would go on to dominate but, pre-Moly, there was Rob Fisher, who took ten wins from just 14 finishes.

Harold Daniell, Jim Moodie, Bill Ivy and Jimmy Simpson – they all deserve a mention, and all have contributed to why the TT is the greatest event, sporting or otherwise, in the world. To all the riders out there, past and present, we salute you.

TT 1907

Rem Fowler becomes the TT's first winner

The Isle of Man government had already started closing the public roads before the TT for cars, but soon the motorbikes followed suit.

The year was 1907 and it would mark the first Tourist Trophy (TT).

It gave manufacturers and racers the chance to put their skills and machines through the ultimate test – one for racers which still cannot be topped today.

The birth of the TT also brought in big business as tourists would flock to the island to catch the races, leaving with postcards and souvenirs of their heroes.

Most of the fan base could usually be found in and around the paddock and start line, hunting for autographs and the occasional photograph.

But as technology developed, soon the first TT stars were being snapped regularly as they hurtled around the track.

The rise of the TT also coincided with the popularity of production motorcycles growing.

Basic bicycles powered by small engines were soon replaced with much more powerful, fully fledged, racing machines in a very short space of time.

And it did not take long for the island to start attracting the best in the business, with the best manufacturers and racers all vying for TT glory.

Practice sessions were originally held early in the morning, and throughout the day eager autograph hunters would be scouring the paddock in search of the stars of the day.

During the early years, the Norton was simply unstoppable and that included claiming the first win at the TT, although it was not then the marathon course we all know and love today.

Back when the bravest motorcyclists first took on the challenge of the TT, they raced around the 15-mile St John's Short Course, which consisted of ten laps.

It wasn't until 1911 the Mountain Course was used and a further eight years before the full 37.73-mile course was introduced.

Norton's story began in a Birmingham factory, which was run by James Norton in 1898 during the height of the Victorian bicycle craze.

It did not take long, however, for the factory to start adding engines with the aim of producing motorbikes, which happened just four years later, in 1902.

Powered by a French engine, the first Norton motorcycle had a maximum speed of 33mph but it was soon being raced during the start of the amateur race scene, which had begun springing up at the turn of the century.

Owner James Norton himself was a keen racer and just as keen to promote his own bikes and brand at the meetings.

In 1907, Rem Fowler entered the first Isle of Man TT on a Peugeot-powered Norton. It became the first bike to win a TT.

Fowler had almost given up on making history because, following a lot of bad luck, he had been left with a flat tyre.

He was ready to throw in the towel until a spectator revealed he still had a half-an-hour advantage over his nearest rival.

It took him 22 minutes to change the front tyre but he still won the race.

The Norton engine, ultimately, was reliable and it was that that helped Fowler create TT history but fast-forward a year and, in 1908, Norton developed their own engine to go in their motorcycle. The Model 9 had been born.

TT 1908

Marshall stars for Triumph

Norton developed the Model 9 in 1908 and 1909, when it was officially released.

There was no clutch with the bike, which used direct power, but the basic engine design remained with Norton for the next 50 years – which coincided with English manufacturers' domination of the TT for the following five decades, until the Italian and later Japanese machines took control of the island.

The bike cost £12,000 in today's money, which made it a lot more expensive than rivals Triumph and BSA, but TT had spurred Norton on to create bigger, better and faster bikes.

Triumph was also on the scene during the early stages of bike manufacturing and, although it was not anywhere near as dominant as the Norton machines, it remains the oldest motorbike brand, having been in continuous production for more than 120 years, producing some of the world's most iconic bikes.

The newest factory opened in Hinckley, in 2006, and now produces more than 65,000 each year.

The Speed Twin, the Thunderbird and the Bonneville set the early standards when it came to motorbike manufacturing.

In 1883, it was a young German entrepreneur called Siegfried Bettmann who moved to Coventry to seek his fortune. Starting out as a translator, he later began importing bicycles and three years later changed the name of his new company to Triumph, to try and make it look and sound more like a global brand.

While bicycles were becoming more and more popular in Britain, across Europe in Germany the motorbike was really beginning to take off.

In 1894, the world's first commercial motorcycle was produced, and when engineer Maurice Schulte came over to join Bettmann at Triumph, they decided it was the right time to start producing their own motorbikes.

Fast-forward eight years and, in 1902, the first Triumph motorcycle was produced. The early Triumph riders called their machines 'trumpets' due to the design of the manufacturer's first logo.

The company still did not have the capacity at the time to build their own engines, so instead they were shipping in from Belgium – the engine size at the time was around two-and-a-quarter horsepower, which meant when travelling uphill the rider would still have to pedal.

But they proved to be very popular and after starting out building a few for those with a bit of cash, suddenly they were being transported all over the world.

During the same time, BSA, Ariel and Norton were also producing but BSA decided to raise the bar by opening a new factory in Coventry.

Immediately, it could produce around 1,000 bikes a year and by 1908 they were building their own motorbikes fitted with their own Triumph engines. Such was the development the bikes were now powered by a three-and-a-half brake-horsepower engine and had a top speed of 45mph.

Within two years, the company was producing more than a thousand motorbikes a year, a figure that tripled three years later.

Jack Marshall, from Coventry, a man of few words, was one of the earliest TT greats and set the motorbike world alight with his cool and calm demeanour, which some of his rivals mistook for being nervous.

He was always in control and constantly performed under pressure. Marshall helped Triumph on the map during the early years of the TT taking a win over the old St John's Short Course in 1908.

He had signalled his intent the previous year, finishing behind Fowler during what was an incredible ten-lap race, which covered just under 160 miles around the shorter course.

Marshall, ironically, had also suffered a puncture during the race, which had cost enough time to lose the win.

However, undeterred, he went on to claim two seconds and a win during the first three TTs, which really helped put Triumph on the map.

The brand was quickly becoming one of the most renowned motorcycle makers despite having only started to produce bikes, using Belgian Minerva engines, at its factory in 1902.

Marshall's win boosted sales and Triumph, eager to build on their Isle of Man credentials, added the stripped-down, single-speed, sports model TT Roadster to the range.

Senior TT 1911

Godfrey crowned the inagural Senior TT winner

It was in 1911 that the Snaefell Mountain Course on closed public roads was first used – and, more importantly, it was the year the Senior TT was first born. Organisation of the races was also handed over to the Auto-Cycle Union (ACU), which announced the use of the longer Mountain Course.

The changes included the addition of a four-lap, 150-mile Junior race and a five-lap, 189 mile Senior race.

It is quite staggering how very little would change with those particular races over the years and the only real difference to hit the Isle of Man TT would be the addition of extra races and classes, the shorter Clypse Course and the introduction of sidecars over the years.

As technology had increased, the decision was made to move the races to the mountain circuit for the first time.

More than 100 racers lined up on the start line for the first laps around the iconic TT course as it is known and loved today – albeit a quarter of a mile shorter that the 37.73-mile track it would eventually become. That was because, in 1911, the riders turned right at Cronk-ny-Mona, rejoining at the top of Bray Hill.

Oliver Godfrey, riding an Indian, became the first winner of a TT on the new course. Tragically, he would later be killed in the First World War but his name would forever be etched in TT history.

He did it in a time of three hours and 56 minutes, averaging 47.63 mph for the entire race. Second place went to Charles Franklin, who achieved his career-best finish in 1911, with Arthur Moorhouse in third. The entire top three were mounted on India bikes.

Frank Phillip also rewrote the record books by becoming the first riders to break the 50mph barrier around the new-look TT course. He rode his 500cc Scott in the Senior at an average lap speed of 50.11mph.

Victor Surridge became the first rider to be killed racing on the island when he crashed at Glen Helen.

Percy Evans claimed victory in the Junior TT, finishing in three hours and 37 minutes at an average race speed of 41.45mph, on a Humber, followed home by Harry Collier and Harold Cox.

In just five years the TT organisers had realised the benefits of bringing in grandstands for the races, which were built by the Douglas Corporation.

However, even back then, the introduction of stands did not always go down well with the race-watching public as one particular stand, in Douglas, restricted what had been popular viewing for the TT's ever-growing legion of fans.

The course also meant the teams and manufacturers would have to try and get more power to climb the mountain, and to get from the Ramsey section to Brandywell.

Norton's Model 9 would soon develop into the 16H, which was introduced to the world in 1911. Unbelievably, it stayed in production for the next 43 years.

The 16H had the same engine as the Model 9 but by now Norton had introduced a gearbox and clutch.

The 16H could be used for commuting and everyday, family life but they would also be stripped down and raced at the Isle of Man TT, doing really well.

Junior TT 1913

Mason's bravery knows no bounds

The record stood for two years until it was broken by another Scott rider, Tim Wood, during the 1913 Senior, when he completed the race in 43 minutes and ten seconds, at an average lap speed of 51.12mph.

The year also saw the races increased in length, which saw the Junior take place over six laps, 226 miles, and riders battle for the Senior over seven laps, or 265 miles. Nearly 150 riders were on the start line, such was the growing popularity of the race even during those very early days.

However, the real drama of the 1913 TT would unfold in the Junior 350cc race, which was won by Hugh Mason, on a NUT, with average lap speed of 43.75mph over the six laps.

Mason was a small, tenacious, confident rider – and he was forced to use all those qualities to claim victory on the island that year. During a practice lap in fog prior to his win, earlier in the fortnight, he had come off his machine so badly it had left him unconscious, lying in the road.

He was eventually taken to Douglas Hospital and slept pretty much for two straight days until racing on the following Wednesday.

Far from taking it easy, he was still feeling the effects of the crash and fell off again early in the Junior TT race, but despite being overtaken by 11 riders, rather than seeing it as a sign to pull over and watch, he instead ploughed on while throwing up, promptly finished the race and then returned to hospital.

When Friday race day rolled around, Mason was still feeling the effects of his two previous spills and continued to throw up and suffer from headaches even during the race itself.

On discovering a rider in front of him was only a minute in front, he angrily questioned why he had not been told. The response was as expected – it was because no one wanted him to push too hard and fall off again hurting himself, or, even worse.

Mason then embarked on a truly stunning comeback, made up the deficit, and eventually won in just over five hours. Speaking afterwards, Mason explained how he knew he had the fastest machine and, as such, knew he was more than capable of taking the win, despite all his issues leading up to the Junior TT.

Amazingly, Mason had suffered a similar fate the year before when he suffered an accident just before the 1912 Junior TT, only that time he had not been able to carry on.

It would appear that was another major factor in why Mason had been so determined to win. Or, perhaps, it was simply because he was a TT rider.

The 1913 TT would also be tinged with sadness as it would claim its first life, when Frank Bateman, riding a Rudge, was killed in a high-speed crash on the mountain.

Senior TT 1914

First dead heat declared during monster battle

The 1914 Isle of Man Tourist Trophy was the last held before the outbreak of the First World War – and it gave the AJS factory team a chance to truly shine before war would wreak havoc on all of Europe and beyond.

Bad weather overshadowed the Junior race, but Eric and Cyril Williams gained first and second place for AJS having passed Irish newcomer Frank Walker who had been leading on the second lap before suffering an accident.

Walker bravely remounted on his Royal Enfield, followed after the two men, but crashed twice more during his furious chase for glory.

Eric's lap speed of 45.58mph over the five circuits would be enough to take the win, with Cyril second.

Amazingly, Williams had somehow done enough to fill the final podium spot despite his previous misdemeanours but his efforts would ultimately end in tragedy as, crossing the finish line for the final time, he misjudged Bray Hill and crashed into the barrier, tragically losing his life in the process four days later.

Howard R. Davies, who raced for both AJS and Sunbeam, had been deprived of victory in the Junior due to a puncture.

However, he would go to make history in the Senior that same year, after an incredibly closely fought race that had raged on for more than four hours, just over six minutes had separated the top three.

And after Cyril Pullin, on a Rudge, had been declared the winner, nothing could separate Sunbeam-mounted Davies and Oliver Godfrey, who was riding an Indian.

It meant for the first time in TT history a dead heat had been declared. Godfrey had also claimed victory in the 1911 Senior, which had seen the US manufacturer claim the top three spots. Godfrey was later killed while fighting in the First World War.

Tim Wood had broken the lap record once again, with a lap of 53.50mph, which was 42 minutes and 16 seconds around the course.

The start-finish line was moved from Quarterbridge Road to Bray Hill in 1914; the huge scoreboard fans know and love first went up in 1926 but the first evening practice sessions would not take place until 1937.

It showed how different the track, setting and layout of the meeting was in those very early days compared with today.

What would not see much change, however, would be the classes, as the 350cc and 500cc races remained in place right up until the 1980s.

The first Senior TT, in 1913, was run over seven laps, reduced to six the following year and then put back up to seven.

Behind the scenes, the First World War broke out in 1914, making Britain and Germany sworn enemies.

Although entrepreneur Siegfried Bettmann was now a British citizen and mayor of Coventry, the Triumph factory was commandeered by the government to help with the war effort.

During this time, Triumph produced their first proper motorbike, which had no need for pedals and needed a kick-start to get it going.

The Model H was eventually given the nickname 'the trusted Triumph' – 30,000 were made during the war alone because it worked so well, particularly in the trenches.

Norton's 16H was also used during the First World War by the military and Norton also built 17 bikes for the Russian army. However, the war ended before they could be delivered overseas so instead they became the first bikes the company ever sold to the British public.

Junior TT 1923

Woods opens his TT account

Tommy de lay Haye would win the 1920 Senior TT on a Sunbeam with an average lap speed of more than 51mph.

It was the first TT to take place after the First World War and, in the Junior TT that year, the winner was Cyril Williams, again riding the formidable AJS, followed by two riders mounted on Blackbourne machines. The result could have been quite different had it not been for Eric Williams – who had set a lap record during the race – suffering a mechanical failure.

The lap records would continue to tumble during the next few years, with George Dance raising the lap record, on his 500 Sunbeam, during the 1920 Senior, to 55.62mph, finishing his circuit in 40 minutes and 53 seconds.

Fred Edmund then pushed the bikes further, riding a 500 Triumph in the 1921 Senior at 56.40mph, taking 40 minutes and eight seconds to finish his lap, before Alec Bennett, on a 500 Sunbeam, clocked a 37 minute 46 second lap, at 59.99mph, in the 1922 Senior, to again raise the bar.

Another major talking point of the 1922 TT was the introduction of Dublin-born Stanley Woods, who went on to finish fifth in the Junior.

However, it was in Junior TT a year later where history was really made, not just because of the result but because it marked the beginning of a truly stellar TT career.

Woods's class had shone through from the start of his bike-racing career and sure enough he won his first TT not long after attacking the course.

His victory was classed as British win at the time because the Irish Republic was yet to be founded. The result, however, may have been different had Jimmy Simpson, riding an AJS,

27

not broken down having set a new class lap record of nearly 60mph before retiring. Instead, it marked the start of one of the TT's truly great careers on the island.

When it came to the main race that year, the Senior TT, the weather had turned once more and the brave bikers had gone out in horrendous conditions.

The knowledge of the course would come into its own and, in the end, with all his know-how and previous experience, Tom Sheard would claim his second win TT.

In the six-lap Lightweight race, Wal Handley had set a blistering pace, but despite setting a new lap record had suffered mechanical problems, which paved the way for Scotsman Jock Porter, who crossed the line in front of Bert le Vacks, to take the win.

And more history was also made, but for all the wrong reasons. Walter Brandish may only have raced the TT twice, but after the Coventry rider crashed during practice he broke his leg at the 1923 TT. That very same corner was eventually named after him. It sits between Creg-ny-Baa and Hillberry.

1923 Sidecar TT

Dixon wins on a Douglas to claim the inaugural Sidecar TT
The introduction of the sidecars did not go down well at first. And yet, as soon as they were eventually realised on the track, they became a real fan favourite from the moment the first flag dropped at the TT.

Despite a fight from pretty much all of the manufacturers against introducing the three-wheeled class, sidecars became involved in 1923 – and it proved an instant hit with the majority of the fans

During the 1920s, post the First World War, sidecars had become a popular mode of transport, and the manufacturers realised racing their machines would make sense too, especially around the TT circuit.

The first sidecar race at the TT was not without incident too. Unsurprisingly, as Freddie Dixon on a Douglas took the win – posting an average lap speed of more than 53mph – after Harry Langman had crashed – Norton's manager, Graham Walker, on a 600cc Norton and Hughes sidecar, took second. A year later, in 1924, there was a rarity with two brothers tasting victory during the same race meeting. Kenneth Twemlow won the Junior and his brother, Edwin, came first in the Lightweight.

The Senior TT was then reduced to six laps the following year only to be increased to seven again in 1926.

The Junior TT was also increased, from five laps to six in 1923 and would remain a 250cc race until 1977.

As the 1920s progressed, big names such as Norton, AJS and Velocette really began taking an interest in the race, which soon led to the privateers being replaced with the first real superstars of the TT.

Armed with factory support and factory race bikes, the lap and race records began tumbling.

Brands like BMW and DKW, from Germany, and Italy's Moto Guzzi, had also tasted success on the island before the outbreak of the First World War.

However, it was Norton that continued to dominate between the years of 1911 and 1939. By the 1920s, Norton was building 100 bikes a week out of its factory in Birmingham.

But rather than mass production, they instead focussed on big bikes capable of fitting a sidecar and also the sportier models for racing.

Soon the OHV, which stood for Overhead Valve, was produced, giving the bike much more power than a side valve. They became the most successful race bikes in the world.

James Norton died in 1925 but his vision of Norton as a racing brand continued to direct company thinking – and the standout rider of the era was Stanley Woods.

The Dublin-born star claimed ten TT wins during that era, with Jimmy Guthrie taking six and Freddie Frith four.

Woods had actually made his debut as a very young 17-year-old but despite his tender age had still managed to finish a very solid fifth in the Junior TT.

It did not take long for him to taste victory, as just a year later he won his TT in the same race. It was just his second year of racing on the Isle of Man and it was clear to fans and fellow riders that a true star had been born.

The lap record had also been pushed up from an average speed of 64mph in 1924, to 81mph in 1932 – nearly a 20mph jump in just eight years.

It had risen even further, to 91mph, when the Second World War broke out, which was set by Harold Daniell on a Norton on his way to victory during the 1938 Senior TT.

Woods had also signed for Norton back in 1926 and it was then his career really began to flourish. He would claim another TT win in the same year he joined the British team but then there was a six-year gap until his next victory on the island.

The Irishman, however, broke his TT duck in perfect style by winning the double, taking both the Junior and Senior crowns in 1932, a feat he repeated a year later, but then split from Norton.

Despite losing Norton's backing he would continue to show he was one of the TT's greats by continuing to achieve success with different manufacturers en route to taking his wins into double figures.

Senior TT 1925

Handley becomes first to win two in a week

By the mid-1920s, the AJS manufacturer was really starting to make headway, and partnership with Jimmy Simpson in the saddle worked wonders.

Simpson would go on to break the record in 1924 in the Junior TT, with an average lap speed of 64.54mph, completing his circuit in 35 minutes and six seconds.

A year later, in the Senior, Simpson went even faster on his 500cc AJS completing his lap in 33 minutes and 50 seconds while averaging 69.97mph. He would raise the bar again in 1926 meaning he had broken three lap records in three years.

The race itself, however, was won by Howard Davies, who was back for more TT victories in 1925.

He claimed the Senior on his own HRD brand, having set up a business in Wolverhampton, after Simpson had been forced to retire having raised the lap record to nearly 70mph.

Davies's win was made all the more remarkable as he had done it while racing works teams.

The boom of the sidecars forming part of the TT was also short-lived as they were stopped after just three years, eventually returning two decades later in 1953.

It meant Freddie Dixon's new lap record on a sidecar of 57.18mph in the 1925 TT would remain in place until Helmut Faith set an 85.79mph in 1960.

The year 1925 was also the final time Isle of Man Tourist Trophy and final year Ultra-Lightweight class for 175cc bikes was run – and it was won by Wal Handley who would make TT that same year.

After numerous retirements the previous year, Handley would win the Junior TT race over six laps at an average speed of just over 65mph.

Later in the week, he went on to become the first TT rider to win two races in a week when he followed his Junior success with victory in the four-lap Ultra-Lightweight TT race, this time lapping just over 53mph, which was good enough for a new lap record after he crossed the line on one of his flying circuits in 41 minutes and 52 seconds, at 54.12mph.

Handley had even been on for a treble and was leading the Lightweight TT after the first two laps by more than two minutes, but after suffering a puncture he fell off at Signpost Corner, which allowed Eddie Twemlow on a New Imperial to take the win.

Handley would go on to four TTs during his illustrious career and his name would become immortalised around the TT track for eternity after Handley's Corner was later named after him.

Having started his TT career in 1922, he continued to compete on the island for another 13 years, notching up 28 TT races. As well as his four wins, he also picked up second-place finish and broke nine fastest laps.

His final TT victory would come in the Senior in 1930, but even after retiring from motorcycles he continued racing on four wheels and enjoyed a second stellar career.

Tragically, he was killed during the Second World War while serving as a pilot with the Air Transport Auxiliary.

Senior TT 1926

Simpson breaks the 70mph barrier

With more manufacturer interest in the late 1920s, the involvement of AJS saw Jimmy Simpson break the record in three successive years – his latest was breaking the 70mph barrier in the Senior with a speed of 70.43mph, before Stanley Woods claimed his first lap record in 1927.

Charlie Dodson would also see records tumble on his 500cc Sunbeam. In fact, between the years of 1924 and 1930, times would increase by almost 12mph. The bikes were going, on average, 2mph quicker every TT.

Wal Handley's 76.28mph lap on a 500 Rudge would see the start of a classic decade on the Isle of Man, with the TT races becoming the premier event on the motorcycle racing calendar, following in the footsteps of Simpson.

Simpson had made his debut in 1922 and, despite breaking numerous lap records, he would only win one TT.

Racing until 1934, it appeared he would finish his career without a Silver Lady but, armed with a Rudge, he finally broke his duck in Lightweight in that same year, as well as coming second in the Junior and Senior on Nortons. It was also one of the most celebrated wins in the eyes of the fans.

His legacy, however, would live on as he became the first rider to post 60mph, 70mph and 80mph laps around the 37.73-mile course. It was some feat and the organisers realised it too, with the Jimmy Simpson Trophy still being handed out annually to this day to the TT rider who sets the fastest lap of the race week.

Much of Simpson's early success came on the AJS, a company that was founded by Joseph Stevens, an engineering blacksmith from Wednesfield, in Wolverhampton, in 1909.

He had already been involved in motorcycle production from around 1897 when he acquired an American Mitchell motorbike.

Stevens was born in 1856 and became a self-employed engineering blacksmith in 1874. His first company was called J. Stevens & Co, with premises in Cross Street, Wednesfield.

He undertook all kinds of metalwork, from making horseshoes and making garden tools, to bicycles and locks, soon gaining a reputation as a highly skilled craftsman.

Stevens and his wife had nine children, and all of them were later involved in the family business.

When his eldest son, Harry, joined, they moved manufacturing to a premises in Tempest Street, near Wolverhampton town centre, where they were soon also joined by Stevens's third son, Joe Junior.

Harry acquired his father's engineering skills and began to design all kinds of machines and tools for use in the lock industry.

Harry and Joe Junior also built an engine in their spare time, which was completed late in 1897 and was an instant success. The finished article also had a surprisingly good carburettor, made from a mustard tin.

Reliable and efficient, Harry and his father were quick to realise a large market existed for such petrol engines, which could in turn prove to be very lucrative in an era of booming heavy industry.

In 1899, the Stevens Motor Manufacturing Company was formed and it soon attracted the attention of Wearwell, a Wolverhampton-based bicycle manufacturer based in Poutney Street, which was branching out into motorcycle production.

Stevens won a contract to produce around 60 per cent of the company's motorcycle engines and the first Wearwell-Stevens bikes rolled off production lines in 1901.

The bikes cost 42 guineas and were well received, helping to establish a solid reputation for Stevens but the shock collapse of Wearwell in 1909 persuaded the family to go into full motorcycle production under the new moniker of AJS.

The new company, named after one of Joseph's five sons, Albert John, moved from Wednesfield to a factory in Retreat Street, Wolverhampton.

The first two AJS motorcycle models hit the shops in August 1910, called Model A and Model B.

The lightweight bikes received glowing praise from motorcycle journals and observers at the Olympia Motorcycle Show in November of the same year and two further models were produced by 1913.

Orders were rolling in by this time and the company acquired a new, larger site at Graiseley Hill in 1914.

Production would eventually be transferred to this factory by 1917. But the biggest boost AJS produced was when it began producing sports bikes for the Isle of Man TT motorbike race.

A handful of bikes had been used between 1911 and 1913 with encouraging results but in 1914 four machines came in first, second, fourth and sixth, enhancing AJS's reputation across the country.

The increased demand for bikes that year persuaded AJS to become a public limited company.

The nominal share capital added an extra £50,000, and new cycle models were produced by 1915 despite a major shift in production towards war munitions and military motorcycle production after the outbreak of the First World War.

In the 1920s, AJS were consistently successful in motorsport and the awesomely fast machines were winning races just before 1939.

The restrictions on commercial production, imposed in wartime, were lifted in 1919 and business was soon booming again. More than 600 people were employed by the company and between 20,000 and 25,000 bikes were being produced each year by the mid-1920s.

However, demand for the cycles fell in the latter half of the decade, as did the share price, and the company lost £89,201 in 1931.

On 22 October that year, shareholders voted to go into voluntary liquidation and sold the motorcycle name and manufacturing rights to London-based Matchless for £20,000 the following year.

The famous 'Porcupines' carried the AJS banner after the war but the firm declined once it gave up racing in 1954.

The only reminder left in Wolverhampton of the once great company is the Lone Rider statue, which stands in Graiseley Hill, while the AJS Big Port is still a favourite among vintage motorbike enthusiasts.

During the 1929 Senior TT, the lap record would go again – only this was achieved by Charlie Dodson on another Wolverhampton-built machine, a 500 Sunbeam.

He clocked a time of 30 minutes and 47 seconds, averaging 73.55mph, on the Sunbeam, a company that was founded by John Marston, born in Ludlow, Shropshire, in 1836, who would turn his business into one of Wolverhampton's most famous companies.

Marston founded Sunbeamland Cycle Factory in 1887 and production of cars began in 1899.

The prototype models were not sold but sales eventually began in 1901, with bikes named the Sunbeam Mabley voiturette.

Ten years on again, and at the outbreak of the First World War, Sunbeam was producing Isle of Man TT racers and the power of their engines had leaped to as high as 200 horsepower.

Built almost 100 years ago, the 1913 Sunbeam motorbike boasted two-and-three-quarter horsepower – 346cc in new money – and was one of the first models to roll off the track at the Paul Street plant in Wolverhampton.

It was the first model they ever made and it marked a golden period for Black Country vehicle manufacture, when firms like Sunbeam, AJS, Diamond, Clyno and Orbit produced the premium motors of the day.

The Sunbeam company, originally a japanning firm which made painted tinware, moved into bicycle manufacture at the turn of the 20th century and made the logical next step to motorised bikes in 1912. Jappanning is a type of finish that originated as a European imitation of Asian lacquerwork.

Legend has it the original colour scheme of black gloss with gold lining was used by the firm to match the Wolverhampton Wanderers football strip.

About 30 motorcycles per week rolled off the production lines in the 1920s, supplying bikes to the British army, belt-driven models to the French army and sidecar ambulance combinations to the Russians.

In the 1920s heydays, Black Country-built models also dominated the race track, with hill sprint champion George Dance and Isle of Man TT winner Tommy de la Haye among the hallowed names who won Grand Prix at home and abroad.

Production continued apace until 1937, when rival firm Matchless Motorcycles bought out the company.

Just two years later, the Sunbeam brand was taken over by BSA which continued to use the name on 500cc shaft-driven models until the late 1960s. After roaring through the first half of the century, the Sunbeam name then slipped out of existence without so much as a misfire.

However, the Sunbeam 90 remains one of the most sought-after motorcycles in the vintage enthusiast world.

Senior TT 1931

Simpson breaks the 80mph and 30-minute barriers

By now, Simpson turned his attention to racing Nortons, and after Wal Handley had raised the lap record to 76.28mph in 1931, a year later Simpson went quicker again with a staggering lap of 80.82mph.

He finished his lap in under half an hour too, finishing it in 29 minutes and one second.

The meeting was again dominated by Rudge and Norton machinery.

Simpson's bike woes would continue as he finished eighth in the Junior because of bike problems in a race won by his Norton team-mate, Tim Hunt.

Rudge got revenge in the Lightweight TT with Graham Walker taking his single win on the island, which all led to the Senior.

Jimmy Guthrie led during the opening lap by just a second from Simpson, with the third Norton rider, Stanley Woods, a further 17 seconds back in third.

Simpson broke the lap record on the second circuit but would later crash on lap four.

Guthrie then came off his own Norton a lap later but was able to remount and bring his bike home in second place, with Woods in third place.

The fast pace and carnage of a truly spectacular Senior was eventually won by Hunt, who was able to complete a TT double win.

Simpson upped his pace again in 1932, lapping at 81.60mph in the Senior in a year when Norton was unstoppable, claiming a one-two-three in both the Senior and Junior TTs.

During the Senior, Simpson, Stanley Woods and Jimmy Guthrie had been given orders to battle for the first three laps but then hold their positions until the chequered flag.

Woods chased Simpson down on the third lap and would eventually go on to take victory, with Guthrie moving his way up to second before the end of the race, which was watched by Prince George, Duke of Kent, who became the first royal visitor to the Isle of Man TT races.

Woods also claimed the Junior win that year, ahead of Wal Handley and Tyrell-Smith, while Simpson was the man who could not stop breaking lap records.

Having become the first rider to break the 60mph lap barrier in 1924, he was also the first to break 70mph in 1926 and 80mph in 1931.

And it was in the 1932 Senior TT that Handley, riding for Rudge, would crash at the 11th Milestone and sustain a back injury which would force him to retire. The place on the TT course where the incident occurred was renamed Handley's Corner. However, despite breaking eight lap records during his career, Handley's only victory came in the 1934 Lightweight 250cc TT.

But it was a special occasion for more reasons than one, because the win was also Simpson's final race before he retired.

During this era, Allan Jefferies was employed as a reserve team rider for Triumph. Despite noting pulling up trees himself, Allan would leave behind one of the TT's greatest dynasties.

His son went on to win the 1971 F750 TT while his other son, Nick, claimed the 1993 F1 TT. Tony's son, David, went on to become one of the finest riders to ever race the TT circuit, winning nine TTs between 1999 and 2002.

Woods would raise the lap record once more a year later in the 1933 Senior TT, with an 82.74mph effort – and a switch to an Italian machine in 1935 did not slow him down either.

Senior TT 1935

Woods does double on Italian machines

Having parted way with Norton, Stanley Woods bounced back with the Moto Guzzi team by again breaking the lap record in the Senior, this time clocking a staggering 86.53mph lap.

Having also set the fastest lap in the 1934 Senior race before running out of petrol, there were no dramas the following year as Woods rode the Moto Guzzi's V-twin to victory over Norton-mounted Jimmy Guthrie.

Norton had dominated the 1930s and had remained pretty much unstoppable at the TT, winning seven out of eight Seniors between 1931 and 1938.

Away from the island, between 1930 and 1937, Norton also won 78 out of a possible 92 GPs, such was their dominance on the race scene. It seemed the 1935 Senior TT would be a foregone conclusion. No one, despite Wood's sublime talent, had really betted on the great Woods doing much with his Moto Guzzi V-twin, let alone win the race.

But after somehow managing to pull back a 26-second deficit on the final lap, that's exactly what he did.

The Norton-mounted Guthrie had started the race as number one and was ahead on the road for much of the race.

After pitting for the final time, he was on his way to what appeared to be a guaranteed victory.

As Woods approached the pits himself, he made a huge decision, which was to finish the final lap without pitting again believing he had enough fuel left in the tank to make it to the finish line.

Of course, in 1935 it was a lot more difficult and complicated getting messages across to the riders compared with today, so by the time the Norton team had realised Woods had decided to go straight through – and having told Guthrie to take it easy on the final lap to ensure he did not suffer any unnecessary bike problems, believing he had an unassailable lead – suddenly, from nowhere, the race was back on.

Guthrie, however, still had a decent lead and when he crossed the line everyone thought he had still won.

But Woods was on one of the most memorable TT charges of all time and after posting a new lap record of 83.53mph, breaking the previous lap record by a staggering 3mph, he proved them all wrong.

Perhaps even more incredibly, after racing for three hours and seven minutes, he had nicked the win by just four seconds.

It was the first time since 1911 a foreign machine had won the Senior and he would complete his double with victory in the Lightweight, setting another lap record along the way.

The victories on different bikes and in different classes showed what a pioneering rider Wood was, and after winning two more TTs in the late 1930s, his ten victories on the island means he remains one of the race's most successful riders, nearly 100 years since taking his first wins. He was TT great in every sense of the word.

The 1936 Junior TT proved to be highly controversial and was marred by disqualification and protest.

Woods rode for Velocette but retired at Sulby on lap one with engine problems.

After leading for five laps, Guthrie was forced to stop between Hillberry and Signpost Corner to replace the drive chain.

Having fixed the problem, he continued in second place while team-mate Frith, who had joined the team after winning the 1935 Junior Manx Grand Prix, took the lead.

At Parliament Square in Ramsey, on lap six, Guthrie was black-flagged for receiving outside assistance and disqualified. However, he continued the race and finished, with Frith taking the win, lapping at an average race speed of more than 80mph.

After the race, the Norton race team protested the disqualification and Guthrie was posted in fifth place in the final classification but awarded the prize money for second.

In the Senior TT race, Harold Daniell and George Rowley rode supercharged AJS V4s, but despite their high top speed, the bikes lacked acceleration. Both riders retired due to mechanical problems.

The Lightweight TT was held after being delayed for a day because of mist and fog but once the race got going it proved to be a closely contested battle between Bob Foster, riding for New Imperial and Woods, who this time was mounted on a DKW.

Woods was forced to retired on lap seven while stopping to change a spark plug, which paved the way for Foster to take the win at an average race speed of 74.28mph.

Senior TT 1937
Frith smashes the 90mph barrier

Simpson and Woods had remained the men to beat – that was until the emergence of Freddie Frith and Harold Daniell, the latest heroes during the era of the pudding helmet before the TT was forced into another following the outbreak of the Second World War.

Frith smashed the 90mph barrier on a 500 Norton, lapping in 25 minutes and five seconds, averaging 90.27mph.

Jimmie Guthrie would go on to take victory in the Junior TT that same year but sadly that would be the last of his six wins on the island as later that year he would lose his life while competing in the German Grand Prix.

A memorial was built at the point on the climb up the mountain where he had retired, at the Cutting, during his last TT race. Guthrie had made his debut in 1923 on a Matchless but his first victory would come seven years later in the 1930 Lightweight race on an AJS.

Guthrie, who was a Norton works rider from 1931 to 1937, completed TT double in 1934, winning the Junior and Senior.

Italian machines and riders had been temporarily banned from racing at the TT in 1936, because their country had invaded Ethiopia, but a year later Omobono Tenni became the first Italian winner of a TT, claiming victory in the Lightweight class, on a 250cc Moto Guzzi.

In 1938, Daniell raised the record again, hitting 91mph during the Senior on a Norton, with Woods second and Frith third; the record would stand until 1950.

Baby-faced, spectacle-wearing Londoner Daniell had taken his first victory on the island while competing in the 1933 Manx Grand Prix.

He entered the Senior TT a year later on a works AJS, finishing ninth and retiring in the Junior race.

Following years of mechanical problems with AJS, he entered the 1937 races with his own three-year-old Norton, finishing fifth in both the Senior and Junior TT, but his standout result for that year was beating Stanley Woods at Donington and Crystal Palace, as well as second following his first race on the continent, in the Dutch TT.

The Norton factory decided to offer him a team place for the 1938 season – and he immediately repaid them winning the Senior race and setting a record lap, overtaking Woods on the last few miles.

When the Second World War broke out, he applied for service but was rejected – on the grounds of poor eyesight.

Instead, he served in the Home Guard, and when the war ended he continued with Norton, and was immediately back to winning ways.

During the Junior TT in 1937, Woods set a class lap record of 85.30mph, on a Velocette, which would also remain in place for another 12 years because of the looming war. He beat team-mate Ted Mellors and Norton's Freddie Frith.

The Lightweight TT was also a memorable battle. Won by Ewald Kluge on a supercharged DKW, he annihilated the race lap record with an 80.35mph, averaging a stunning 78.48mph for the entire seven-lap race.

He went on to beat the sixth British OHC Excelsiors behind him by more than 11 minutes.

The 1939 Senior was dominated by Georg Meier, on loan from the Auto Union GP team, who beat Jock West into second place, becoming the first rider outside the UK to win a TT while riding a supercharged BMW 'Kompressor' machine.

The race was dominated by German-made BMWs with West adding to the German manufacturer's success with his second-place finish, also on a Type 255 BMW RS 500.

To properly handle high revs, the BMW engines featured side shafts leading into the two cylinder heads, and two overhead camshafts in each cylinder head controlled the gas cycle.

Benefiting from low weight, the bikes could hit nearly 140mph, but despite the speeds neither was able to beat Daniell's lap record.

Meier, who started out as an off-road rider and had only completed his first season in road competition the previous year, recorded an average speed 89mph on his way to victory.

It proved to be a fruitful year for foreign manufacturers in general too as Ted Mellor went on to win the Lightweight on an Italian-built Benelli, beating Ewald Kluge into second place on a DKW. Woods had set the fastest lap of the race before retiring.

A plaque was also placed around the track at Ballaugh Bridge to remember Karl Gall, a winner of Dutch and German GPs, who died during practice in 1939.

Following the outbreak of the Second World War, racing on the island would be halted for seven years with many of the riders called into action while motorbike manufacturers also turned their attentions to the war effort.

Thursday, 14 November 1940 was the night when Coventry was targeted by the German war planes – and when they hit the Triumph factory it was completely destroyed.

However, undeterred, Triumph opened a new factory in Meriden, Warwickshire, in 1942 and would play a major role in war, which would also shape the development of the company in years to come.

Again, the company did its best for the war effort and produced the 3SW, which was just what the army needed at the time. The technology went backwards but it was what was needed.

Following the end of the war, a golden era began at Triumph. The 6T, known as the Thunderbird, was produced, and helped the company break into the American market because it had more horsepower. They could hit more than 90mph.

And when Marlon Brando rode a Thunderbird in the classic flick, *The Wild One*, in 1953, it really took off in the States. It also singled the start of 'the biker' and, despite Triumph not really being on board with the outlaw image, the US was soon taking 70 per cent of Triumph output.

On 6 September 1956, Jonny Allen from Texas set a new land speed record of 214.4mph. And he did it on a revamped Thunderbird, which gave the brand even more publicity in the US.

In 1958, Triumph released the Bonneville, as homage to Allen. The bike could reach speeds of 115mph. Many Hollywood A-listers by this point were lining up to be seen on a Triumph but none did the brand more favours than Steve McQueen.

Racing them and using them in his movies, including *The Great Escape* – that had big connections with the Second World War – it would go down as Triumph's most famous moment on the big screen.

Triumph's most famous win, however, would come at Daytona in 1966. The Texan Buddy Elmore, rose from 46th to win the Daytona 200 on a Triumph Trophy and, one year later, the company released the Daytona Supersport 100 R.

Triumph went on to win at Daytona for the second time but complacency – especially when the Honda CB754 arrived on the market – marked the demise of the British motorbike industry. The new Honda was a superbike and Triumph – and the rest of the British brands – simply could not keep up with Japanese development.

In September 1973, Triumph announced it was closing the Meriden plant due to falling sales. After two years of strikes the factory was reopened but as part of the workers' co-operative.

Despite making thousands of bikes once more, the US market had slipped between its fingers and UK sale soon began plummeting too.

By 1983, Triumph had been closed, the factory put up for sale and the brand sold to British businessman John Bloor.

A few Triumphs were made for the famous White Helmets display team but the last Les Harris Triumph was built in 1988 by which time Meriden had been replaced by a housing estate where road names honoured the once iconic brand.

It would be years until Triumph troubled the TT podiums again.

Senior TT 1947

Daniell straight back to winning ways

Following the outbreak of the Second World War in 1939, the TT was finally reinstated in 1947, two years after victory had been declared in Europe and Japan.

The programme remained the same as it had during the pre-war years when the TT returned, with a 500cc Senior race, 350cc Junior race and 250cc Lightweight race, all competed over seven laps.

Freddie Frith suffered a crash on his Moto Guzzi during practice, much to the dismay of his fans who had been so eager to see him race.

He broke his collarbone following a spill at Ballacraine, which ruled him out of the entire TT race week.

The AJS E90 was one of the rare post-war machines to make the TT grid in 1947, which became known as the Porcupine, due to its spiky fins.

The bike, which was originally designed to be supercharged, was ridden by Les Graham and Jock West.

However, the TT authorities had banned supercharged machines the previous year, which meant the bike had to go through major alterations.

It meant that despite the AJS team's potential, lap record holder Harold Daniell still remained one of the favourites.

His long-standing lap record, set before the outbreak of the war, looked certain to remain intact too because all the racers had been forced to use low-grade petrol following the ravages of the war.

There were only 14 finishers during the 1947 Senior TT, which was won by Daniell, who claimed the second TT win of his career. In second place was Norton with Artie Bell while in third was Peter Goodman, on a Velocette, who was two minutes behind.

Les Graham, despite having his rear chain dislodged before the finish, still managed to finish ninth on his Porcupine.

Lightweight TT was won by Manliff Barrington, after TT great Stanley Woods had persuaded Giorgio Peroni, boss of Moto Guzzi, to provide him with a bike.

Barrington's win, however, would come under controversial circumstances as he was adjudged to have beaten Maurice Cann but a review of the timing sheets since has revealed there may have been a discrepancy of up to a minute between the pair.

Despite a protest from Cann and his team, judges ruled that the result should stand.

Third-placed Ben Drinkwater was more than eight minutes behind the top two Moto Guzzis on his Excelsior in third place but it was still seen as an excellent result.

Cann, however, would gain revenge in the 1948 Lightweight TT. A lot of the riders were still racing pre-war machines during 1947 and the Junior TT was won by Bob Foster, with David Whitworth second and Jock Weddell in third. All were on an AJS.

Peter Goodman had been going well before he ran out of fuel and was forced to roll his bike home in fourth place.

The Clubman races, set for riders entered by club racers or dealers on road machines, were held between 1947 to 1956.

Those who could enter must have already claimed a TT replica, or finished in the top three at the Manx, as a minimum.

It helped bring new riders into racing and gave some of the British brands a big boost too, particularly those that had steered clear of the main TT races.

The Clubman's Lightweight was won by AJS's Basil Keys while Clubman's Junior, where there was no age limits on the bikes, was won by five-time Manx GP winner – and later a renowned commentator – Denis Parkinson on a Norton.

Fellow Norton rider Bob Pratt was second, with Wilf Sleightholme, on an AJS, third. The bike was similar to the one raced by the great Les Graham. Clubman's Senior was won by Norton's Eric Briggs, who was followed home by Triumph's Allan Jefferies and Ariel's George Parsons.

BSA would become the dominant force of the Clubman races, while machine regulations and rumours of factory support behind the scenes for some of the racers and manufacturers also meant the races were never too far from some sort of controversy.

By 1954, the 'TT' name of the Clubman's race would be dropped and a year later races were moved to the Clypse Course, before returning to the mountain in 1956.

Finally, after being dropped from the programme altogether for the Golden Jubilee meeting in 1957, they never returned. But during those few years, BSA had claimed 11 victories, Norton six, Vincent-HRD four, Excelsior three, Triumph two and Velocette one.

The 1000cc Vincent-HRD, which had been ridden to victory by John Daniels in 1948, was also one of the most dominant machines of the era in that class and, ultimately, contributed to the class's demise.

Junior TT 1949

Frith rolls back the years again as TT gains GP status

The year 1949 was one of the most important in the history of the races as it marked the inauguration of the TT into the FIM World Championships.

Not only that, the race would also become known as one of the most demanding – and most important – on the racing calendar across the globe.

After the FIM had sanctioned a world championship for motorbike racing, the TT was chosen as the British round.

It had begun following a meeting in 1948 when the FIM decided there would be a motorcycle world championship along Grand Prix lines. A six-race annual series, with points being awarded for a placing and a point for the fastest lap of each race, was launched in five classes – 500cc, 350cc, 250cc, 125cc and 600cc sidecar.

The Isle of Man TT would be one of those races and would become a mainstay on the GP calendar until 1976.

Daniell, on a Norton, won the first GP in the 500cc Senior TT at an average speed of 86.93mph.

Les Graham, on an AJS Porcupine twin, had led the Senior until the last lap when his magneto drive sheared. He pushed the bike past the finish line in tenth place.

However, his earlier efforts would prove vital in terms of the world title as Graham – who had been an RAF pilot during the Second World War and had started racing motorbikes once he had been demobbed – gained one championship point for recording the fastest lap.

With wins at the Swiss GP and Ulster, it meant the championship would be decided at the final race in Monza.

Graham found himself in a direct battle with Nello Pagani, who was riding a Gilera.

Pagani would go on to win the race after Graham had been taken out by another Gilera rider but, as it was the days when riders could lose their three worst results, following some calculations, Graham was eventually handed the title by just a single point.

Sadly, he would lose his life at the TT in 1953. Having started working with MV, it had appeared he might be back on the championship trail but sadly he died after crashing at the bottom of Bray Hill.

Daniell's career came to a close in 1950 when he made his last appearance on the island, finishing third in the Junior race quite a distance behind the emerging new star of the sport, Geoff Duke, who himself finished behind Artie Bell.

On retirement, he became a Norton dealer in Forest Hill, London, but would continue racing on four wheels in Formula 3.

There were more memorable races during the TT too as a romantic story unfolded in the Junior.

Freddie Frith, who had sealed his first TT win way back in 1936, may have been a veteran by the time racing on the island returned but he still had the pace.

And his skills showed through once more in the 1949 Junior TT, when he took victory on board a KTT MKIII.

A stylish rider and five-times winner on the island, Frith was one of the few riders – along with the likes of Daniell – to win TT races before and after the Second World War.

Having won the 1935 Junior Manx GP, he joined the Norton team later for a year and it turned into a winning combination as he won the Junior and finished second in the Senior.

In 1937, he claimed his first Senior TT, setting the first 90mph lap, finished third in the 1939 Senior and then missed the 1947 TT following a crash.

Returning to the island on a Velocette a year later, he won the Junior, repeating this success a year later becoming the first 350cc world champion.

Senior TT 1950

Duke wins on a 'feather bed'

At the turn of the decade, a new star was born as Geoff Duke announced himself on the world stage in the 1950

Senior TT, setting a lap record of 93.33mph – continuing the Norton's domination.

During the 1930s and 1940s, Norton was beginning to be beaten by the likes of AJS and Velocette but not for long because, in 1935, it had produced a works machine and also started creating a bike using overhead camshaft machines.

Norton's race bike engines were also by this stage being made with ultra-light magnesium. It meant the entire package was simply faster and more efficient than any of their racing rivals.

At the same time, on the road, the Model 30 International was being produced. The 1934 roadster may not have had the magnesium engine or the same racing spec as the TT winning bikes, but they were still fast enough for privateers to enter in races across the country and the continent, and even on the Isle of Man TT.

When the Second World War broke out, Norton became one of the biggest motorcycle suppliers to the British army. The Norton Big 4 was used to haul a sidecar with a machine gun on it.

The 16H proved itself to be reliable, which was why the army was so keen to use it. With the two brands combined, Norton produced 100,000 bikes for the war effort – a quarter of all bikes supplied to the military.

It proved Norton could mass-produce machines, but following the war the company set its sights on a twin-cylinder machine, which became the Dominator.

The Model 7 Dominator became a direct competitor with Triumph's Speed Twin but the brand, like their UK rivals, had its eyes set on the US market.

Targeting the Daytona 200 in the 1950s, they headed to the States – and despite the best efforts of the Americans, they could not stop the British manufacturer from winning when Dick Klamfoth claimed three wins in 1952 on a Manx Norton, the latest unstoppable race bike.

Armed with a 'garden-gate' frame, the Nortons were quick but could not properly compete on the European circuits.

Enter the 'feather-bed' frame, which had no lugs and was just a tube that was much stiffer. It was an instant success and helped Norton claim the top three places at the 1950 Senior TT.

Harold Daniell had given the frame its famous name after saying it rode 'like a feather bed'. Modern bikes still use the same steering geometry to this day making it one of the most important developments in motorcycle chassis-making.

The single-cylinder Norton 500cc engine was also as good as it got, because it was able to compete with the Italians' newer four-cylinder engines. With the frame, it was the perfect combination – especially when Duke was at the helm.

Having already won the 1949 Senior Clubman and 1949 Manx GP, 20-year-old Duke was one of Norton's rising stars.

By 1950, he was racing a 500cc version of Norton's revolutionary bikes, which had the unique chassis designed by Rex McCandless.

And it proved to be a great match too because, after finishing second in the Junior TT, he went on to win Senior, setting a new lap record of 93.33mph.

The 'feather-bed' Norton had certainly played its part in his success too. McCandless would later design and ride Norton's 350cc machine, which became known as the 'Kneeler'.

He also went on to push the uniquely designed 350cc and 500cc machines to new levels, breaking records. In Montlhery, France, he maintained a speed averaging 133.7mph for one hour. Another section of the course was also renamed in 1950 following another accident, which thankfully had not been fatal.

Bill Doran crashed on a section of the course, a long left-hander that comes immediately after Ballig Bridge, breaking his leg. The bend would be renamed Doran's Bend in his honour.

* * *

In an article in the *Shropshire Star* newspaper, his widow, Peggy, revealed her husband's pride in having a bend named after him:

With his trademark jutting chin and ready smile, who is immortalised at the Isle of Man TT with a bend named in his honour – Doran's Bend.

With his trademark jutting chin and ready smile, Bill Doran was Shropshire's motorcycling ace who is immortalised at the Isle of Man TT with a bend named in his honour – Doran's Bend.

He came a cropper there in 1950, riding for the AJS works team. He escaped with a broken leg.

'He was so proud of it because he was the only living person at the time to have one named after him,' says his widow Peggy.

It was by no means the last of his scrapes during an illustrious career which began at the age of 32 with the 1946 Junior Manx Grand Prix and ended at Rouen in 1953 when he slid on cobblestones and had a head injury.

Among the other spills (and there's a bit of a list) was a crash in the 1952 Dutch TT in which he suffered a damaged back which left him in plaster from his armpits to his thighs.

Amid the spills and tragedy – Les Graham, who had been his team-mate at AJS, was killed at the 1953 Isle of Man

TT – there was glory. Ten victories against top-class fields, including wins in the Belgian GP in 1949 and at Silverstone in 1953. Fastest laps. Third place in the 1951 350cc world championship table. Seventeen world records in the AJS team. A whole cupboardful of silverware.

It's probable though that most Salopians who remember him will have known him from his post-racing years in business in Whitchurch Road, Wellington, firstly in partnership with Matt Wright – the AJS development engineer – from 1954 to 1967, and then as Bill Doran Garages Ltd after Matt retired.

After living fast on the edge during his racing career, Bill Doran was destined to die of a heart attack in September 1973 aged 58.

Mrs Doran, 85 (and, incidentally, the pronunciation she uses is an un-stressed 'doorun'), carried on with the business until closing it in 1987.

'Bill was lovely, a happy guy, always smiling,' she said.

'I met Bill while he was racing. He said, 'We shouldn't get married.' It was too dangerous. And in those days, it was. We had lost so many friends.'

She met him at the annual dinner dance of Wolverhampton Motorcycle Club, of which her father Herbert Ratcliffe was vice chairman, at Beatties in Wolverhampton just after Bill had won the Belgian Grand Prix.

'People think that when I met him that I didn't know anything about motorcycles. But I knew what motorcycling was all about.'

Her father had ridden motorcycles – winning a cup in 1913 for riding from Birmingham to Carlisle and back. And she had a sadder reason to know all about motorcycling.

'My brother, Eric, was killed on a motorcycle. A post office van came out of a side road and he went straight over the top. There were no crash helmets in those days. That happened at Wollaston, near Stourbridge, in 1946.'

Thereafter she was, understandably perhaps, 'wrapped in cotton wool', and not encouraged to ride herself.

She and Bill married in October 1955.

'When Bill and I married, Bill said, 'You are going to pass your test. I want you to become independent.' I thought that was a funny thing to say after about three months of marriage. I took my test and passed it, in an Austin pick-up, I think it was an A90.

'The main reason he wanted me to pass my test was to go to Birmingham to pick up motorbikes. I used to go and pick up BSAs, Velocettes, Watsonians, side cars and all sorts of things.'

In the business she would serve petrol, and help in the shop while Maud Wright, Matt's wife, did the office work.

'I used to go to Birmingham for the spares and bikes. We did a seven-day week.'

Soon they had another filling station further up Whitchurch Road, and another at the Red Lion on the Holyhead Road.

There was a sort of pattern to sales. 'People would start with a BSA Bantam and then go up to something larger. Then they would get married, and have a sidecar. Then we went into Messerschmitt and Isetta bubble cars. Bill and I used to go down to Gatwick airport and collect them and drive them back.

'Then the explosion happened. The Mini came in. That virtually put an end to them.'

Motorcycling continues in the family blood. Daughter Jayne rides a Ducati Monster. Granddaughter Emilie Weaving is a mechanic at Ducati Wolverhampton Ltd and rides a Yamaha R6.

Mrs Doran is happy about it: 'You can't wrap them in cotton wool.'

* * *

Jayne still wears the watch (it still works) engraved for her father after his ride in the 1952 Swiss GP and, when watchmakers Tissot found out, they invited Bill's wife, daughter and granddaughter as honoured guests to the Grand Prix at Silverstone a few weeks ago. The trio were presented with Tissot watches and given a framed photograph of Bill.

'We had a wonderful day. It brought back lots of lovely memories. I was so proud he is still remembered,' said Jayne.

Frank Sheene had also started racing around the same era and, although he never troubled the podiums, his son would go on to become one of motorsport's biggest stars – and one of the most controversial figures in the history of the TT.

Barry Sheene, who won the world title in 1976 and 1977, first raced at the TT in 1971 but after two DNFs he never returned.

He became one of the most vocal riders against racing the TT because of how dangerous he felt the race was. His words and actions eventually contributed to it being removed from the GP calendar in 1977.

Italian machines would also become the dominant force during the 1950s, led by the Moto Guzzi factory, although the German-based BMWs and NSUs were also are the front end of most races.

However, it was the Norton-Duke combination that once again claimed the 1951 TT. Lapping in 23 minutes and 47 seconds, breaking the record with an average lap speed of 96.22mph, he claimed back-to-back Senior wins.

And things would get even better for Duke as he claimed his first TT double, taking the Junior title too, this time increasing the lap record to 95.22mph.

Norton were simply too strong in the Junior class, with Johnny Lockett, a factory team rider between 1947 and 1951, finishing second. Fellow Norton rider Jack Brett ensured it was a podium lockout for the British manufacturer.

Meanwhile, AJS rider Doran had finished second in the Senior, which gave the E90 Porcupine its best-ever result around the Mountain Course. Lapping at 93.83mph, he was the only non-Norton rider to finish in the top 14.

FB Mondial Factory of Bologna took first, second, third and fourth during the first 125cc TT race, with Cromie McCandless followed home by Carlo Ubbiali, Gianni Leoni and Nello Pagani.

However, the brand would completely withdraw from racing in 1957, closely followed by the once-dominant Gilera and Moto Guzzi teams.

In races during this era, practice sessions saw the bikes set off with white plates and black digits on the front, while the side plates had the class colours, which made it easier for race organisers, adjudicators, officials and even photographers to understand better who was racing and what in which class.

The Ultra-Lightweight TT was lengthened from two laps to three in 1952, while the Lightweight race was reduced to four.

Fergus Anderson went on to win the Lightweight 250cc TT in 1952, which was dominated by the Moto Guzzi garage. He finished ahead of team-mate and 350cc champion of that same year, Enrico Lorenzetti.

The Scot, who was based in Italy, would himself go on to claim the championship between 1953 and 1954. Sadly, he later died while racing a BMW in 1956.

Cecil Landford claimed the 125cc Ultra-Lightweight race on a four-stroke MV Agusta but when it came to the Senior it was more of the same. Geoff Duke, mounted on a Manx Norton, rode it to victory once more, breaking the lap record and posting a time of more than 90mph.

The Manx Nortons were so good they are still raced today but it was with Merseysider Duke, and his unique, smooth riding style that the combination proved to be so lethal.

Ash was the first rider to wear a one-piece racing leathers, he first burst on to the scene in 1949, winning the Clubman's TT and Senior Manx GP.

And it did not take him long to claim his first TT either as a year later, as a fully fledged Norton works rider, he claimed victory in the Senior having come second in the Junior.

Such was his talent he continued to get faster while his riding style remained the same, taking a double win in 1951 and then a fourth TT in 1952 in the Junior, only missing out on yet another double after being forced to retire while leading the Senior.

Such was Duke prowess and national appeal, he was soon made an OBE and then decided to switch to the Italian Gilera team in 1953.

The move proved to be a success on the world stage, as he claimed three 500cc titles in a row, but he crashed out of the Senior in 1953 and was forced to pull in due to bad weather in 1954, but in 1955 he would once again stamp his authority all over the TT.

Despite Duke's run of bad luck, it was becoming increasingly clear the MV Agusta and the Gilera were very fast bikes, while the Matchless G50 was also a contender, and the Manx Norton seemed to handle all track conditions better, both abroad and at home. But it wasn't just on two . wheels where Nortons dominated. During the 1950s, sidecar racing was also seeing a boom in popularity across Europe and the leading British pair of Eric Oliver and Stan Dibben took many victories on a Manx Norton combo.

Renowned for his aggressive riding style, Oliver would become a four-time world sidecar champion missing out on just one of the opening five titles.

Norton was taken over by Associated Motorcycles in 1952, and in 1962 the Birmingham factory was closed, with production being moved to three AMC factories in Wolverhampton, Manchester and Plumstead.

Senior TT 1953

Amm wins in record-breaking fashion

The biggest change for 1953 was seeing Geoff Duke leave Norton for Gilera. Once there, he helped the factory team develop a four-cylinder machine but despite the pairing things did not start so well when racing on the island.

While leading the Senior, on lap four Duke crashed, which left the door open for Ray Amm to seal another win for Norton. And he did it in style too, lapping in 23 minutes and 16 seconds, while Jack Brett ensured it was a one-two for the British brand as he claimed second place.

Behind the scene, German manufacturer DKW, which had won a TT in 1938, returned to the island 15 years later with the aim of adding to their solitary victory.

Factory rider Siegfried Wunsche rode his DKW to third place in the Lightweight TT, behind Werner Haas, on an NSU, who came second.

The double podium, however, showed the revival of German-made machines was well and truly building momentum following the end of the Second World War.

The Lightweight race was eventually won by Fergus Anderson, who also finished third in the Junior TT.

There was even more movement behind the scenes. Les Graham, now based in Italy along with his family, had been busy working hard with Domenico Agusta to help develop his machines.

Graham's hard work would pay off too as he went on to win the Ultra-Lightweight TT on a 125cc Agusta, setting a lap record of 78.21mph However, joy soon turned to despair as Graham, riding a 500cc Agusta in the Senior TT, crashed at the bottom of Bray Hill and died.

The year 1954 was also significant as it marked the second time John Surtees had entered the TT.

Having won his first competitive race aged just 17, his father had persuaded him to take up the motorsport, particularly as he had raced sidecars himself.

Surtees went on to claim 15th in the Senior and 11th in the Junior, aged 20, but of course it would not be long before he was breaking records on both two and four-wheeled machines.

Amm had continued to raise the bar during 1954, increasing the Junior TT lap record to 94.61mph.

However, he would not claim the victory in that particular race as he was forced to hand the win to Rod Coleman, who was riding for the AJS team, after retiring at Barregarrow on lap five. Coleman, in turn, became the first New Zealander to win a TT.

But it was not all bad news during the 1954 race week as Amm would go on to claim victory in the 1954 Senior TT, which had been reduced to four laps due to weather.

Once again, it was the genius of McCandless who helped Amm claim victory, this time with his Ant Easter-designed motorbike, which ingeniously used side panels to carry extra fuel in the tanks. That, in turn, helped keep the weight low.

It was a great year for NSU in the Lightweight category too. The race was won by Werner Haas, who smashed the lap record with a 91.22mph effort, while team-mates Rupert Hollaus and Reg Armstrong ensured it was one-two-three for the NSU team.

Sidecar racing returned to the island again in 1954 but, instead of using the mountain circuit, it was raced around the shorter Clypse Course, which was 10.79 miles long. The circuit was also used by Ultra-Lightweight machines for a time too.

Senior TT 1955
Dominant Duke falls just short of 100mph lap

Eventually, the switch to Gilera machinery would reap the rewards for Geoff Duke who, rather than slowing down, was simply getting faster. He pushed towards the magical 100mph mark but the six-time TT winner would fall agonisingly short with a lap record of 99.97mph.

The result was not without controversy as Duke had in fact believed he had broken the 100mph lap barrier for the first time.

However, after his lap had been properly checked, it turned out he had registered a 99.97mph effort – about as close as you can get.

Duke, however, humble to the end, said after the race he was just pleased to have given Gilera its first TT win.

Seventy-seven riders from nine countries were lined up on the grid, with the greatest of all, the number 50, Duke, the favourite to win the Senior TT once again. Some 264 miles of twisting and turning mountain road awaited them, demanding the utmost from man and machine.

Duke was away on his Italian Gilera, one of the foreign bikes made for the event, which fans and commentators had already realised was competing well against the factory-line British models.

Duke was joined by Ken Kavanagh on a Gilera, while Reg Armstrong, on a Moto Guzzi – who would come third – was another British rider mounted on an Italian bike. The simple reason was because British-manufactured bikes would prove to be too slow to compete, and the top riders knew it.

After the opening lap, Duke was already leading – and the crowd, fans and commentators were all wishing him well as his last win had come way back in 1951. Plagued with bad luck, it appeared he had persistently been robbed of victory.

But there would be no bad luck on this occasion and Duke was followed home by his team-mate, Armstrong – who actually crossed the finish line first on the road – to make it a one-two for Gilera.

After six wins in six years, the 1954 Senior TT proved to be his last success on the Mountain Course and, although he continued racing at the TT until his retirement in 1959, he was unable to challenge for the race victories.

Duke would eventually set up home on the island and lived there until he passed away at the beginning of 2015, aged 92.

John Surtees had stuck with Norton and finished fourth in the 1955 Junior TT to show the watching world he was getting better and better with each passing year.

In the Clubman race of 1953, BSA-mounted army captain Eddie Dow rode the 500cc Gold Star single to victory, winning by more than a minute ahead of Ian Atkinson, who was riding a Triumph.

In third place was Manxman Raymond Kelly, on a Triumph Tiger 100.

There was more movement behind the scenes as Bob McIntyre left AJS to ride for Joe Potts, riding his 350cc Potts Norton, complete with dustbin fairing, to second in the Junior TT, which was won by Bill Lomas.

He then finished fifth in the Senior TT and decided to stay with the Glasgow-based racing team for another year.

Meanwhile, Lomas, backed by the factory Moto Guzzi team, had been in imperious form, again raising the Junior lap record, this time to 92.33mph, beating McIntyre in the process by a minute.

The year, however, would end in tragedy as the great Ray Amm, who had left Norton to join MV Agusta, would be killed at Imola, Italy, having only made his debut in the April of that same year for the Italian manufacturer.

A year later, Italian rider Carlo Ubbiali would continue to dominate the smaller classes, taking victory in the 125cc and 250cc classes in 1956, both on MV Agustas. He would eventually win five TTs and nine world championships.

Meanwhile, the sidecar race of that same year, won by BMW-backed Fritz Hillebrand, was not without its incidents.

Pip Harris and Ray Campbell came second on their Norton but were only handed the podiums after German Willi Noll was forced to pull in, despite having just set the fastest lap of the race.

Walter Schneider, winner the previous year, was also forced to retire.

John Surtees had, by this point, made the switch from Norton to MV Agusta. And after failing to finish the Junior TT he went on to take Agusta's first Senior TT victory in the process – beating John Hartle and Jack Brett.

The year 1956 was marked by the notable absences of Geoff Duke and Reg Armstrong. They had been given six-month bans by the FIM governing body for speaking up for riders who had agreed to strike following a ballot to get start money pay at the Dutch TT, in 1955, which had opened the field up even further – and Surtees had pounced.

And the good news just kept coming for Italian manufacturers as Ken Kavanagh – who had become the first Australian to win an FIM World Championship race with his victory in the 350cc Ulster GP race – riding a Moto Guzzi, claimed victory in the Junior TT, amazingly by completing the entire seven laps without refuelling.

Team-mate Bill Lomas had led before being forced to pull in after five laps. Surtees had then taken over at the helm only to run out of fuel on the final lap while leading over the mountain.

Junior TT 1957

Bob Mac claims his first TT win

The golden jubilee would turn out to be a very special meeting, with the Steam Packet ferries having to work harder than normal to bring the fans on to the island, such was the anticipation of what they knew would be a glorious occasion – and they were not disappointed either.

As the visiting motorbikes were lifted off the ferry with cranes, visitors had to buy their tax discs from the Manx government for riding on the roads.

The TT also celebrated its Golden Jubilee welcoming 15 different manufacturers to enter races across the fortnight.

As in further celebration, the Senior TT was raised to an eight-lap race to mark the special occasion, with races around the Clypse Course also extended to ten. Meanwhile, the Junior was held over seven laps, which was 264 miles – and taking his first victory on the island, riding a Gilera, was Bob McIntyre.

McIntyre not only won the race but did so with a new lap record of 97.42mph on his 350cc Gilera Four, averaging 94.99mph across the entire seven laps.

Victory was made a little easier when Dickie Dale and John Hartle both crashed, but Bob Mac would go on to create even more history later that week, becoming the first person to ever break the 100mph lap barrier.

In second place was Keith Campbell, who went on to become the world champion of 1957, riding a Moto Guzzi.

Australian Bob Brown would finish third in the Junior and Senior TTs, behind team-mate McIntyre and Moto Guzzi's Keith Campbell in the Junior. He also came third in the record-breaking Senior later that week, this time behind McIntyre and Surtees.

One for the home crowd was seeing Manxman Dennis Christian finishing 11th, to win a silver replica.

Wednesday's race action that same year was held on the Clypse Course, which had formally been a cycle course before housing the sidecar and Lightweight TTs for a number of years, from 1954 to 1959 to be exact, until all the races then returned to the Mountain Course. It had received its name because it circled the Clypse reservoir.

The first race round the Clypse Course that year was the Lightweight TT, and it seemed as though Carlo Ubbiali was heading for victory, especially as some of the fastest riders had discovered they could keep their corner speed even higher by using the pavement while travelling through Park Field.

Unfortunately, Tarquino Provini, who had taken the same line, eventually ran out of fuel, and Ubbiali was later forced to retire. It paved the way for eventual winner Cecil Sandford, who seemed to have a more orthodox line than his Italian competitors through Park Field, to take victory, winning by nearly two minutes in the end from Luigi Taveri and Roberto Columbo.

Sandford had led for most of the race, while Taveri and Columbo had worked their way through the field to each claim a podium spot.

Sammy Miller had been leading the Lightweight on the final lap before falling off his Mondial at Governor's Bridge but still managed to push the bike home to finish fifth.

The Ultra-Lightweight TT, a ten-lap race, had again been led by Miller on a Mondial, with Taveri and Ubbiali on MVs, close behind.

Again, the Italians decided to use as much of the road – and pavement – as possible to keep their speeds up. Provini would eventually claim the TT and was followed home by MV riders Ubbiali and Taveri.

Provini would also end the year as Ultra-Lightweight world champion. He was recruited by MV once Mondial had decided to withdraw from GP racing.

Another standout ride that year was from Swiss star Florian Camathias, who rode both in the Lightweight TT and the sidecars during his debut on the island.

He finished ninth in the Lightweight on an NSU, despite accidentally being flagged off after nine laps.

Officials decided to give him an aggregate time on his final circulation because of the error, which meant he was awarded a silver replica.

An hour later he was out racing on three wheels, around the same Clypse track, in a class dominated by BMWs, which took the top three places, with fourth to sixth positions going to Norton-mounted riders.

In the end it was Fritz Hillebrand and Manfred Grunwald who took top honours, with Walter Schneider and Hans

Strauss in second while third place went to Camathias and Jules Galliker.

Hillebrand would also go on to claim the world title that year but sadly Hillebrand would later die during a practice session at the Spanish GP.

Senior TT 1957
Bob Mac breaks the golden 100mph barrier

The Gilera team looked formidable and was originally supposed to contain the stellar line-up of Geoff Duke, Bob Brown and Bob McIntyre, but because Duke had suffered two crashes at Imola, he did not race.

Brown had started practice on a G45 Matchless but later swapped for the Gilera Four, while Stanley Woods, by now a ten-times TT winner, was out on a Moto Guzzi.

McIntyre, known to his legion of fans simply as Bob Mac, also entered the Lightweight race on a 250cc Norton but after practising on the Clypse Course decided to turn all his attention to making sure he could ride the Gilera to the best of his ability.

And the Scotsman would go on to the make the occasion extra special and extra memorable by breaking that elusive 100mph in the Senior TT on his unique and distinctive-looking Gilera 500, circulating in 22 minutes and 23.2 seconds, at an average speed of 101.12mph.

Bob Mac may have been helped on his way to immortality by being chased by motorsport legend John Surtees – the only man to win a world title on two wheels and four – who was riding an MV Agusta at the time.

Surtees, humble to the core, said that if anyone was going to break the 100mph barrier, 'it was someone like Bob' and he explained how he had been very happy for him at the time, particularly as the Scotsman, by this time, already had great experience of racing on the Isle of Man. Members of the vintage motorcycle club took their pre-1930 machines out for a lap of the course before the Senior TT got underway.

Jack Brett then went off number one, heaving his Norton off the start line, much to the delight of the eager crowd.

Despite being the fastest Norton rider for most of the race, he slid off at Quarry Bends on the sixth lap.

Keith Campbell was riding a Guzzi Single and finished fifth, although happier times would come his way later in the season as he won the 350cc world title.

Bob Mac started his race in truly stunning fashion, hitting 99.99mph on his opening lap.

Thousands of fans had made the pilgrimage to the island for the Senior, thanks to excursions laid on by the press, which meant a coach or train journey to Liverpool, with a ferry to Douglas, before another coach then took them to a place on the track. Most returned back home that same day.

During that era the 'bungalow' still sat on the track on the mountain section, right on the racing line, before it was finally demolished a year later. Many a rider had suffered scary moments heading towards that building while travelling at speed.

Eventually, averaging just under 99mph, Bob Mac ensured the huge crowds were treated to something truly special as he took the chequered flag to be crowned the winner, followed home by Surtees and fellow Gilera rider Bob Brown.

Bob Mac would only claim three TT race victories but he was still revered as one of the UK's finest riders as there had been many an occasion when, leading the field in blistering fashion, his machine had broken down. And yet, like all riders of his generation, he would never complain, being a hard-riding, tough Scotsman. He was simply happy to win when he could.

Having won the Manx GP during his debut in 1952, it set the scene for what was about to come. After taking second, his first podium, in 1955 Junior TT, he split from the works Moto Guzzi and instead focussed on racing as a privateer.

His big break really came when Duke was injured early in 1957 and he was asked to replace his close rival in the works Gilera team.

McIntyre paid their faith back in superb style, and ensured his name would forever remain in the record books, as he became the first man to lap the Mountain Course at more than 100mph during the gruelling eight-lap Senior, having also won the Junior TT four days before.

When the Italian manufacturers decided to pull out at the end of the 1957 season, he returned to Norton.

Bob Mac picked up his third TT win a year later, in 1959, again ensuring his name would forever be in the record books as he claimed the inaugural 500cc Formula 1 race.

He switched to Honda for the 1961 and 1962 campaigns and, despite still having the pace, nearly breaking the 100mph lap record in Junior, bike problems continued to plague him.

A crash in pouring rain at Oulton Park in August 1962 saw him sustain serious injuries and he succumbed to the injuries nine days later but would always be remembered as a true star of the TT and motorcycle racing world.

Senior TT 1958

Surtees wins the first of two back-to-back doubles

Surtees may have missed out on the first 100-plus lap, but he did do the double in 1958 and 1959, when he also claimed his own lap record – which he again increased the following year.

He explained how his record-breaking effort had not left him tense and he had not gone out to try and prove any points; instead they had just been occasions when the bike was working well and he had managed to create a partnership with the machine – and of course with a further year's knowledge of the circuit, it had helped bring it all together.

Surtees's first priority was always to try and simply win the race – but he admitted having some cream on the cake by also having the lap record making the win even nicer.

Behind the scenes there was also a lot of change too as, despite dominating much of the 1957 TT, Gilera withdrew from the GP scene, which forced the likes of Bob Mac to return to British manufacturers, namely Norton.

With FB Mondial and Moto Guzzi following Gilera out of competing, it opened up the playing field a little more once again.

Bob Mac lapped at 99.98mph on the Norton during the 1958 Senior only for engine failure to scupper his chances on the third lap while sitting second.

Meanwhile, Dickie Dale had moved from Moto Guzzi to BMW to take on the might of John Surtees and the MVs.

But it proved to be an unhappy hunting ground for BMWs that particular year as Dale finished 11th in the 500cc while team-mate Geoff Duke, racing in his first TT since 1955, broke down on the opening lap.

The year was also highly significant because it marked the debut of a certain Mike Hailwood, who went on to finish the Junior TT in 12th, on a Norton Manx. He also finished third on an NSU Sportsman in the 250cc Lightweight TT.

In 1959, the 350cc and 500cc, for standard racing machines – used by non-factory teams and privateers – was added to the programme and would take place over the Mountain Course.

That same year marked the second time a future TT star, Southern Rhodesia's Jim Redman, had raced at the TT. Before switching to Hondas, he rode to seventh in the 350cc class in the Formula 1 TT.

The 1959 sidecar race proved to be an intriguing affair as BMW factory rider, Walter Schneider – who had also won a TT in 1955, and was the world champion in 1958 and 1959 – beat Florian Camathias and passenger Hilmar Cecco, who were also BMW-mounted.

Both would sadly lose their lives in the years ahead, with Cecco being killed at Modena in 1961 and Camathias at Brands Hatch in 1965.

Schneider's domination would continue into 1959 as he claimed back-to-back Sidecar TT wins.

His fastest lap of 74.04mph in 1958 remains a TT lap record to this day, because sidecars were raced around the Clypse Course at the TT for the final time a year later. Sidecars returned to the Mountain Course in 1960, which meant the German's record around the much shorter circuit would remain in perpetuity for ever.

But it was Surtees who remained the dominant force, upping the lap record once more in 1959 to 101.18mph in the Senior TT.

He went on to collect his fourth and fifth titles, adding another in the 350cc class.

The Senior had proved to be a torrid affair with terrible weather conditions blighting the race and riders.

It had already been cancelled once, moving from the Friday to the Saturday, but once again poor weather moved in.

Surtees had broken the lap record on the opening lap, when he broke the 101mph barrier, but was soon lapping

4mph slower because of the atrocious conditions. But he persevered and eventually claimed the victory while his team-mate, John Hartle, crashed out.

Surtees walked from motorbike racing in 1961 and signed for Ferrari in the Formula 1 World Championship.

He took the F1 title just two years later and went on to win six F1 races before retiring in 1972. He passed away in 2017.

Surtees competed in 15 TT races in total before concentrating on racing cars, finished in all except the 1956 Junior.

He rode Norton's first in 1954 and then turned to MV Agusta in 1956 – and his records on the Italian machines were truly spectacular as he claimed four wins and a second in the Senior TT between the years of 1956 and 1960, as well as two firsts, a second and a fourth in the Junior.

The only thing that equalled his speed on track was his sportsmanship off, which made him one of motorsport's genuine heroes and icons.

Japanese manufacturer Honda made its first foray into European racing in 1959 and chose the TT to showcase its latest machines, with Suzuki following closely behind along with Yamaha. Despite being down on pace in the Ultra-Lightweight class, their reliability shone through.

It was 7 May 1959, when Honda arrived on the Isle of Man for the first time.

Little did the public know the manufacturer would go on to smash pretty much every record going on the island.

After finishing sixth during their first visit, they would go on to win another two (1983 and 2019).

Among those wins would be Joey Dunlop's victory in 2000, Hutchy's record five TT wins in a week in 2010, Honda's own 100th win in 1998 and numerous race and lap records, including John McGuinness's first 130mph during the century year in 2007, Steve Hislop's 120mph lap in 1989 and even Michael Rutter's 121mph lap on an electric bike in 2019.

The records have tumbled across all classes in every decade since the team first set foot on the island in 1959.

When Honda first started out, they purely focussed on 125cc machines. Two years later there would be a small sign of what was to come, as the team dominated both the 125cc and 250cc classes at the TT.

Soichiro Honda had travelled to the island prior to his team's visit on a fact-finding mission when he discovered what it took to take a TT-winning machine.

After deciding against competing between the years of 1954 and 1958, he finally set sail for the island with his team a year later.

Honda entered five racers in the Ultra-Lightweight class, who had all studied the course intensely referring to a guide that had been written by Geoff Duke.

However, most of their revision had appeared to be in vain – because at that time the Ultra-Lightweight class was raced around the Clypse Course and not the Mountain Course.

Honda also wanted to double the power of the bike's output. After replacing the bike's single-cylinder machine with a brand-new twin, they were then forced to fly in some new valve heads to get them to work effectively.

The Hondas had beautiful engines but it was the chassis that were letting them down.

However, with the team squashed together in a little hotel, the riders put their spare time to good use by getting to learn the Clypse Course, as well as working on their bikes and preparing for the first practice session.

Although the bikes ran well, they needed a lot of adjusting, which meant buying parts locally on the island.

Naomi Taniguchi was the fastest qualifier out of the team, posting the 12th quickest time. Experienced riders like Bob McIntyre were already starting to take an interest in these new, exotic machines too.

Come race day and Tangiguchi had managed to make up managed to make up half a dozen places finishing the race in a very impressive sixth.

Behind him were his team-mates Giichi Suzuki and Tanaika, with Junzo Suzuki in 11th. Their results were enough for Honda to claim the overall team prize on their first visit to the island.

That was the carrot they really needed and it marked the beginning of a truly remarkable dynasty. The manufacturer would become part of the fabric of the TT.

Two years later, in 1961, Honda claimed victory in the 125cc class, with Tom Phillis piloting the winning machine, while Mike Hailwood claimed victory in the 250cc class too.

And if that was not impressive enough, Honda also took the top five spots in both races for good measure.

Hailwood would also win the 250cc world championship while Phillis dominated the 125cc class.

In 1977, Honda went on to claim all three class wins in the new road-based world championship, once the TT had lost its GP status, with Phil Read winning the Formula 1 race, Alan Jackson the Formula 2 and John Kidson the Formula 3.

Joey Dunlop claimed his first Formula 1 TT on a Honda, which would mark an era of total domination in that class as the rider and manufacturer remained undefeated for a further six years.

In 1988, Honda won three TTs in a single week, courtesy of Joey in the F1 and Senior, while Hislop would take victory in the Production TT.

Honda's 100th win on the island came in 1998 courtesy of Jim Moodie. The year 2000 would be filled with absolute joy and despair as Joey, in his 25th year of racing on the Isle of Man, would take three TT wins in a week, all on board Hondas, before tragically losing his life while racing in Estonia later that same year.

Another TT legend who stepped in to keep Honda's winning streak going was McGuinness, who set the first 130mph during the TT's 100th anniversary.

And the Dunlop name would also remain synonymous with the Honda brand when Michael Dunlop, Joey's nephew, clocked an average lap speed of 129.197mph during the opening 2018 supersport race. It also marked Honda's 170th victory on the island.

Lightweight TT 1961

Hailwood's victory sets up first three TTs wins in a week
During the 1960s, the TT was seen as one of the most prestigious races on the FIM World Championship calendar, due to its challenging, unique and dangerous nature of the 37.73-mile track.

The grids were also bigger than most due to the fact it included non-championship riders. And riders also came from all corners of the globe, with 25 manufacturers from seven different countries also all vying for top spot on the TT podium.

Honda and Suzuki had withdrawn from the championship by 1967 but Yamaha continued to compete and sold many of its bikes to privateers, helping to keep such championships afloat.

By the 1960s, the Japanese manufacturers had begun entering their machines to contest the TT and immediately began making their mark, which was a sign of the complete domination that would follow in later years.

The Clypse Course had also been dropped altogether with all races now taking place over the mountain. The Ultra-Lightweight and sidecar races were held over three laps and the Lightweight over five, with riders battling for six laps in the Junior and Senior races.

Gary Hocking, riding an MV Agusta, would go on to win the 1960 Lightweight TT, beating team-mate Carlo Ubbiali.

Ubbiali set a new lap record on a 250cc-class machine, lapping at 95.47mph during the race, knocking Tarquinio Provini, who was riding a Moto Morini, into third place.

It marked the beginning of another truly dominant year for MV, with the manufacturer going on to win every solo race in 1960, a repeat of its stunning performance in 1958.

Another notable finisher in the 250cc race was Bob Brown. He had switched from Gilers to Norton, once the Italian manufacturers had pulled out of GP racing, but by 1960 he had been drafted in by Honda to compete in the 250cc race. He went on to finish fourth, becoming the manufacturer's highest-placed racer.

Brown also jumped back on a Norton to finish fifth in the Senior TT. And yet the year would end in tragedy as Brown would lose his life riding a 250cc Honda during the West German GP.

Over in the MV Agusta garage, John Hartle went to victory in the Junior TT, finally beating his rival and team-mate, John Surtees.

Surtees had, in fact, been leading the race, breaking the lap record in the process with a 99.20mph effort on his 350cc machine, only for gearbox problems to end his hopes of a win and knock him back to second place.

Hartle, who would leave MV at the end of the season, pounced to take the win with a new record of his own, averaging 96.70mph over the course of the entire race.

However, Surtees would gain revenge in the Senior TT, taking the win over Hartle while once again breaking the lap record in the process with a time of 104.08mph. Mike Hailwood brought his Norton home in third place.

Another big move saw the return of the sidecars to the Mountain Course, having moved from the Clypse Course to join the solos on the 37.73-mile track

It was the first time since the 1920s the three-wheeled machines had been able to compete on the same circuit as the bigger solos machines – and the sidecar racers were still using standard-framed motorcycles at the time.

The race was eventually won by Helmut Fath and his passenger Alfred Wohlgemuth – with the passenger playing a pivotal role in the win.

On the final lap, the fuel pump on their BMW had failed, but rather than panic or retire, Wohlgemuth blew down the tube to supply the engine with petrol. Sadly, a year later, while racing at the Nurburgring, he was killed in a crash.

The accident had also left Fath, the 1960 world champion, with serious injuries. Yet he was still able to make a comeback, building his own engine and racing it to his second world title in 1968.

The year 1961 saw more of the best racing from Hailwood and Phil Read, who were both aged 22 at the time.

Although Hailwood was not on a works Honda for the TT that year, his father had made sure he had the best Hondas for both the Lightweight and Ultra-Lightweight TT races.

And the investment paid off too as Hailwood went on to give the Japanese manufacturers their first TT wins on the Monday of race week.

The Lightweight TT had been the first race of the week for the riders, as they prepared to head back over the island's Mountain Course in anger.

First off the line was Jim Redman on his Honda, followed by Naomi Taniguchi riding for the same manufacturer.

Luigi Taveri, from Switzerland, was also on a Honda and, along with Hailwood, they had both caught Redman by Sulby on the opening lap.

By the Guthrie Memorial, both had passed Redman and Taveri was doing his best to lose Hailwood as they continued circulating together as they reached Signpost Corner, with Redman just behind on the road.

Taveri had narrowly taken the lead by Governor's Bridge on the roads but it was Hailwood leading on time as he broke the lap record by nearly 2mph.

A truly epic battle for the outright lead commenced, with Taveri and Mike the Bike neck and neck heading into Ginger Hall. On lap two, Hailwood's truly wondrous skills on a motorbike had again come to the fore as he broke the lap record for a second time, this time nearly hitting 88mph, again taking the outright lead in the process.

Honda-mounted riders completely dominated the Lightweight TT that year throughout as Hailwood eventually went on to take the win from Taveri by just seven seconds, eventually raising the lap record to 88.45mph.

Read, from Luton, had won the Senior Manx GP the year before and wasted no time notching his first TT win, taking the Junior TT on his debut, riding a Norton.

Gary Hocking had been leading the race, while raising the lap record to 99.80mph, until he suffered mechanical problems. Hailwood had also temporarily taken the lead too but his AJS 7R's engine failed on the final lap.

Read's win would also be the last time a British bike would win the Junior TT for 20 years.

However, it would not take long for Hailwood to make amends as he would pick up his third TT victory in the Senior and, in doing so, became the first racer to ever win three TTs in a week – having already claimed the Ultra-Lightweight and Lightweight TTs.

Averaging 100.60mph on a Norton, he beat fellow Norton-mounted Bob Mac into second place.

Again, the win would be a significant one for the British manufacturer who would have to wait another 31 years for another Senior win, when Steve Hislop would beat Carl Fogarty in 1992, in one of the most intense and memorable battles ever seen on the island.

Hislop's win would also be the first time any British-built bike had won a TT since Hailwood's victory in 1961.

Another standout performer in the 1961 Senior TT was Tom Phillis, who had taken over from Read to ride the factory Norton to a podium spot, coming third.

Finishing behind Hailwood and Hocking, he had lapped at 101.36mph, becoming the first racer to lap the TT course over 100mph while riding a twin-cylinder machine.

Lightweight TT 1962

Minter a surprise but worthy winner

The Lightweight TT had a surprise winner in the form of Derek Minter, who took victory ahead of a race that had just seven finishers.

Having been loaned a Honda 750cc for the race, he claimed a stunning win while his fellow competitors dropped all around him like flies.

Bob McIntyre had set a new lap record of 99.06mph during the race before being forced to retire, while a fuel cap problem meant Honda's leading rider, Jim Redman, was also forced to drop out.

Tom Phillis also suffered a misfire, which ultimately cleared the way for the Minter to take the win after six gruelling laps.

The race nearly ended in disaster for Minter too but he was just about able to hold his bike together to cross the finish line despite his engine beginning to break up.

Another surprise followed in the sidecar race as Chris Vincent and passenger Eric Bliss took victory.

Vincent also worked for BSA at the time and his victory gave the Birmingham manufacturer its first TT win.

BMW had been expected to dominate the sidecar race but Florian Camathias crashed and another race favourite, Max Deubel, was forced to retire.

BMW, however, did manage to salvage second place thanks to the efforts of Otto Kolle, while in third was Colin Seeley and his passenger, Wally Rawlings, on a Matchless 50. They had managed to beat three BMWs to claim the final rostrum position. He also broke the lap record for a single-cylinder machine, with an average lap speed of 83.13mph.

In 1962, the two-lap 50cc race was added, which was won by Ernst Degner of West Germany, ahead of Taveri and Tommy Robb.

The Junior TT that year was also hard fought with Hailwood – who by now had lost the support of the Honda garage, having decided to ride for MV Privat Equip, a rival to the Japanese company, in the 1961 350cc TT race – enjoying numerous race-long battles.

But he still managed to claim yet another win, setting a lap record of 101.58mph after first beating away the advances of Honda-mounted Bob McIntyre and Tom Phillis, and then pipping his fellow MV Privat Equip rider, Gary Hocking.

Third-placed rider in the Junior TT was Czech racer Frantiser Stastny, on a 350cc Jawa. Stastny, who had ridden for the Czechoslovakian team since the 1950s, had also shown his stellar by winning the 1961 West German GP.

The Privat name had come about after Count Agusta, who had two years previously said he would no longer be running teams in GPs, had been convinced to change his mind.

And the decision proved to be a fruitful one too as Hocking went on to claim the 350cc and 500cc titles, despite suffering a 120mph crash during the TT race fortnight.

Gary Hocking would also reign supreme in the Senior TT, breaking the lap record with a lap of 21 minutes and 24.4 seconds, at 105.75mph, while Hailwood would only manage to finish 12th.

The MV had proved to be a formidable machine on the island between the years of 1947 and 1962, taking 21 TTs, while Norton had claimed 17, Moto Guzzi eight, BMW seven, Honda four, FB Mondial three, Gilera three, Velocette three and NSU two during that same period, while AJS, Benelli, BSA and Suzuki all claimed one apiece.

During the 125cc race, Taveri had broken his own lap record, becoming the first rider to break 100mph in that class.

The Swiss star would become known as the Ultra-Lightweight TT king after being followed home by four fellow Honda riders.

Phillis had managed to finish third in the Ultra-Lightweight race behind team-mates Taveri and Tommy Robb before suffering a tragic accident, as the reigning Honda 125cc world champion would lose his life after crashing at Laurel Bank in the Junior later that same week.

Phillis, a motor engineer from Marrickville, New South Wales, began his successful racing career in his homeland winning six major event between the years of 1953 and 1957.

A year later he had first raced outside Australia and stunned the paddock by winning four events at Thruxton, in Hampshire. That same year he entered the Junior and Senior TTs, coming 32nd and 18th respectively, which earned him two silver replicas.

Phillis continued to dominate racing back home claiming the 350cc and 500cc class titles in the Australian TT, which was raced at Albany, Western Australia, as well as 500cc class at Victoria GP.

His stunning performances continued in Australia during the 1959 campaign and on his return to the island he had no luck, as he was forced to retire from the Junior and then finished in 16th during the treacherous Senior TT, which was good enough for a bronze replica.

Undeterred, he returned a year later to compete in all four solo classes, finishing 10th in the Ultra-Lightweight and fourth in the Senior, while retiring in the others.

But his talents were there for all to see as after finishing second at the Ulster GP he went on to win three races in a week at the Pyynikin TT, in Finland, winning the 125, 350 and 500cc races.

In Europe he also scored numerous podiums the Spanish, Austrian and French GPs.

He would come closest to winning a TT at the Isle of Man during the 1961 campaign, coming second in the Lightweight 250cc and third in the Lightweight 125cc and Senior TTs before losing his life a year later.

The Australian's death would also have a tragic knock-on effect because later that same year Hocking, who was a close friend, had been hit particularly hard by Phillis's fatal crash in the Junior TT and had decided to switch from motorbikes to racing cars instead.

However, he would also lose his life while racing on four wheels in South Africa in December of the 1962.

It left Hocking, a Welsh-born Rhodesian, with a brief but impressive TT career that had lasted just four years.

Opening his TT account with a 12th-placed finish in the 1959 Junior TT on a Norton, he returned to ride MV Agusta the following year and took a superb win in the Lightweight TT, despite the challenge from Honda and its growing reputation.

Hocking suffered plenty of frustration in 1961, with a best of second in the Junior behind Read, and he went on to claim a second TT win TT in the Senior before the series of tragedies claimed the lives of both him and his friend.

The 1962 TT campaign was also significant because Beryl Swain became the first woman to race on the Mountain Course when she entered the 50cc race on board an Itom.

Swain went on to first finish 22nd but, aside from her performance on a machine that was suffering with mechanical problems, she later had her licence revoked by the male-dominated elite.

The ban stayed in place for 14 years and was only lifted when Hilary Musson competed in the Formula 2 TT.

Lightweight TT 1963
Redman opens his TT account

With safety slowly becoming more of a priority, helicopters to airlift injured riders and spectators were first introduced in 1963 – the same year Honda's Jim Redman won the first of his six TT wins by claiming victory in the Lightweight race.

The race had been led by Fumio Ito, of Japan, on a Yamaha – who would claim the Ultra-Lightweight TT –

but a long pit stop cost him and he had to settle for second place behind Redman, who in later years would also become known as a voice for getting better pay for all the riders.

Bill Smith, also riding a Honda, came third. Smith's affiliation with the Isle of Man TT would eventually see him enjoy a lengthy and successful TT career as he continued competing between 1957 right up until 2000, picking four superb wins along the way.

Tommy Robb, who had been signed by Honda, had to settle for fifth place due to exhaust problems. Redman would also claim the Junior title to make it two in a week.

But when it came to the Senior, Hailwood reclaimed his title as King of the Mountain, as he dominated from start to finish while raising the lap record to 106.41mph.

John Hartle, on a Gilera, came second while Tom Arter, who had broken the 100mph lap barrier the previous year, took the final podium spot.

The sidecar race was won by Florian Camathias and fellow Swiss competitor Fritz Sceidegger, with the Birch brothers, Alan and Peter – not to be confused with today's sidecar stars, the Birchalls – coming third in only their second TT. All were powered by the dominant BMWs.

Redman was also back at it again in 1964, as he reclaimed the Lightweight TT on a Honda, ahead of Alan Shepherd, who rode his two-stroke MZ to second place.

Shepherd, who was riding with a collarbone injury, had shown he was no slouch too having won the US 250cc GP Daytona.

He would sign for Honda later that same year but after being left with head injuries following a crash in Japan he decided to retire soon after.

The sidecar race was won by Max Deubel and passenger Emil Hoener while Colin Seeley, passengered by Wally

Rawlings – who had been lent Florian Camathias's BMW in return for supporting the Swiss rider's championship bid – came second.

Camathias, meanwhile, had borrowed four-cylinder engines from Gilera in a quest for the title but instead had a race to forget.

Despite losing factory support, he was still leading the sidecar race before losing fourth gear and hitting bank at Creg-ny-Baa, slightly injuring passenger Alfred Herzog in the process, on his way to a very disappointing 15th-place finish. Deubel would go on to claim his fourth straight sidecar title.

It was business as usual in the Senior TT, which was won by Mike Hailwood, who took victory by more than three minutes from his nearest rival, Derek Minter.

Even more amazing, Mike the Bike had been battling illness throughout the week too.

Norton-mounted Minter, meanwhile, had enjoyed a race-long battle with Matchless riders Fred Stevens and Derek Woodman en route to second place. His rivals would finish third and fourth respectively.

In the 125cc TT, Luigi Taveri followed up his success in 1962 with another victory two years later.

The Swiss rider had also claimed the 125cc titles in both of his TT-winning years, as well as claiming a third in 1966.

Sandwiched in between was another TT success in 1965, in the 50cc class, all while riding for Honda following his switch from MV Agusta.

Lightweight 250cc TT 1965

Redman and Honda a match made in heaven

Jim Redman rode the six-cylinder Honda to its first victory during the 1965 Lightweight TT.

Taking the lead after Phil Read's Yamaha had seized, Redman clocked speeds of nearly 145mph and went on to break the 100mph lap for the second time in a 250cc race en route to his win.

Mike Duff, on a Yamaha, came second, with Suzuki's Fred Perris third and Benelli rider Tarquinio Provini fourth, meaning four different manufacturers were in the top four.

Provini returned in 1966, but after badly injuring his back following a nasty crash it ended his career as he was forced to retire.

Behind the scenes, Italian 350cc champion Giacomo Agostini had decided to swap teams and was now riding MV Agusta's 350cc, which would see him go on to completely dominate the championship in years to come.

Under the guidance of Mike Hailwood, he was soon into the swing of things, finishing third in the Junior TT with a lap of 98.5mph.

Hailwood had again broken the lap record in the same race, with a 102.85mph effort, but he was unable to follow up his impressive pace with a win after his drive chain broke.

The race was won by Redman, who made it two in a week, while Phil Read managed to come second on his water-cooled Yamaha 250cc despite having a smaller engine size than most of his rivals.

Read had also broken the 100mph lap barrier in the Lightweight TT, becoming the first rider to do so in the process, but this time Lady Luck decided to abandon him as mechanical problems on the mountain section scuppered any chances of adding to his TT wins tally.

Read, however, got to give Yamaha victory in the Lightweight 125cc TT.

The Senior TT was a memorable race for all the wrong reasons as bad weather plagued the entire race.

Even greats like Hailwood and Agostini slid off during the race, but such was the slow pace – due to poor conditions – Hailwood was still able to remount, head back to the pits and go on to claim yet another victory.

German Georg Auerbacher and Brit Peter Ryders rode their BMW to third in the Sidecar TT in 1964, behind winners Max Deubel and Emil Horner, which was a sign of things to come.

Auerbacher would continue to show his talent for racing and also engine building in later years, reaching the podium several times before taking his first TT win in 1971. He was also a world championship runner-up in 1967 and 1968.

The year 1965 was also a significant one because it marked Tony Rutter's debut at the TT.

He would go on to become one of the TT's finest competitors and became known as the rider who could win on anything – and few could argue during the years of 1973 and 1985 when he picked up all seven of his TT wins.

Rutter also claimed four Formula Two world championships but his career was cut short by a terrible crash at Montjuïc circuit, Barcelona, Spain, in 1985, when he was still at the peak of his powers.

He bravely raced on after recovering but decided to retire from racing at the TT in 1991, only a few years before his son, Michael, would take up the mantle.

Sidecar 500 TT 1966
Close race fuelled by controversy
In 1966, the TT was delayed until August because of a seaman's strike but when it finally got underway the Ultra-Lightweight race would prove to be a fascinating affair as Bill Ivy, racing at just his second TT, on a Yamaha, set a new lap record of 98.55mph on his way to a stunning maiden victory.

He beat fellow Yamaha rider Phil Read into second in the process, with Suzuki's Hugh Anderson in third and fellow Yamaha rider Mike Duff in fourth.

In the Senior, it was business as usual as Hailwood won and set a new lap record of 107.07mph. He was simply unstoppable. However, it was the sidecar race that claimed all the headlines during the 1966 Isle of Man TT.

But rather than the race itself, it was what went on behind the scenes that made it such a memorable one.

Swiss driver and reigning world champion Fritz Scheidegger took the chequered flag, along with British passenger John Robinson, ahead of Max Deubel, who was less than a second behind – 0.6 seconds to be exact – in second place.

However, it transpired Scheidegger had used Esso fuel rather than Shell, which was against race regulations.

After an official ruling, Deubel was initially given the win but months later, and following two appeals, Scheidegger was finally awarded his first TT victory. Sadly, he did not have much time to celebrate his win as he was killed just a year later during a race at Mallory Park.

History had also been made before any of the riders had even lined up, because 28 August 1966 saw the 500cc sidecar race became the first TT to ever be held on a Sunday.

Deubel and passenger Emil Horner had led the field at the end of the first lap – in fact, their lead over world championship Scheidegger and Robinson had been raised to a formidable-looking 12 seconds.

A lap later, Deubel had increased his lead to 15 seconds, but on the final circulation Scheidegger was on the charge and closing rapidly. By the Bungalow, the Swiss driver had amazingly taken the lead and then it became a nervous waiting game for Deubel as to who crossed the line first.

The German was forced to wait for 40 seconds to see if he had done enough to claim the win but as Scheidegger and Robinson stormed past the chequered flag he claimed the win by one of the closest margins in TT history.

And to make matters even worse for Deubel, after Scheidegger had been stripped of the win only to claim victory once more following his double appeal, the extra eight points were also enough for him to take a second World Sidecar Championship crown.

The Junior TT, which had been held up until 4pm after fog had delayed the 125cc race, was won by Giacomo Agostini on his 350cc MV.

Behind the dominant Italian, Australian Jack Aharn had found himself in a great three-way battle with Peter Williams and Chris Conn for second place.

In the end, Aharn eventually slotted into fourth at the finish line, behind second-placed AJS rider Williams and Norton's Conn.

Hailwood had failed to trouble the podium positions having been forced to retire without even completing a single lap.

But the Junior TT was not without its controversies too as Czech rider Frantisek had been temporarily placed on the podium only for it to later be confirmed the CZ rider had in fact finished fifth.

The 50cc victory went to Honda's Ralph Bryans, from Ulster, who had claimed the 50cc world title the previous year. The reigning world champion also finished third in the 125cc race.

The year was also significant as, in 1966, Redman announced his retirement from motorbike racing following a crash at the Belgian GP, which left him with a badly damaged arm.

Redman would go down in TT folklore for many reasons, but perhaps his greatest achievement came in winning three doubles on the island, in three back-to-back years.

During the years of 1963, 1964 and 1965 he won both the Lightweight Junior TT races – a stunning record.

Between 1958 and 1960, he mainly raced on Norton machinery but was only able to get a best result of seventh in the Junior TT, which came in his debut year.

Honda, however, had noticed his drive and potential early on, so much so he was recruited to join the factory team in 1960.

Redman was immediately on the pace too, riding the four-cylinder 250cc machine to third in the Lightweight, followed by a fourth in the 125cc class.

A year later, he improved further to second place in the 250cc class and then secured his first of six TT wins in 1962. That win would be the beginning of his three TT doubles in three years.

He also claimed further doubles too, claiming the 250cc and 350cc world championships in 1962 and 1963, as well as retaining the 350cc championship in 1964 and 1965 – making it four in a row on the bigger bike.

Redman certainly enjoyed six-of-the-best throughout his racing years, winning six TTs and six world titles during a career that saw him awarded an MBE in recognition of his achievements in later life.

ISLE OF MAN TT MEMORIES

John Dickenson, from Laxey, on the Isle of Man, competed in the Manx GP between 1980 and 1985. He has lived on the Isle of Man all his life:

I'm going back over 50 years to when, aged 12, I can still remember watching what turned out to be one of the most famous and memorable races in TT history, namely the 1967 Diamond Jubilee Senior TT. Back then, if my memory serves me correctly, each race day would consist of completing my paper round as early as possible, then meeting up with my friend, Roger Luckman, who used to stay at our house during TT week when his parents went on holiday.

We would then go to Laxey tram station to see which driver or brakeman would let us hitch a ride on the back or front steps of one of the Snaefell mountain trams, a practice I'm sure must have been discontinued many years ago.

Once arriving at the Bungalow we would 'watch' the morning race there while collecting any empty lemonade bottles from the many spectators who also watched on the mountain, in order to reclaim the old three pence deposit, I think it was, paid on the bottles at the Bungalow café.

After collecting more empties during the break, between races we would then walk over to the Graham Memorial bend, or as it was more commonly known by the locals in those days, the Stone Bridge, not Bungalow Bridge, as it is now referred to.

The Friday morning race in the mid-60s was the three-lap massed start 50cc race, which I must admit to having no recollection of back in 1967.

The records show it was won by Stuart Graham from Hans-Georg Anscheidt on the works Suzukis.

I do remember those little bikes being a tremendous feat of Japanese engineering with a twin-cylinder two-stroke disc valve engine and a 500rpm wide-power band, between 17,000 and 17,500 rpm.

To make these tiny machines rideable they were fitted with a 14-speed gearbox to keep them in the power band.

It's hard to imagine the number of gear changes required per lap!

The much anticipated Senior race was the classic duel between Mike Hailwood, on the more powerful but harder to ride four-cylinder Honda, and Giacomo Agostini on the lighter better handling three-cylinder MV Agusta.

I remember there being a cine film crew located at the Graham Memorial and I think we appeared very briefly on the official film of the race.

The race itself has been well documented in the past but the most memorable moments for me were the anticipation, waiting for the first bikes to arrive, as you could hear the multi-cylinder machines from a long way off down the mountain.

Then there were the tremendous corner speeds of the riders on the bumpier, less well-surfaced roads, with the added problem of melting tar in places.

And, finally, listening to the Manx Radio commentary, especially during the pit stops with the frantic work involved in attempting to repair Mike's loose twist-grip throttle.

Of course, the announcement Ago's chain had come off on the approach to Windy Corner while narrowly leading the race on the fifth lap soon followed.

Being a Hailwood fan in those days, I was happy he won the race but still felt sorry for Ago who had ridden so well in a tremendous battle that resulted in Mike's outright lap record of 108.77mph lasting for eight years.

On a personal note, Roger and I still often go to the races and practices together.

After all these years our enthusiasm for the TT, Manx GP and Classic TT still continues.

Incidentally, Roger became the first rider to lap at more than 100mph in the Newcomers MGP on his way to winning the 1979 350cc race, narrowly beating Rob McElnea, who was a few years later destined to be a TT winner and works 500cc Grand Prix rider.

Senior TT 1967

Ago and Hailwood go toe-to-toe

Fifty years ago, two of the greatest-ever TT riders moved the lap times around the Mountain Course up to speeds some riders today would be happy with.

Hailwood had switched to Japanese machinery by moving to Honda in 1966 but would face a challenge from an Italian rider on an Italian bike, with the great Giacomo Agostini pushing him on to yet another lap record during one of the most memorable TT races of all time.

When the greatest riders of their generation are pitted against each other and go head-to-head, on the world's toughest and most exhilarating track, it's safe to assume there will be some fireworks.

Hailwood and Giacomo 'Ago' Agostini would dice for the lead throughout the 1967 Senior TT, shattering records while racing at a breathtaking pace.

Ago set the benchmark early on, smashing the lap record on the opening lap with 108.38mph.

The race also marked a battle between two of the biggest manufacturers, with Hailwood mounted on a Honda and Ago thrashing an MV Agusta.

All in all, seven riders would go on to break the 100mph barrier, such was the blistering pace in perfect conditions.

Williams had managed to smash through the barrier from a standing start, which would eventually help him to finish second behind Hailwood, following Ago's breakdown late in the race on lap five.

Hailwood had started the race 30 seconds ahead on the road. It meant the 25-year-old Italian knew he had his work cut out to chase down the master, who had already claimed victory in the 350cc TT – but that was exactly what he did.

Ago had soon established an eight-second lead having smashed through the 21-minute barrier as his record-breaking lap came to an end.

Hailwood had also started very quickly, posting an opening lap of 107.37mph, but he knew he would have to push even harder, especially with Arter, Blanchard, Williams and Spencer also nipping at his heels.

Hailwood really tried to put the hammer down at the start of lap two but Ago still managed to maintain his eight-second lead.

Both were averaging 108mph as they pitted for the first time but Ago's lead was soon down to just two seconds as they began lap three.

However, Hailwood was forced to make some adjustments to his Honda in the pits, which cost him precious time and saw Ago extend his lead to ten seconds, which had increased by a further five at the start of lap four. Pasolini was the first of the real big hitters to experience mechanical problems, as he was forced to retire his Benelli, which moved Williams into third and Malcolm Uphill, who by now had also lapped at 100mph on his Norton, was in fourth.

Up front, Hailwood had cut Ago's lead to 11.6 seconds and then somehow brought it down to just two seconds at Ballaugh. He even briefly took the lead at Ramsey, only for Ago to respond and retake the lead at the Bungalow.

A final duel to end all duels looked on the cards as the warriors began their fifth laps but sadly it would come to a premature end as news filtered through that Agostini had been forced to retire his MV at Windy Corner.

A broken chain had scuppered his chances of securing a famous win and it also left Hailwood, who by now was well and truly in the groove, with a huge lead.

Eventually he discovered his rival was out of the race and he decided to play safe and nurture his Honda home for the win, with Williams in second, Spencer third, John Cooper fourth and Fred Stevens fifth.

The sidecar race was won by Siegfried Schauzu, which marked his second TT victory, but again it was not without incident as Schauzu's passenger, Horst Schneider, had actually fallen off on the last lap before remounting. The pair went on to win the race adding to what was a very successful TT career for Schauzu, who would go on to take nine wins on the Isle of Man.

In fact, Schauzu would go on to become the most successful continental sidecar driver in the TT's history, claiming all of his victories between 1967 and 1975 – and all on BMWs.

The German, who became affectionately known as 'Sideways Sid' due to the unique way he took corners, also won the German championship no less than five times, although the world crown eluded him.

In second place was Klaus Enders and passenger, Engelhardt, who was competing in just his second TT.

His efforts, however, helped him claim the 1967 World Sidecar Championship, as he had also won five races over the course of the year. Enders would also go on to become a very successful sidecar racer, claiming six world titles during an illustrious career.

Behind the scenes, the three-class Production TT had been launched for the first time in 1967 while the final 50cc race was held a year later.

It was won by Australian Barry Smith on a factory Deri. Smith, having tasted success, would also compete in TTs during later years, picking up three wins in three years while competing in the Formula III race, from 1979 to 1981, all while riding Yamahas.

Sidecar 750cc TT 1968
Arnold first lady on TT podium

The year 1968 also saw the introduction of the first 750cc sidecar race, which was won by Essex driver Terry Vinicombe and passenger John Flaxman, who were using a 654cc-capacity engine.

The 750cc race, which took place alongside the 500cc race for the first time, was also memorable for another important reason.

Norman Hanks and his passenger, Rose Arnold, had experienced difficulties during their first TT outing as a pair in 1967, but returned triumphant a year later coming second in the 750cc race.

In the process, Arnold – who would marry the driver's brother, Roy, whom she would also passenger for in the 1970s – became the first woman to stand on the TT podium.

Meanwhile, Helmut Fath had managed to finish the Sidecar TT in fourth place, which had been enough to secure the world title on his URS machine.

Another mentionable competitor was Mick Boddice and his passenger, Dave Loach, who failed to finish the 1968 race.

However, it would not be long before success would follow because, following in the footsteps of his father, Bill Boddice, Mick would go on to claim nine TTs between the years 1983 and 1993.

Mick's first race had come two years earlier in 1966 but he had been forced to retire before going on to finish eighth in 1967.

After his fourth place in 1968, it would be another 15 years before the Kidderminster star claimed his first TT win.

Mick would go on to share the same number of wins as fellow sidecar TT greats Siegfried Schauzu and Dave Saville. Mick would also claim a staggering 40 silver replicas during his long and successful career.

However, his 35-year affiliation of racing on the island and around circuits would come to an abrupt end as this article in the *Express & Star* newspaper, in 1998, pointed out:

British racing champ Mick Boddice was forced to make a dramatic retreat from the Isle of Man TT.

After winning three British championships and competing in sidecar races for 35 years, he was drummed off at the end of the second lap.

Mick and his passenger, Dave Wells, held ninth place at the end of the 37.73-mile lap but a pit stop at the second lap dashed all hopes of the pair making it a record 10th TT win.

Mick, 50, said: 'I hit a puddle on the mountain first time around and I think I'd taken water on board. It got into the electrics and that was the end of the race for me.'

Mick, known to friends as Mick Senior, was in the competition with his 26-year-old son Mick Junior, or Michael, also from Kidderminster.

Michael, 26, who works in Stourport, said all his energies would now be focussed on winning the British championships in a fortnight's time in Leicester.

He said: 'I am over the moon, I finished sixth in the TT race but obviously I'm disappointed for my dad.

'The first thing I did was call my wife and then I celebrated down the pub. But it's a pretty good achievement considering 80 pairs around the world entered,' he added.

Due to bad weather most of the races were postponed leaving the dynamic duo more time to work on their car, which was having clutch trouble.

The pair believe if the car had been working 100 per cent the final positions could have been very different.

The week's events were marred at the start when a young racer was killed in a practice run last Friday.

Michael added: 'Luckily we didn't know the chap but it was very upsetting. We just had to put it behind us.

'The course isn't easy and it is very rough but it's the thrill of that and the speed – without getting caught by police – that drives me.' He described the course, for anyone who missed the biggest bike race this year, as speeding through the streets of Bewdley at 120mph.

But for now the father and son racing duo must put the memories of the TT race behind them and concentrate on winning the British championships on Sunday, June 28. Mick's son, Mick Boddice Junior, would also continue the family tradition by racing sidecars from 1994 to 1999.

Lightweight 125cc TT 1968
Read's controversial win

By 1968, Phil Read and Bill Ivy had developed a fierce rivalry, despite being team-mates at Yamaha.

Ivy had won the Lightweight 250cc TT race, setting a lap record of 105.51mph.

Yamaha had wanted Read to win the 125cc race too as he was top of the world championship table in that class at the time.

Ivy, however, had other ideas and took the lead with a lap of 100.32mph on the smaller machine.

On his third and final lap, however, Ivy stopped near Creg-ny-Baa to ask the fans who was winning the race at the time, which was long enough for Read to catch him and then controversially win the race.

He took victory with an average lap speed of 99.12mph, finishing in one hour, eight minutes and 31.4 seconds, which was just over a minute quicker than Ivy.

Then 1969 saw the likes of Alan Barnett and Irishman Brian Steenson try to wrestle wins from the formidable Giacomo Agostini but he was simply unstoppable across most classes on his fearsome MV Agusta.

The 750cc Production race was won by Malcolm Uphill on a Triumph Bonneville and then riders from Caerphilly went on to repeat that feat on a 750cc Trident a year later.

Yamaha had withdrawn from GP racing by 1969 but their bikes continued to be snapped up by privateers

John Molyneux and driver Ernie Lee failed to finish the 1969 sidecar race but would recover to finish third in 1970.

Separate 500cc and 750cc sidecar races were run that year and it also marked the final time the 50cc machines would be raced on the island at the TT.

Molyneux and driver George Oates would sadly lose their lives while racing eight years later at the Ulster GP in 1977.

John's son, Dave, would go on to become one of the TT's most successful ever racers, claiming 17 TT wins. He continues to race to this day.

By the 1970s, some of the biggest racers in the business had begun to boycott the TT due to its dangerous nature – and it would lead to a decade of real change in the history of the event.

The year 1970 was one of the most devastating for the sport when six riders died, which marred the entire fortnight.

One of the most high profile to boycott the TT was Giacomo Agostini, who had made the decision following the death of his compatriot, Gilberto Parlotti. He was killed after crashing in wet conditions while trying to win the 125cc world championship in 1972.

Ago, himself the reigning 350cc and 500cc world champion, was also backed by the likes Phil Read and Barry Sheene, who at the time was one of the sport's rising stars.

As pressure grew, the FIM finally decided to remove the world championship status from the TT in 1977.

But the TT managed to not only maintain its popularity but even began to thrive once again during the late 1970s.

Its popularity was helped by the likes of Read and also Mick Grant being convinced to continue competing on the island, while the winning return of Mike Hailwood towards the end of the decade also helped boosted its popularity.

A new set of FIM TT Formula championships were created for the production-model machines, which by 1986 had been expanded to include the San Marino motorcycle Grand Prix, in Misano, Italy; Hockenheim, Germany; Assen, in Holland, Jerez, Spain; Vila Real, Portugal; Imatra, Finland; Dundrod, Northern Ireland; and the Isle of Man.

Hailwood had set a lap record of 108.77mph during his epic battle with Agostini in 1967, which had remained in place for the next seven years.

But once the bigger capacity bikes started being introduced, the records began to tumble once more.

Mick Grant raised the average lap speed to 109.82mph on his Kawasaki 750cc in 1975, while Pat Hennan, who was part of the Suzuki GB garage, became the first rider to finish a six-lap race in under 20 minutes, while riding a 500cc machine, with a lap of 113.83mph in 1978.

Senior TT 1972

Agostini wins then retires after friend's death

The sea of change had continued during the early part of the decade with 1971 marking the first time clutches had been used to start the race.

In the Formula 750 race – which had just been introduced and would run for another four years – Tony Jefferies, on a Triumph Triple, beat Ray Pickerell, who was riding a three-cylinder BSA.

What was more significant about the result was the fact both machines had been built in the BSA-owned Triumph factory.

Pickerell's bike had also previously been raced at the Daytona 200 by none other than Mike Hailwood.

During the same year, Alan Bennett became the first privateer to lap at more than 100mph on a 350cc machine during practice week, namely a Yamsel, with a Yamaha engine and Seeley chassis.

In what would be his final year of racing at the TT, he had also held second place in the Junior TT before crashing on lap three but enjoyed a podium finish in the Lightweight 250cc TT on a Yamaha, coming home in third.

A year later, the TT would again change forever when Giacomo Agostini, most successful world championship rider of all time, announced his decision to retire from the TT.

Having made his debut on the island in 1965, he became one of the TT's true greats over the next eight years by claiming ten wins.

He had a big advantage racing as a factory MV Agusta rider throughout his TT career but he was one of the few who could compete with the likes of Hailwood.

After claiming his first TT podium in the 1965 Junior TT, he claimed his first win a year later in the same race, breaking the lap record in the process.

Another standout moment for Agostini was when he smashed the outright lap record from a standing start in the 1967 Senior TT, which would remain one of the most talked about races in the history of the TT.

With MV Agusta dominating, he took a Senior and Junior TT double for the next three years, won the Senior in 1971 and then did another double in 1972 – the year that marked his final year of racing at the TT.

He made the decision after his good friend Gilberto Parlotti tragically lost his life in that year's 125cc race.

Parlotti, the Italian Morbidelli works rider, was killed at the Verandah on the last lap with the race eventually won by Chas Mortimer, with Charlie Williams second and Bill Rae third.

Weather conditions were atrocious at the time, and Agostini was ready to boycott that afternoon's Senior TT in protest at what had happened to his friend.

In the end the weather conditions improved and Agostini won the race. It was to be his last TT.

Ago had only ridden the race after much persuasion but, once out on the roads, his last appearance brought yet another commanding victory.

He took the win ahead of team-mate Alberto Pagani with Yorshireman Mick Grant moved up to third spot.

Peter Williams had ridden brilliantly to push Pagani back into third place but was agonisingly forced to retire on the final lap at the Bungalow with the podium in sight.

Agostini and Phil Read proclaimed that the TT course had become too dangerous for the modern motorcycles and, although the TT circuit maintained its position on the Grand Prix calendar, the star riders of the day shunned the course. The writing was on the wall.

Earlier in the week, Read and Agostini had done their talking on the circuit for the MV team during the Junior TT, which would make the start of another double win on the island for the Italian.

Read had led early on but dropped out on the second lap paving the way for Ago to take the win, with Tony Rutter – who produced his first 100 mph – beating Grant, who ran out of petrol on the line, into second.

However, the 1972 TT had been far from a total loss for Read as he claimed victory in the Lightweight 250cc TT, leading from the start, while Gould finally beat John Williams into second.

Another standout ride came from Siggi Schauzu, who became the first sidecar racer to win both the 500cc and 750cc races in the same week, to claim his sixth and seventh victories.

But the meeting was dominated by the retirement of Agostini who, during his illustrious career, would go on to win the 500cc world championship seven times in a row, as well as six successive 350cc titles on MVs. His record included 62 wins on 500cc machines and 48 on 350cc bikes in Grand Prix races.

He formed his own team with backing from tobacco company Marlboro in 1976, the year he claimed his final 350cc race win at the Dutch TT, which also marked the last time a four-stroke engine won a race in the same class.

Ago may have refused to continue racing at the TT but he did continue to support the event from a distance. Following his retirement, he would take part in numerous parade laps, including the 2019 Classic TT.

Junior TT 1973

Tony Rutter backs up his 'fastest road racer' title with a victory

Tony Rutter wrote his name into motorcycling history when he claimed a fantastic victory in the Junior TT in 1973.

Already considered one of the sport's greatest road racers, his victory in the Junior had been truly special as he joined the likes of Giacomo Agostini, Mike Hailwood, Phil Read, Jim Redman, Bob McIntyre and Geoff Duke as Junior TT winners.

Rutter had an average lap speed of 101.99mph over the five laps. He showed his complete superiority by also setting the fastest lap of the race when he clocked a 104.22mph effort, lapping in 21 minutes and 43.2 seconds, beating Ago's previous best of 103.34mph the year before on his all-conquering MV Agusta.

Rutter had entered the five-lap, 188.65-mile race as one of the favourites as he had previously been the rider to have been able to lap the course at more than 100mph on a 350cc machine.

He had come second to Ago the year before but, with absence from the TT, having refused to race on the island due to its dangerous nature after the 1972 race meeting, it had thrown the field wide open.

However, despite not winning the previous year's TT, Rutter had set the fastest lap of the race, clocking an average speed of 100.90mph.

While many of the top riders also refused to race the course, results still qualified at the time for the world championship – and Rutter had always enjoyed racing around the island too.

Rutter rode a 348cc Yamaha to victory, which had been entered by Bob Priest, and his success in the Junior TT had also followed him becoming the world's fastest road racer.

During the North West 200, he had covered the 9.73-mile circuit in Northern Ireland in 36 minutes and 54.4 seconds, at an average lap speed of 110.56mph. His quickest lap had been 112.44mph, so he had come to the TT in seriously good form.

And he proved far too hot to handle as he romped to victory ahead of Ken Huggett and John Williams. The entire top 20 was also made up of Yamaha riders.

ISLE OF MAN TT MEMORIES

Chris Lewis, from Shrewsbury, Shropshire, is a former Wirral 100 club champion:

I'd been giving my most memorable TT race some serious thought and one that sprung to mind was my first visit in 1974, when Mick Grant won the Production race on a Triumph called 'Slippery Sam'.

In 1975 we were watching at the Bungalow when Grant kicked up dust at the edge of the road on the way to beating Mike Hailwood's eight-year-old lap record with a 109.82mph average lap on his 750 Kawasaki Triple.

On the next lap his chain snapped at the Gooseneck so he didn't finish the race.

I missed 1977, when Joey Dunlop won his first TT, but was there for most of his other 25 wins, including his last three in 2000.

The electric atmosphere in 1978 was the best I remember for Mike Hailwood's comeback after 11 years and his Formula 1 win on the Sports Motorcycles Ducati. That was simply amazing!

He also returned in 1979, winning the Senior race.

Another highlight was 1992 when Steve Hislop – who was my all-time TT favourite – won the Senior TT on the 'White Charger' rotary Norton, beating Carl Fogarty in an epic battle.

Then 2007 was another memorable year, with it being the centenary of the TT – and with John McGuinness breaking the 130mph lap record barrier.

The year 2010 was also another huge year with two spectacular crashes involving Guy Martin and Conor Cummins, and of course Ian Hutchinson winning five races in a week, a record that still stands today.

The highlight of last year was Peter Hickman setting an incredible new lap record of over 135mph.

As I look back through the yearly records, more and more memories just come flooding back.

Production TT 1974

Grant takes his first TT win on 'Slippery Sam'

Bad weather wreaked havoc with the 1974 programme – but that did not stop Mick Grant from grabbing his first TT win in the new 1000cc class of the Production race.

And he did it on board the now-famous 'Slippery Sam', the Triumph Trident that had won the race for the previous three years.

The Yorkshireman swept aside the opposition, with the BMWs of Hans-Otto Butenuth and Helmut Dahne second and third respectively.

Peter Williams was in third place in the early stages on the Gus Kuhn Norton, but retired on lap two at the Highlander.

The Production event was increased to ten laps a year later, making it the longest TT race yet.

Alex George and Dave Croxford continued Slippery Sam's amazing TT success exploits by winning the 750cc class, as the race was so long it was shared by two riders.

It meant Sam had won every Production 750 TT between 1971 and 1975. Triumph, meanwhile, would win the class for seven straight years on different bikes.

It had all started when Malcolm Uphill set the production bike best at 100mph on a Triumph Bonneville Thruxton in 1969 and the following year Uphill won again, this time on a tuned three-cylinder 750cc Trident, which marked the dawn of the Slippery Sam era.

The bike had been given its name after experiencing engine issues, particularly during the Bol d'Or 24-hour production bike race in France, but after sorting those early problems the likes of seven-time TT legend Grant would go on to taste TT success on the machine.

The year 1974 was also special because it marked the year when the Formula 750 race temporarily replaced the Senior as the main event, becoming the final race of the week too.

The Formula 750 turned out to be an exciting race as well as, on the final lap, Chas Mortimer beat Charlie Williams by just over eight seconds with Tony Rutter third. All were mounted on Yamahas too, such was the strength of the manufacturer in that particular class.

Behind the front three, Norton riders Peter Williams and Dave Croxford had retired on the first lap, Grant had struggled with the power of the Kawasaki and Percy Tait had finished fourth on a Triumph Triple.

Weather had also plagued the Senior TT, which was reduced to five laps because of the weather, and was dominated by the 352cc Yamaha twins.

Williams had tried early on to compete with the Japanese bikes in dry conditions but then rain fell, leaving the path open for Phil Carpenter to take the win, followed by Charlie Williams – who also took victory in the Lightweight TT – and Rutter.

Mortimer and Austin Hockley would hit problems in the 125cc race, leaving Clive Horton to take the win followed by Ivan Hodgkinson and Tom Herron.

Rutter would also leave the island a TT winner taking his second Junior win on the bounce on a 350cc Yamaha after Charlie Williams had retired on the third lap and Mortimer was also forced to pull out.

Grant and Paul Cott came second and third.

In the 500cc world championship race, BMW's Heinz Luthringhauser secured his one and only TT victory while in the 750cc race Rolf Steinhausen smashed the lap record from a standing start but was forced to drop out allowing Siegfried Schauzu to take the spoils.

Classic TT 1975

Grant breaks Hailwood's eight-year record

The man who finally removed Hailwood from the top of the records list, and became the next King of the Mountain, was Mick Grant.

The Yorkshireman admitted he thought the lap record would have been broken before he did it – and he also claimed it had not bothered him too much at the time. The most important thing was always winning. Riding his 750 two-stroke triple Kawasaki, Grant lapped in 20 minutes and 36.3 seconds, raising the lap record to 109.92mph.

However, soon after, his chain broke as he came round the Gooseneck, but he still went on to break the record – he did not know at the time; all he knew was he was not going to win the race.

However, Hailwood had in fact later been in the press box with Ted Macauley when, from the grandstand, it was announced Grant had just broken the long-standing record.

Legend has it, Hailwood simply turned to his friend and released a four-word expletive, which Grant admitted was the best accolade he had ever had in his career.

Grant had waited until the second lap of the final race of the week to beat the record during the six-lap Classic TT, in a race that was ultimately hit by breakdowns towards the front end, which changed the complexion of the race.

First Grant's chain broke on the third lap and Yamaha's John Williams took the lead for a short while, only to be overtaken by Tony Rutter.

However, Rutter too saw his race ended early, on the fifth lap, when the chain came off his Yamaha at Ballaugh Bridge.

Williams would soon retake the lead for the final time and take victory over second-placed Percy Tait and Charlie Sanby, in third. However, Grant had tasted success earlier in the week, claiming the postponed Senior TT, again on a Kawasaki.

Chas Mortimer had been the early pace setter but after a long pit stop Williams had taken the lead only for Grant to move ahead on lap five, ahead of Williams, while a charging Mortimer recovered to take third.

Charlie Williams took the Junior TT after his battled with Scotsman Alex George ended when the latter crashed at the 33rd Milestone on the last lap but luckily was not seriously injured.

Two riders shared the duties over the ten-lap Production TTs, with Alex George and Dave Croxford taking victory in the 750 class on a Slippery Sam, Charlie Williams and Eddie Roberts won the 500cc class on a Honda, and Chaz was triumphant when paired with Billy Guthrie in the 250cc class, giving Yamaha victory on the smaller bike in a race that took place over nine laps rather than ten.

Junior TT 1976

Mortimer wins battle with Rutter to complete TT double

The 1970s was a significant decade for Charles 'Chas' Mortimer, who would go on to win eight TTs in eight years, starting with the Production 250cc race in 1970, and ending with the victory in the Junior 250cc TT in 1978.

However, it was in 1976 when he did the TT double, winning both the Junior 350cc TT and Production TT, both on Yamahas.

Because of the postponements, the Junior had been moved to become the opening race of the week that year – and it was a race that Mortimer, ultimately, controlled throughout despite a late surge and a lap record from Tony Rutter.

Mortimer's main challenger, Charlie Williams, had been delayed in Liverpool prior to the race due to the fog that had caused the races to be switched around, which had forced him to start at the back of the field.

And to make matters worse for Williams, he was forced to retire on the second lap with mechanical problems.

Instead, it was Rutter who mounted the strongest challenge and set a new lap record of 108.69mph but fell just seven seconds short in second place at the chequered flag, with Billy Guthrie in third.

The Production race was once more run over ten laps, with smaller 250cc machines again running over a lap shorter.

Mortimer and Bill Simpson, having won the 250cc class, were eventually declared overall winners despite completing less laps. The victory would be one of Mortimer's eight career TT wins.

Best known for his world championship exploits in the 125cc class, Chaz's success began in 1970 when he won the Production Lightweight event.

However, such was his skill on a bike he also went on to claim TT wins in Ultra-Lightweight, 750cc, Lightweight and Junior classes.

Another double TT winner during the 1976 meeting was the great Irish racer Tom Herron, who claimed both the Senior and Lightweight TT wins.

The Senior had been topsy-turvy where the lap record had once again been beaten with John Williams knocking an incredible 3mph off his previous best, until he was ultimately forced to push his bike home having run out of petrol, collapsing on the finish line. However, he had already become the first rider to break the 110mph barrier on his 500 Suzuki lapping in 20 minutes and 9.8 seconds, in 112.27mph.

He had led Yamaha-mounted Herron by almost three minutes going into the last lap, but after losing power he was spotted pushing his bike from Governor's Bridge all the way to the finish line in pure frustration.

Herron, who won the Senior ahead of Ian Richards in second and Billy Guthrie third, also took the four-lap 250cc Lightweight race.

Charlie Williams had been chasing him, sitting two seconds behind, but when he retired Herron was able to win comfortably from Takazumi Katayama and Mortimer.

Lap record holder Williams was also able to claim a much-deserved win later in the week when he took the Classic TT ahead of Alex George and Tony Rutter.

It was a classic year in general that saw the lap record go and two riders win two TTs in a week.

Ulsterman Herron competed on the island between 1970 and 1978, claiming three wins.

Having shown real potential with a silver replica during his debut campaign in Lightweight 250 TT, he then suffered a bad crash in the Junior at Ballacraine, which ended his season.

A further crash a year later in 1971 at the North West 200 in Northern Ireland meant he would miss the TT for a second successive year.

He returned in 1972 and was unable to finish any of his three races but a year later he was back showing some of his true potential taking ninth in 1973 in the Lightweight 250 TT and then four silver replicas in 1974.

Finally, after a few relatively injury-free years, he claimed a podium in the 125cc class, coming third, and achieved the same result a year later in the Junior TT.

However, he still craved a win and it duly followed, in style too, when in 1976 he won the Lightweight 250 and Senior TT.

Two further podiums followed in 1977 and a year later, fresh from two victories at the North West, he was battling with the great Mike Hailwood on his return to the TT only to break down on the third lap.

However, he would taste victory again in the Senior, beating Pat Hennen to claim the win and then took third in the Junior.

Sadly, another crash at the North West in 1979 would prove to be fatal as extremely popular rider Herron would lose his life. Such had been his burgeoning talent during his final year he had even been picked to be Barry Sheene's GP team-mate during the 1979 world championship.

Herron would be as fondly remembered for his TT double as Mortimer but that same year would be the start of a huge change on the Isle of Man.

And that was because, later in 1976, the FIM decided to strip the TT races of its world championship status.

Officials, under mounting pressure, had agreed the mountain circuit was too dangerous and then British round of the series was switched to Silverstone. Many thought this would signal the end of the TT. How wrong could they be?

Another significant part of the 1976 TT was also the first appearance of one William Joseph Dunlop, who was to rewrite the record books over the next 20 years and would do as much as anyone to ensure the races would remain as popular as ever.

There would be some rocky roads ahead but the TT would not only survive – it would thrive.

The motto that goes with the three legs of man means, it will stand wherever you throw it, which is particularly poignant when it comes to the TT races.

A total of 141 lives had been lost by the time the TT had celebrated its 80th year but, despite more than one attempt to destroy it, the races continued to be as popular as ever.

Ten years after the island had been stripped of its world championship status, the lure to pure road racing, privateers and out-and-out enthusiasts remained as strong as ever. The thrill of the race, the risk and everything that came with it remained the same.

A four-hour journey separates the North Irish riders, teams and machines – and in later years the sea would take the bikes of Joey and others following a particularly choppy trip. Brian Reid was among them too but they dragged what they could from the bottom of the ocean, washed everything in diesel and put together everything they could.

But none of them ever wanted to miss the TT, such a thought had never entered their mind, and of course they were back in the years to come.

In fact, ten years after losing its Grand Prix status, many of the classes were oversubscribed and more fans than ever were making the pilgrimage to see their heroes in action, and just to take in the atmosphere and what the TT was all about.

No one could argue the consequences of TT being struck off the championship calendar would be huge but the island immediately fought back, which was to be expected of a community so fearlessly protective of its traditions – and used to going its own way.

The Manx government stayed committed to supporting the races, realising the effect trade during the TT week had on the rest of the financial year.

It has also been such a boost to the people and businesses on the island, as well as being a superb spectacle for its adoring fans across the globe.

Finances were increased, with nearly £250,000 being ploughed into the 1978 TT by the government, which of course was in itself boosted by the heroic return of Mike Hailwood.

The other idea was to specialise in production bike racing, which helped bring a whole host of new motorbiking heroes to the fore on the island. It helped preserve its legacy.

The time trial remained and little had changed over the years, with the 226-mile course still intact. Some sections had been widened and some of the surfaces were made smoother, but the fact remained nothing much about the hardest, toughest and most respected course in the world had needed to change – and nor would it.

Equipment would be pushed to the limit, where roadside hazards were around pretty much every corner.

Bikes still had to be set up differently for the TT. The grip was different, the mindset was different – everything was different.

For most people who race the TT it is a labour of love. There isn't much money in it but they cannot stop coming back. It's a mecca for all road racers and so it would remain.

And a lot of the riders would continue to pass on their experience to the next generation, following in the footsteps of Billy McCosh, who rode a Matchless at the TT during the 1960s.

He had passed his skills onto the great Mick Grant, one of the most successful TT riders of his era and one of the saviours of the TT during the early years when GP status had been removed.

He, in turn, passed his knowledge on to Neil Robinson. Grant loved the constructive talks about the circuits, where both he and Billy could be completely right and completely wrong over the course of the 37.73-mile circuit – not everyone can agree where to go fast, change gear or keep it flat out.

All riders know certain tricks, racing lines and where and where not to use brakes, gear changes, etc. Such is the size of the challenge, everyone has their own gems.

And it was the quirkiness that remained too – such as Roger Marshall once being caught by a speed gun doing more than 80mph in a 30mph on the island, which led to a fine and a ban, but luckily for him only on the open roads, which meant he could still race.

Grant believed strongly at the time that a way of making the TT safer would be to raise the standard of those who raced it, and also try to increase the marshals, especially at a time when the TT was receiving a record amount of entries.

And that, really, has remained the crux of the races for so long. While some call for the event to be banned forever, there is always such a huge interest and passion of racers wanting to enter it, who are all aware of the risks, and yet they still yearn to compete.

Organisers had also argued at the time that only those who could race at a certain standard – qualified with an international licence – were able to race at the TT.

However, they also believed that if times during practice were raised to ensure only riders of a certain ability were able to compete during race week, it would simply make practice week more dangerous, forcing everyone to push harder just to make the cut. There were, and still are, always details that need ironing out but the TT would remain a haven for racers, bikers and fans.

Classic TT 1977

Grant breaks lap record again as TT rebuilds

Once the TT had been stripped of its GP status, the races began to change pretty quickly, which included a new format being introduced with the Production TT being dropped.

The Junior TT was also raced on 250cc machines instead of 350cc, while both sidecar TTs were back on 1000cc machines.

However, in the Classic TT, it was business as usual for Mick Grant as he again reclaimed the lap record.

His previous best had only lasted a year with John Williams making Suzuki's first mark on the island – but the seven-times TT winner restored Kawasaki's pride in 1977.

Grant realised by this stage that if he was going to win on the island, which had always been his priority, he was probably going to have to break the lap record.

But he had never started a race there thinking the prime concern is to beat it – his prime concern was simply to finish and to win.

And he did it in style too, taking the Classic TT win on his 750 Kawasaki lapping in 20 minutes and 4.4 seconds, at an average speed of 112.79mph, blowing the competition away.

A further three minutes behind was Charlie Williams, with fellow Yamaha rider Eddie Roberts third.

Perhaps more ominously, lying back in seventh place, was Joey Dunlop, who had also been riding a Yamaha.

The year would be very significant for the future of the TT races as it marked the first time Joey had ever won around the mountain circuit.

He achieved the first of his 26 wins in the Jubilee 1000cc TT, some 51 seconds ahead of George Fogarty.

The 1977 meeting was only the second time Joey had raced at the TT but on board his 750cc Seeley, which had been built by John Rea, he overcame a stop at Parliament Square to check on his rear tyre to claim the win in the Jubilee 1000 classification.

Lapping at 110.95mph, it was a very early indication about what was to come as, over the next 25 years, he would pick up another 26 TTs while competing in a staggering 100 races on the Isle of Man.

He would take his second win three years later at the Classic TT in 1980, with a record-breaking 115.22mph lap before going on to dominate for the rest of the decade.

The 1978 Classic TT produced more of the same for Grant as he not only beat his own lap record, with a speed of 114.33mph, he also dipped under the 20-minute mark.

It was an era completely dominated by Japanese manufacturers who had all begun to take over pretty much every aspect of motorcycle racing, both on the roads and around the circuits.

However, the Japanese teams did not have everything their own way. It would in fact be Ducati who would claim all the headlines in 1978 as Mike Hailwood marked his return to TT racing when he entered the Formula 1 TT 1978 – the link between Hailwood's win and the future success of Ducati would also be inextricably linked forever.

The world-famous Italian manufacturer's story had all started way back in 1926 when Antonio Cavalieri Ducati and his three sons set up the first factory in Bologna.

Ducati started as a precision electronics company and had nothing to do with motorbikes, instead making intercoms, projectors, razors and cameras.

The company built a whole new factory on the outskirts of the city in the 1930s as business continued to boom, employing thousands of people.

When the war broke out, Italy had joined the Nazis, but by 1943 had surrendered, with Germany using the Ducati factory for the war effort.

By 1944, Allied Forces had destroyed the factory with their bombs. It was eventually rebuilt under state ownership but because money was tight there was no calling for their previous electrical work.

And because of the poverty, most Italians were getting about on bicycles – and Ducati saw a market where they could attach an engine to the bike to make it easier to travel, with a whopping one-and-a-half horsepower.

But because it was cheap and efficient and it could be attached to any bicycle, its popularity took off. A total of 200,000 had been produced in just six years.

The Ducati 60 soon followed in 1949, the manufacturer's first motorbike.

When the Moto Duro d'Italia was launched in the 1950s, in Bologna, Ducati realised it had to be a part of it and went about creating a better, faster and more beautiful machine to race in it.

In 1954, designer Fabio Taglioni was hired and would change Ducati's fortunes and direction forever.

The 125 Grand Sport, known as the Mariana, was the first bike he produced, especially for the Moto Duro, which it would go on to win in 1956. The 175 and then 250cc machines followed in the 1960s, such as the Ducati Diana to cater in part for the American market.

The drive to make it big in the US saw the Scrambler produced and it proved to be very popular both on the roads and for racing, particularly off-road and even in the desert.

The L-twin design again changed the direction of Ducati, as it could compete with the Japanese manufacturers with its 750cc engine.

Five 750 Desmodromic L-twins were entered into the 1972 Imola 200, which was seen as Europe's Daytona.

Ducati needed some top riders to race their new machines and called up Paul Smart, the brother-in-law of Barry Sheene, who at the time was a works rider for Kawasaki.

Smart eventually agreed to race at Imola, against the likes of Giacomo Agostini and Phil Read, and all the hard work paid off as, without a first gear, he claimed the win – and a one-two for Ducati – after Ago's MV Agusta had broken down.

Despite their success on the track, production did not take off – that was until Mike the Bike got involved with the manufacturer in 1978 in one of the most memorable TT races to ever take place.

Formula 1 TT 1978

Hailwood stuns the world and helps save the Ducati brand

Once Mike Hailwood had decided to make his great return to the island, he immediately began training at his home in New Zealand to get fit.

Despite a lapse of 11 years, he still had the edge and single-mindedness required to win on the island. There was simply no one like him on a motorbike and although he knew the task that lay ahead, if anyone could pull off such a remarkable comeback, it was him.

He had left the island with one of the TT's greatest-ever races, when he battled with Agostini to claim the Senior win in 1969. Not only that, his lap record had stood for eight years so it was fair to say he had already truly left his mark on the island.

Having tried his hand at Formula 1 racing, which included varied success and a terrible crash that nearly cost him his career, Hailwood felt he had unfinished business at the TT and decided he wanted to mount one of the greatest comebacks in motorsport history – plus he was looking forward to renewing his rivalry with the likes of Phil Read, who was still on the pace himself and had won a TT the previous year.

Hailwood said publicly that, after 11 years away, he could not return the same rider – but secretly he knew he could, and he took advice from the likes of Mick Grant and Tom Herron as he began planning his winning return.

Of course the bikes had changed considerably too – the tyres were slicker, brakes were sharper and the engines much more powerful.

Grant admitted to being worried about Hailwood falling off and did not think he would even make the top six but he soon changed his mind after seeing how he performed during practice week in 1978. Hailwood would ride the bumps, forget the fancy GP lines, go with the camber regardless, brake late and attack the corners.

Grant ended up admitting it would make his week just to keep pace with him.

Behind the scenes there was also another intriguing battle taking place, with the Read versus Hailwood battle now becoming a fight for superiority between Yamaha's power and Ducati's handling.

Just in case anyone was in any doubt whatsoever about whether Hailwood could make a successful comeback, he set the perfect early marker by breaking the record on his first practice lap, with a 102.69mph effort, while Read had posted a 101.74mph effort.

The problem for all of Hailwood's rivals was, however, he already knew he could go quicker.

Hailwood then clocked a 105.70mph lap on his Yamaha 500cc and then two nights later set a personal best time of 111.04mph, just shy of Grant's record 112.77mph on a 750cc Kawasaki. Hailwood by now was a bald 38-year-old who was suffering with a cold and had to limp on to his bike each time following his terrible crash at the Nurburgring, during the 1974 F1 German GP, which had ended his career racing four-wheeled machines.

And yet, even after all those injuries and all that time away, still no one on the island could touch him.

Going into the Formula 1 TT in 1978, Hailwood had given Read a 50-second start off the line for the opening race of the week but used all his natural skill and flair to dominate, keeping a watchful eye on John Williams after Read and Herron, both racing Hondas, either had to pull in or faded away.

Hailwood set a new lap record of 110.27mph and race record of 109.51mph, completing the 226 miles in two hours, five minutes and 10.2 seconds.

He admitted his eyes were so full of tears he could barely see when he crossed the line to claim the victory. Hailwood later said it was also his fondest memory in racing.

It was Steve Wynne who had prepared the Ducati that helped Hailwood win the race – and he, like many others, knew Hailwood could have gone even quicker during the race, despite winning the race by two minutes, such was his pace. Racing the Yamahas during the same year, however, was not such an easy ride with the manufacturer being blamed for not giving Hailwood the support he needed and costing him any chance of claiming another TT that week. The 500cc, 250cc and 750cc Yamahas all let him down.

Despite finishing 28th in the Senior, he still lapped at 112mph, just shy of the 113.83mph outright record. He also finished 12th in the Classic.

However, 1978 would also be remembered for another tragedy, when Malcolm 'Mac' Hodson lost his life.

Having begun his career racing solos at the Manx GP and TT, he later turned his attentions to sidecar racing in 1964, finishing 17th a year later.

But his times improved over the years and he made the podium during the mid-1970s, eventually taking his first victory in 1976, in the 1000cc sidecar race, followed by another victory in the second leg of the 1977 Sidecar TT meeting.

A year later tragedy would strike, as both he and his passenger, Kenny Birch, lost their lives following a crash at Bray Hill.

Despite the fatality and the Yamaha's letting Hailwood down, after his astonishing win on the Ducati, the manufacturer immediately went to work releasing the Mike Hailwood replica, which helped to save the company for the time being. But the Italian giants knew further changes were needed to stop the company from disappearing.

The belt-drive engine followed, which was much cheaper to produce. In 1980, the Panta 500 arrived, which developed into a more powerful model with a 650cc engine.

The company was again saved during the 1980s, which enabled it to start producing even more powerful race bikes that would become the benchmark for all its future developments and, ultimately, successes.

The 888 was one of the more successful designs, especially when Ducati signed up none other than Carl Fogarty.

He started off as a privateer, riding the 888, and because it allowed Foggy to keep a lot of corner speed, it soon became a match made in heaven. The 916, released in 1994, was perhaps the most famous design in Ducati's history. With Foggy at the helm, on both the 916 and 996, he would win the World Superbike Championship a then-record four times, between 1994 and 1999.

Behind the scenes, the Ducati Monster was produced for the roads and it proved to be a huge hit – selling 300,000 to this date. The brand was sold to an American investment fund in 1996 and eventually it led to Casey Stoner winning the MotoGP in 2007.

However, on the island, things went pretty quiet after Hailwood's win, with Michael Rutter the last rider to have made a serious effort on a Ducati, finishing 10th in the 2011 Senior TT with an average speed of 123.632mph on a 1200 Ducati.

However, the brand did a little better on the circuits, winning the World Superbike title with Carlos Checa at the helm, while Casey Stoner also claimed the MotoGP crown on a Ducati in 2007.

Before Rutter, the great John McGuinness ran a 998 Ducati in 2003, finishing second in the Senior TT with a lap of 123.93mph, and third in the Formula 1 race.

The company changed another four times during that period until 2012 when it finally gained some stability when it was bought by Volkswagen Audi.

Yet the heart of the brand remained in Bologna and now employs more than 7,000 people. The Panigale is one of the latest and most popular models.

Now competing at the front end in MotoGP and World Superbikes, you would never bet against the manufacturer making a successful comeback at the TT once more.

Senior TT 1979

Hailwood wins again, this time on a Suzuki

Ducati took the following year, following Hailwood's winning return, more seriously and brought over a bigger team and crew to aid his efforts – but straight away he was not happy with either the handling or the speed of the bike.

He crashed the Ducati while testing in Italy and then Tom Herron, who had helped him with his return to the TT, died at the North West 200. The two accidents almost convinced Hailwood to quit but out of loyalty and the buzz of joining Suzuki he decided to carry on.

In the F1 race he was blown away by Alex George's works 997cc Honda. He was also up against a works Honda-backed Ron Haslam and Charlie Dixon, who was riding a master-framed Honda.

When Hailwood's gearbox went on the final lap, despite a monumental effort, he was overtaken by Haslam who moved into third place.

He later had to pull over and reconnect the battery leads, which gave New Zealand's Graeme Crosby the chance to pass, leaving Hailwood to cross the line in fifth.

However, Hailwood was buzzing with his Suzuki and did not want to make any real changes to the bike. He was happy to get on it and ride the wheels off it, which was in complete contrast to what the team had been used to with the likes of Barry Sheene, who usually rode the bike.

Suzuki had also agreed to paint the bike in Hailwood's famous red, white and gold colours. It just felt like something special might be about to occur once again.

Hailwood had not ridden the 500cc Suzuki since Friday's practice, but when it was started up the night before the Senior a problem with the oil-seal spring and crankshaft was discovered.

Mechanics worked on it all night but no one was sure how it would go the morning of the race.

An injured Mick Grant would eventually break down on the third lap, and a fired-up Alex George took the lead early on, but Hailwood had overtaken the Scotsman by lap two and stretched his lead to 8.8 seconds by lap three, beating Pat Hennen's lap race record in the process with a time of 19 minutes and 51.2 seconds.

George was also later forced to retire, which left Tony Rutter and New Zealand's Dennis Ireland in pursuit, but Hailwood was more than two minutes ahead of both at the finish line.

The victory was Hailwood's 14th and last TT win. He completed the race in two hours, one minute and 32.4 seconds, averaging 114mph.

Classic TT 1979

George strikes back to beat Hailwood

George took revenge over Hailwood in the Classic TT when the veteran admitted to racing far closer to the edge than planned, such was the stunning pace throughout a race that turned out to be another truly classic battle around the Mountain Course.

The Classic TT had pitted Hailwood's 500cc Suzuki against George's 998cc Honda, and it was the Scot who had taken a 9.2-second lead by the end of the first lap. But

Hailwood, who had opted to stick with his 500cc engine rather than the 652cc in his Suzuki, had reduced that time by five seconds going into lap three.

They both went on to complete the first 113 miles in under one hour, the first time that had ever been achieved, with George now 4.2 seconds ahead once more.

Amazingly, Hailwood had somehow managed to sneak in front by the end of lap five by just four-fifths of a second, a lead he held going into Ballacraine that marked there were just 30 miles of the race to go.

The veteran still led with 20 miles remaining at Ballaugh, but by the time they both came into Ramsey, George – with the more powerful machine – had edged back in front.

A back-marker accidentally held Hailwood up while he was charging up the mountain, which ended any real chance he had of getting the time back leaving George, with the momentum, to take the win by 3.4 seconds.

George described beating his idol, in one of the most hard-fought and frantic TT races of all time – as both the happiest and saddest day of his life. He was delighted to have won, but gutted it had to be against his hero.

Pleased to have won, beating his hero in such a superb race had left a bittersweet taste in his mouth, such was the respect all the riders, fans and commentators gave Hailwood.

The winner would later reveal how his rear shocks had gone towards the end of the race, he had nearly crashed into the crowd at Creg-ny-Baa and just missed clipping the bank at Signpost, such was the effort he was putting in to win the titanic battle.

Another secret to his victory was using the extra 500 revs his more powerful bike could offer, which he had in reserve, that could make him go faster along the straights.

Hailwood would eventually announce his retirement at Donington Park in July 1979. And it would be a bit of an anti-climax too, as a crash during practice on the Saturday would result in a painful broken collarbone, meaning he would not compete on race day in front of the 60,000 fans who had made the pilgrimage for their hero's swansong.

Still, Tom Wheatcroft, Donington's multi-million owner, called the send-off the best experience of his life, despite the fact he could not race.

Hailwood even tried to turn down the £12,000 he had been offered as payment for his appearance because he felt he had not given the fans or the owner their money's worth.

MIKE HAILWOOD

HAILWOOD'S FIRST race was on a 125cc Agusta at Oulton Park, Cheshire, on 22 April 1957, just after his 17th birthday. Two months later he secured his first win in the 125cc class at Blandford.

Another four months later, he qualified for his international licence having picked up four wins, four seconds, four thirds and four fourths in just his first 18 races.

Chasing another protégée in John Surtees at Oulton Park, he crashed and broke his collarbone.

After being sent to South Africa to work on his education, as well as his race craft, he returned to England for the 1958 world championship campaign. He would enter his first TT aged just 18, with his racing career barely 14 months old.

The TT was a world championship race at the time and Mike rode a 350 and 500 Norton, a 250 NSU and 125 Ducati.

He finished all four races with an amazing best finish of third in the 250 race, which was ridden over the old ten-and-three-quarter-mile Clypse circuit.

He also finished seventh in the 125cc race, 12th in the Junior 350 race and 13th in the Senior.

Mike would go on to win the 125, 250 and 350 British championships, and came fourth in the world championships.

A year later, he won his first world championship race at the Ulster GP, at Dundrod, on a 125cc Ducati. That same year he had claimed the 125 and 500 British championships, as well as picking up four wins at Aberdare Park in Wales, while breaking the lap record.

After four years of racing, he lifted his first 250cc world title on a Honda – as well as winning the 250 TT – and finished second in the 500cc class on a Norton. By the age of 21, Mike had won more than 200 races and broken 150 lap and race records.

The mid-1960s were the halcyon days, which saw top battles between the likes of Hailwood, Phil Read, Bill Ivy, John Redman, Frank Perris, Ernst Degner, Hugh Anderson, Alan Shepherd, Ralph Bryans and Tommy Robb.

Mike started racing an East German 250cc MZ before joining Redman at Honda as part of a really special class, which included the Suzuki known as 'Whispering Death'.

Mike was a gentleman but also the bravest and most skilled rider of his era – but he could also fight and knew how to lose.

During his entire racing career, Mike was backed by his father Stan, who believed 100 per cent in his ability but never spoiled him, despite his huge personal fortune. Sadly, Stan died in Miami just before Hailwood's comeback in 1978.

But he did see his son claim multiple titles and championships, which included when Mike made history in 1961 by becoming the first racer to win three TTs in one week.

Mike's record-breaking week saw him beat Luigi Taveri and Tom Phillis in the 125 class, Phillis and Jim Redman in the 250cc class, and Bob McIntyre and Phillis in the Senior – he also picked up the 250cc world title for good measure.

His success attracted the interest of Count Agusta who offered him the chance to ride the works MV at the Italian GP, in Monza. He went on to win the 500cc title and came second in the 350cc class behind Hocking.

Hailwood would go on to dominate the series from 1962-65, collecting four world titles along the way.

Redman beat him to the 350 title but their battles would see numerous race and lap records tumble.

In 1966, having switched to the Honda, he won ten of the 12 250cc GP races and beat Agostini to the 350cc title, which he again won the year after, but not the 500cc title.

The Honda was big and dangerous but he was still able to race it to victory over Agostini's MV at the 1967 Senior in one of the TT's greatest-ever battles.

Constantly swapping positions over 226 miles, they were often separated by a tenth of a second.

Mike won when the chain broke on Agostini's bike but he admitted being scared the whole way round. He was gracious enough to say that without the DNF, Ago would have won.

Agostini and Hailwood had maintained a healthy, friendly rivalry throughout the mid-1960s.

It really all began in 1965, when MV had given Ago a bike for the Italian GP and, having taken Mike by surprise, he had won the 350cc race. Shortly after, while racing at the Riccione race track, Mike was now ready and he took his revenge – but not only did he win, he was lapping two seconds faster than all his rivals in the 500cc race.

That was when Ago realised he was the greatest and they remained friends for life, as they respected each other's skill, sportsmanship and honesty.

Ago would also later mark the 1967 TT the greatest race of his life, despite losing due to a mechanical fault.

Because of the time trail nature of the TT, they never actually saw each other during the battle and had to rely on signals. Ago was also suffering chain problems while Mike's throttle was being held on by a handkerchief at one stage, but both were riding harder and faster than either ever thought was safe, hitting their shoulders off the walls while at Ballaugh Bridge. It was all good, clean, fast racing and it was why Hailwood's competitors were so respectful of him, win, lose or draw.

By his first retirement from bikes in 1967, Mike had 76 GP wins as well as claiming 25 second places, 11 third places, 12 fourth places, nine fifth places and two sixth places.

He had finished in the top six 135 times in world championship competitions, while riding a Mondial, AJS, NSU, Ducati, Norton, MZ, EMC, MV and Honda.

Thirty-seven of his GP victories were on a 500cc, 16 on a 350cc, 21 on a 250cc and two on a 125cc.

Hailwood was awarded an MBE in later life and was also recognised for his bravery when, during the 1973 South African Grand Prix, he went to pull Clay Regazzoni from his burning car after the two collided on the second lap of the race.

Hailwood's driving suit had caught fire, but after being extinguished by a fire marshal he returned to help rescue Regazzoni, an act for which he was awarded the George Medal, the second-highest gallantry award that a British civilian can be awarded.

Picking up the George Medal from the Queen, he realised he had left his suit jacket in Brazil, 5,000 miles away. It was one of the few times he was seen visibly panicked, but he managed to find someone to bring another one in time.

After his winning exploits during the 1978 and 1979 TTs, his friend and journalist, Ted Macauley, received the Segrave Medal because, without him, Hailwood said, his comeback would never have happened.

With a record of 76 GP wins from 152 starts, ten world titles and 14 TT wins, there are few, if any, who compared to

Hailwood. Winning half of the 700 races he took part in, he was regarded as the greatest of his era, and perhaps greatest of all time on two wheels.

His ability to switch classes and continue winning races set him apart from everyone else. He could ride any bike, in any class, and win.

During the 1960s he dominated, and even when he made his sensational comeback in 1978 he found a way to win two more TTs.

Honda agreed that no one had ever ridden their machines better than Hailwood, who was also seen as a fine ambassador for the manufacturer and the sport in general.

As well as claiming wins during his GP career all over the world, including Assen in Holland, Spa in Belgium, Suzuka in Japan, Brno in the Czech Republic and Inatra in Finland, he also broke the one-hour record at Daytona in America.

Phil Read, the winner of 52 GPs and eight TTs, said Hailwood was the greatest of all time and also his inspiration, while seven-time TT winner Mick Grant – who took years to break Hailwood's lap record of 108.77mph, set in 1967 on his Honda 500-4 – also admitted Mike the Bike was the best.

Even six-time TT winner Geoff Duke agreed Hailwood had done more for the popularity of the TT during his two stints than anyone else. He was simply the finest to ever grace two wheels.

And after all those races on two and four wheels, he tragically lost his life as a result of a road accident on 23 March 1981, just two years after taking his final TT win.

Driving his family Rover saloon, he crashed into a lorry not far from his home in Tanworth-in-Arden. Doctors spent two days fighting to save his life but despite their efforts he died aged 41.

Classic TT 1980

Joey beats Grant and breaks lap record

Mick Grant believed, and rightly so, that riding the F1 Honda, he was the man who was going to win the Classic TT in 1980.

Grant, however, experienced a few problems within the Honda team and the man who would go on to win the race would be Joey Dunlop, setting a new lap record for good measure. Afterwards, the Yorkshireman admitted, with hindsight, despite the problems, he would not have been able to go round at the speed that Joey had – and what made it all the more remarkable was the fact it was the first time he had really taken notice of the Northern Irishman.

Joey did not just beat the likes of Grant to win the race, he also became the fastest man in history to have raced around the TT course. Not content with breaking the lap record once, he did it five out of the six laps including a final lap time of 115.22mph.

It was the year Dunlop had sailed to the island in a fishing boat and eventually departed the TT leaving the factory Honda team scratching their heads.

Riding a John Rea 750 Yamaha, he simply kept up the incredible pace he set during the opening lap for the entire race. In Grant's defence, he was only able to use four out of the five gears available during the race due to a mechanical problem, but whether that made any real difference to the outcome remains to be seen.

The Honda mechanics had decided to fit a 1063cc chassis between the F1 race, which Grant had won, and the Classic – but their plan did not pay off.

Dunlop himself was forced to hang on to his own eight gallon tank for most of the 226-mile race after the tank strap had broken on the opening lap.

Despite Dunlop's blistering pace, Honda had threatened to steal the win from Dunlop following a lightning-fast pit stop, courtesy of their quick-fill fuelling system.

And it nearly worked, because at Ballacraine just 0.3 seconds separated the riders, but Dunlop managed to increase the pace further still, and had established a 7.5-second lead by the start of the final lap, breaking Grant's lap record in the process.

He eventually crossed the line 21.6 seconds ahead of his nearest rivals having become the first person ever to set a 115mph lap.

It was an emotional day too because Dunlop had been contemplating retirement following the death of his brother-in-law Mervyn Robinson, the man who had turned his head towards road racing in the first place in a crash at the North West.

The result could also have been different for other reasons too because, very early in the race Jeff Sayle and Graeme McGregor had been setting the pace.

Sayle, riding a 750 Yamaha, posted a 111.66mph lap from a standing start, McGregor also clocked his first 110mph-plus lap for good measure too.

Unfortunately for the Aussie pair, McGregor was forced to retire at Crosby after suffering an electrical problem. Sayle suffered a huge tank-slapper, which he survived, but the near-crash gave Ron Haslam enough time to take third place behind his team-mate Grant.

ISLE OF MAN TT MEMORIES

Tony Else, from Weston-on-Trent, in Derbyshire, is a photographer at the Darley Moor Motorcycle Road Racing Championship:

Of my many TT memories, the events of 1981 stick in my mind, with the Honda, all-in-black protest. Earlier in the week, there had been drama on the start line when Australian Graeme Crosby experienced a technical issue with his Heron Suzuki RG500, so didn't start at his allotted time and position.

He was due to be one of the first away. From memory, I think it was a puncture.

The race itself was won by Ron Haslam, with Joey Dunlop and John Newbold finishing second and third respectively.

Crosby finished in a faster race time; however, his race time was adjudged to have started at his original start time, and consequently he finished far down the field.

It didn't take Suzuki long to lodge a protest, which they subsequently won, relegating Haslam and Dunlop to second and third, and Newbold into fourth.

Honda were clearly unhappy about this. For in the Classic TT, later in the week, the Honda team of Ron Haslam, Joey Dunlop and Alex George turned out on all-black Hondas, with black leathers, helmets and boots.

That is, with the exception of George, who was wearing his original Honda red boots, which made for quite a spectacle.

Another strong memory, but for the wrong reasons, was in 1984, when I decided to attend with my recently renovated BSA A65 Thunderbolt.

It actually performed admirably and I loved trundling around the island on it.

Unbeknownst to me though, the final drive seal had blown.

Our hotel was on one of those steep side streets off Douglas Promenade and, on one particular morning, I stepped out on to the street to several angry bikers complaining about an oil slick that had run down the steep road, and under around 15 bikes.

Whoops! Refilling the gearbox, the bike was actually fine upright but not parked on its side stand.

Formula 1 TT 1981

Protests galore as Crosby wins controversial TT

Protests, anger, dismay, new winners, all-black attire – it's fair to say the Formula 1 TT of 1981 had pretty much everything.

It appeared to all and sundry that Ron Haslam had claimed his first TT win – but that was only until a Suzuki protest resulted in their late-starting rider Graeme Crosby being awarded the win.

It meant victory had been taken away from Honda's Haslam and, in a retaliatory protest, his team-mates decided to dress in black for Classic TT as part of their own protest – as well as painting their machines black too for good measure – under team orders.

The arguments were all started when Crosby could not set off at his allocated time because of chain problems on his Suzuki.

Officials allowed him to start at the rear of the field, but with no time allowance.

Joey Dunlop was the early leader on a Honda, but after being forced to change a tyre at his pit stop, Ron Haslam took over at the front and would win the race with the Ulsterman in second – or so everyone had thought.

Crosby had bravely fought his way back to third and that was how most of the riders, punters and team thought the race would be forever recorded in the history books.

However, there was plenty going on behind the scenes and it was not long before Suzuki had put in an official protest.

They believed Crosby should have been given a time allowance for what had gone on before them, which would promote their rider to the winner's spot relegating Haslam to second in the process.

And sure enough, two hours later, Crosby was declared the winner.

Understandably, the entire Honda team was left furious and decided to take matters even further.

In a protest, they dressed their riders in all-black leathers and even painted their bikes black for the Classic TT, which was held at the end of the week.

But if the team thought its stunt would have a positive outcome, they would be very much mistaken.

Away from all the drama, Joey Dunlop had continued to raise the bar, taking his 1023 Honda around the TT course in 19 minutes and 37 seconds, in a speed of 115.4mph, during the Classic.

However, after running out of fuel, it paved the way for Crosby to complete an even more contentious double, with team-mate Mick Grant second and Alex George on the only all-black Honda to finish.

Meanwhile, the Senior had also been delayed due to bad weather that same year, which saw Crosby out on the first lap leaving the field open for Grant to claim victory in heavy rain, followed by Donny Robinson in second, TT newcomer John Newbold in third.

Tony Rutter dominated the Formula Two race on his Ducati, setting a new lap record, while in the Formula 3 class Barry Smith completed a hat-trick of victories on his Yamaha.

As the results were declared across the race week, it was certainly a strange meeting for New Zealander Crosby, who had started his racing career in 1974, in his home country.

His talent had blossomed early, and two years later he was racing in the Australian Superbike Championship before heading to Europe to compete in Britain.

His first TT success came in 1980 when he won the Senior TT as he competed in the 500cc road racing world championship on a Yamaha. However, he was also formidable on a Suzuki and went on to win the Suzuka eight-hour endurance race a year later – the same year he reclaimed the Formula 1 TT in such controversial and memorable circumstances – while also finishing fifth in the 500cc championship.

Such was his talent, he joined the great Giacomo Agostini at his Yamaha factory racing team, winning the 1982 Daytona 200, eventually finishing second in the 500cc championship.

He returned to his home country after walking away from GP racing that same year and went on to run motorcycle businesses while also racing in Touring Cars.

Such was his pedigree, he was inducted into the New Zealand Sports Hall of Fame in 1995 and the New Zealand Motorcycling Hall of Fame in 2007.

ISLE OF MAN TT MEMORIES

Paul Biddulph, from Telford, Shropshire, is a former Classic Racing Motorcycle Club champion who has also competed on the roads at the Chimay races in Belgium:

The first time I went to the Isle of Man was in 1982; five of us went in a Ford Transit van. We called it the Hotel Transit. It broke down at Hodnet so we fixed it with a coke can and got there. The van was boarded out in the back bunk-bed style, two on the top, two on the van floor and one across the front seats. It was mainly parked at night on the front at Douglas next to the toilet block for washing etc.

The weather, as I remember, was great and you could watch from most places then as long as your feet were not on the road or path if there was one.

It was great to see all the legends of that time: Joe Dunlop, Ron Haslam, Phil Read, Mick Grant, Steve Parrish and Alex George.

In those days they set off from the grandstand in twos. The TT Formula 1 was the highlight event as it was part of the World Championship then, with Joe Dunlop and Ron Haslam going head-to-head on the works Hondas.

We watched that race from the lawn at Governor's Bridge. Ron Haslam was popping big wheelies while still in the gutter nearest us coming out of Governor's dip. He went on to win, just pipping Joe with a 113.33mph record lap.

One of the lads bought a brand-new Yamaha RD350LC from Pagett's Shop on the island as you could register it over there and save paying the VAT, then he rode it home.

While outside the shop, Norman Wisdom walked by. My mate started his Mr Grimsdale routine and Norman went into character and did a small routine. We all fell about laughing, then we had a sensible chat with him about the TT. What a great guy he was!

On one afternoon we were in a crowded pub and I was chatting to two nurses from Noble's Hospital. The lad who bought the bike wanted my seat so he jangled the bike keys in front of me and said, 'Thought you wanted to ride it?'

I looked at the girls then the keys and I was off on my first lap of the TT course on a bike. Great, but when I got back to the pub the girls had gone home! The next time I went was in 2006 and then I was there every year until 2015 when I started racing. The 2007 centenary year was great with so many people and racing legends, and the racing was brilliant. Guy Martin was just pipped into second place by John McGuinness, both doing 125mph laps in the Superbike TT.

I was there to see John McGuinness do the first 130mph lap. Great days and fond memories.

Sidecar TT 1982

Hanks continues the family tradition

By the 1980s, Yamaha technology was being used far more widely in the sidecar machines, which in turn also helped to increase their speeds.

And two of the grateful recipients of the extra power were Roy Hanks and Vince Biggs, who were the aggregate winners of the two sidecar races in 1982.

Roy's father, Fred, had also raced the TT between 1955 and 1970, while his brother, Norman, raced from 1964 until

1970. Roy's nephew, Tom, was his passenger before going on to race sidecars himself between 1995 and 2006.

Roy later married his brother's passenger, Rose Arnold, and their daughter would even continue the tradition of sidecar racing at the TT, taking up the motorsport from 2008 to 2015.

Back in 1982, the two sidecar races were for machines with engines of 351cc to 1000cc, most of which were two-stroke Yamahas.

The opening race had been won by Trevor Ireson and passenger Donny Williams. Ireson had previously won both 1000cc TT races in 1979 and claimed another in 1980.

The pairing had been pushed by Dick Greasey and his passenger Stuart Atkinson who had come second in the first race before being forced to retire from the second with a puncture. Greasey had previously written himself into the record books in 1977, setting the first official lap of more than 100mph in a sidecar.

The second race, however, was won by Jock Taylor and passenger Benga Johannson, who broke their own lap record of 108.29mph. It would remain intact for another seven years, only being bettered in 1989.

Second in the second sidecar race, behind Taylor and Johannson, was husband and wife team Dennis and Julia Bingham, who were more than one minute behind.

However, the overall victory from the two races went to Hanks and Biggs, who were fifth in the second race.

The F3 class for smaller machines was dropped in 1982, followed by the F2 class in 1987.

The Formula 1 class would prove to be even more popular as, having helped launch and eventually establish modern superbike racing, it would only be replaced by the Superbike TT as late as 2005.

Meanwhile, the TT fortnight was increasingly being sold to its huge following as a motorcycling festival, rather than just a selection of races.

The races themselves, while still attracting some overseas interest, would be dominated by UK and Irish riders, with the lap and race records consistently being broken as the machines continued to get more and more powerful. The TT remained as unique as ever and began to thrive once more.

The lap record would go again in the Senior Classic TT when Norman Brown, riding a 500 Suzuki, raised it to 116mph in 1983.

Honda later reclaimed the record with Dunlop, and then Steve Cull, having being usurped by Suzuki's Brown.

And then came the arrival of Scotsman Steve Hislop. Making his TT debut in 1985, the 'Flying Haggis' was notable for his distinctive pink helmet.

After winning a TT for the first time two years later, it would eventually mark the beginning of yet another era of great racing on the Isle of Man.

Formula 1 TT 1983

Joey joins Honda and makes immediate impact

By 1983, Joey Dunlop's performances were making the factory teams take notice and that same year he became a works rider for the Honda team for the first time – and it proved to be one of the most successful pairings in the history of the TT.

He took his first Formula 1 victory that year and his win was filmed for the movie *V for Victory*, which would also go on to become part of racing folklore.

Joey had suffered no problems at all at the TT that year; it was just the perfect combination of winning machine being ridden by a hugely talented racer.

The F1 had become a three-round competition, with the likes of Mick Grant and Rob McElnea of Suzuki competing against the likes of Honda's Roger Marshall to claim the spoils.

And yet it was Honda's use of Dunlop tyres and Shell Oils that had also helped to made Joey's bike a winning combination.

First off the line in the F1 race was New Zealander Dave Hiscock and Geoff Johnson, with Joey and Malcolm Lucas following behind ten seconds later. Charlie Williams and Alan Jackson went off as the third pairing.

Joey had the lead as he came into the pits for the first time to take on fuel, followed by team-mate Marshall. But Joey never looked back and, despite having had a poor practice week, the win gave him his second successive world title.

And it was more of the same in 1984, with another F1 victory, closely followed by reclaiming the world title once more.

ISLE OF MAN TT MEMORIES

Kevin Morgan, Ruyton-XI-Towns, near Shrewsbury, in Shropshire, competed in his first TT in 2019 with his brother, Steve, as passenger, in the sidecar class. They followed in the footsteps of their TT-winning father, Kevin, who died aged 59, following an accident at Ballacrye during a qualifying session on 31 May 2011:

The idea of writing about my most memorable TT really got me thinking.

I have been to the TT almost 20 times in the past 35 years, but I can honestly say I don't really remember a particular race.

Maybe it's different when you have a family member competing, or maybe it's just that my memory is rubbish! But either way, I don't recall a specific race.

However, one that does stand out is the first Formula 2 sidecar race, which was held in 1984 alongside the F1 sidecar race.

It's special for me because it was won by my dad, on his debut! He was the passenger for Cliff Pritchard, who still lives in Shrewsbury and helps Steve and I now.

I can't say I can remember it probably because I was only three, but I was there and I do have a couple of photos from that year.

The result is listed in some books but others just have the combined results, which I think placed them around 35th.

They should have won race two as well but they changed piston rings between races and it seized.

Senior TT 1984

McElnea pulls off an unlikely win as Joey runs out of fuel

Having seen the lap record broken in five out of the six laps, it is fair to say the public thought Joey Dunlop might win this one.

However, digging away behind the scenes was Rob McElnea, who himself had been circulating under the previous record lap times during the race. But even his valiant efforts were not enough to reel in Dunlop, who held a 40-second lead.

However, everything would change on the sixth and final lap as Dunlop's Honda started to hit trouble. It was because, just ten miles from the finish line, his bike had started running out of fuel.

Dunlop had knocked six seconds off Charlie William's old record on the opening lap to lead McElnea by 1.8 seconds. McElnea himself was on a flyer and pushing as hard as he could.

By lap two the deficit had been reduced to just one second at Ballacraine and then McElnea had taken a three-second lead at the Bungalow, lapping at 118.23mph.

But, as is often the case at the TT, the pit stop would play a crucial role in the outcome. Dunlop had pulled a 17.5-second lead gap at Ballaugh by lap three but then pulled in for a surprise pit stop himself.

It was all part of a plan that ultimately failed. As Dunlop screamed past, McElnea pitted, which gave his rival a 22-second lead by the start of lap five.

The lead had jumped to 34 seconds by the Bungalow, as Dunlop again posted a new lap record of 118.48mph but more drama was to follow as he ran out of fuel, paving the way for McElnea to steal an unlikely win.

McElnea admitted during interviews after the race he could not understand why he had been so far behind at the start of lap four – he had no idea about the pit stop strategies.

Such had been the pace set by the battling front two, rider Roger Marshall, who had come in second following Joey's disastrous end, was three minutes behind – lapping more than 3mph slower too. Trevor Nation rounded out the top three.

Junior TT 1985

Reid and Joey go toe-to-toe

On the Wednesday of race week, the weather was wonderful and the crowd was waiting in anticipation for the six-lap Junior TT to start. Always seen as one of the most competitive and dramatic races, this one seemed especially close to call with Brian Reid on the EMC and Joey Dunlop on the Honda.

The fact they were both Ulstermen just seemed to add to the occasion. Reid had been fourth fastest in practice but had not received much luck in his earlier two races in 1985.

And early into the Junior he was being chased hard by Joey, who had left the start line just ten seconds behind after setting off with Steve Williams.

Steve Cole and Gerry Brennan, another pair of Ulstermen, were close behind too – but Joey was on a real mission from the first corner and looked in ominous form.

By the end of laps one and two, Joey had already managed to take the lead from Reid, who still led on the road, but this race was far from over and Reid hit back, retaking the lead on lap three.

The reason for that, however, was the fact the bike Joey had rescued from the sea earlier that week, when their boat had sunk during their trip from Ireland to the Isle of Man, had sprung a leak from its fuel tank.

Joey was still in no mood to give up first position because, after Reid had pitted himself, he had somehow managed to retake the lead again.

Gary Padgett by now had worked his way up to fifth while Steve Cole had stayed in the top three throughout the race.

But it was all going on at the front of the race as Reid – who had been out of fuel when he pitted – again retook the lead on the penultimate lap, signalling once again to Joey he really had a fight on his hands.

Heading into the final lap, it was as you were, with Reid, Joey and Cole holding the three podium positions, but who would be standing where on the rostrum was still up for grabs. Then disaster struck, for Reid anyway, as he cruelly ran out of fuel just two miles from the finish line, paving the way for Joey – who would later call the victory his luckiest TT win – to claim his win number two of the week, with Cole promoted to second and Eddie Roberts in third, three minutes adrift.

Graham Cannell, Gene McDonnell and Johnny Rea rounded out the top six while the small consolation for Reid was the fact he had set a new lap record of 112.088mph, finishing his lap in 20 minutes and 11.8 seconds.

Joey had also started his week in superb fashion, reclaiming his world title for the third successive year while winning the Formula 1 TT once again, which would eventually see him become one of the few racers to claim three wins in a single week on the island.

It was this year that Joey and 12 fellow passengers nearly sank, along with their machines, when the fishing boat they were travelling in went down en route to the Isle of Man.

After recovering one bike during low tide, divers prepared to rescue seven others they thought may still be on the fishing boat, which had sunk 100 metres to the seabed.

As the first bike was pulled ashore, Joey was first on the scene to assess how badly the bikes had been damaged.

Frightened and left shaken, he was soon back racing his motorbike at the TT, which began with the F1 race he had become so accustomed to winning.

It was a title he had held for the past three seasons with Honda and he was straight on the pace, setting the fastest times during practice.

Joey's competition, however, was fierce with the likes of GP racer Klaus Klein, from Germany, although he was feeling a little battered and bruised after suffering a crash during practice.

Klein and Andy McGladdery were first off the line, followed by Joey and Tony Rutter, on a Suzuki Four.

Marshall and Gary Padgett were following behind on the roads but Joey was leading the race by two seconds at Ballacraine, which had been extended even further at Ballaugh Bridge, having already overtaken Klein and McGladdery on the roads to lead the race on the road and on time.

In hot pursuit were Steve Parrish, Mick Grant, Marshall and Rob Vine. By Ramsey, Joey was pulling further away from second-place Marshall, with Grant holding on to third.

By the start of lap two, as Joey stormed down Bray Hill, he had opened up a 30-second lead on Marshall, with McGladdery third on the road but fourth overall.

Into Quarter bridge, and Joey still led McGladdery and Marshall on the road as he headed back towards Braddan and Ballaugh Bridge, Parliament Square and up May Hill before heading over the mountain on his way to his second pit stop.

Behind him, Grant had moved into second place with privateer McGladdery in third after Marshall had stopped at the Mountain Box, eventually being forced to retire.

Rutter had really been pushing on, and his efforts had paid off too with the retirements of both Grant and McGladdery moving him into second and Parrish into third.

However, all those breakdowns had given Joey a staggering lead of nearly four minutes.

And as he neared the end of his final lap, cheered by the crowds through the Gooseneck and at the Creg, Joey and Rutter brought their bikes home safely to take the top two positions.

But there was bad news for Parrish, who was disqualified for having an oversized tank, which promoted Sammy McClements on to the final podium spot.

Joey had won the F1 TT again and showed his unstoppable form early on breaking the lap record from a standing start on the opening circuit, despite his bike leaking brake fluid, which meant his race boots could not stay planted on the foot pegs, but it mattered not as he claimed his first win of the week.

After adding the Junior, and with two wins already in the bag, Joey headed into Senior TT full of confidence as warm weather once again greeted the riders.

Only Mike Hailwood had managed three wins in a week before, in 1961 and 1967, and Joey had Marshall nipping at his heels, while newcomer Roger Burnett was also looking in fine form, and Tony Rutter, racing in his 21st year on the island, was also one to watch out for. Steven Cole had also looked good throughout the week.

Joey was on the pace immediately and had the lead at Ballaugh Bridge, closely followed by Marshall and Trevor Nation. But it was Joey who led Klein and Nation, with Mark Johns in fourth during the early stages of the race. Mick Grant had crashed at Black Box and broken his thumb.

Marshall moved into second by the start of lap two, while his team-mate held a 33-second lead as the riders came into the pits.

Joey continued to lead Marshall – who would set the fastest lap of the race with a 116mph effort – and Johns as the race progressed with Sammy McClements in fourth. He would take his third TT of the week, 16 seconds ahead of his team-mate, taking his seventh victory in all on the island.

However, the race would be clouded in tragedy as Rob Vine, from Dover, who had a best-ever finish of second in the Classic Manx GP the year before, died after crashing in the Senior TT in 1985.

The Rob Vine Fund was set up in his memory to provide equipment and training that would benefit Manx motorsport, which continues to this day.

ISLE OF MAN TT MEMORIES

Andy Davies, from Stourbridge, West Midlands, is a former classic bike club championship winner, who has also competed in endurance racing and at the Classic TT:

It was 2013, I was 42 years old and I was sat watching my first Manx Grand Prix on the Isle of Man – and that's when the bug really bit me.

Seeing the classic and more modern machines fly past as I sat there on the bank by Signpost Corner, it had me thinking, 'I'd love a go at that.'

Having club raced for ten years, winning a couple of championships along the way, I felt I would be capable of giving it a good go.

What followed in the next 12 months was late nights in the garage, preparing a bike that had last seen action in the 1986 Formula 2 TT. It was a Spondon 350 YPVSs that needed lots of fabrication, repairs and renovation of every single component, which I discovered while I was preparing the bike.

Visiting the Isle of Man to learn the course, I was soon amazed by the support behind the whole event, which included the TT and the Manx GP

From residents of the island, to a guy round the corner who could ally weld the next bracket, the knowledge and history just has so many people hooked – like myself.

Twelve months after I'd sat watching the Manx Grand Prix, I was now sat in the paddock queuing up to go out for my first timed practice.

I was ready to head down Bray Hill flat out on my very own machine. The next 37 miles blew my brain – there's no feeling in the world quite like that TT course.

But from a TT fan's point of view, the race that sticks in my mind is when Mat Oxley did a 100mph lap on a Production 250 TZR in 1986. It was truly incredible.

Production Class D TT 1986

Mat Oxley becomes first rider to top the 100mph barrier on a 250cc production machine.

Mat Oxley was in record-breaking form in the Production Class D TT of 1986 but unfortunately, despite smashing the 100mph barrier, would not win the race.

After sliding off his Yamaha at Governor's Bridge, he left the gate open for Barry Woodland to take the win.

Oxley's crash would be one of many during the 1986 TT, which was plagued with terrible weather and led to four riders being killed, including Gene McDonnell. Joey had become so accustomed to winning the F1 TT it almost seemed inevitable he would add to it again – and so it proved as he claimed his eighth TT and fourth straight F1 TT victory and fifth consecutive F1 world title.

The early part of the 1986 race week had been hit by bad weather, but as the mist eased the racers were finally ready to hit the track on the Monday, although it was put back until the afternoon and cut from six laps to four.

Joey admitted that building up to a race for three days had been nerve-wracking, especially with riders still unsure of what tyres to choose and where the track might be damp or dry as they lined up on the grid.

One of his biggest rivals was once again Roger Marshall, who was yet to win a TT, but first off on the start line was Klaus Klein and Brian Reid, followed by Joey and Andy McGladdery, Trevor Nation and Steve Parrish, Geoff Johnson and Steve Cole, Roger Burnett and Phil Mellor, and Marshall and Gary Padgett.

Dunlop was still too strong once again in the early stages, taking a seven-second lead, while his team-mate's Honda began to misfire.

Reid was soon forced to retire with Johnson holding second place and McGladdery third at the end of lap two, as Joey pitted for fuel and a new tyre.

Marshall had moved up to third but was well behind the front two as the third lap began, with Nation in seventh and Burnett all the way back in 30th.

With a change of tyre, Joey had increased his lead to 40 seconds by May Hill and then almost a full minute on the final lap, with Johnson in second, McGladdery third, John Weeden fourth, Mellor fifth and Nation sixth. Marshall had been forced to retire on the final lap.

Joey spoke frankly after the race saying both he and the fans would have preferred a six-lap race, admittedly with a wry smile, while a beaming Johnson said he ranked his second place in the F1 TT over his two Production TT wins.

But it was circumstances during the Junior race that would lead to one of the worst and most unfortunate accidents in the history of the TT.

Brian Reid led all the way on his Yamaha, establishing new race and lap records, in the Formula 2 TT with John Weeden second and Neil Tuxworth third.

Reid, however, crashed at Ballaugh Bridge during the Junior, which saw the helicopter being despatched.

The noise frightened a horse, which ran on to the course after jumping several fences and gates, colliding with McDonnell's bike, ending both the animal and rider's lives.

Steve Cull went on to win the race ahead of Phil Mellor and Graham Cannell but they had only continued because they had been completely unaware of what had happened to their fellow rider.

The Senior TT was won by surprise package Roger Burnett after Marshall, Nation and Dunlop were all forced into long pit stops or retirements, with Geoff Johnson second and Barry Woodland third.

Another standout win came in the three-wheeled format as Lowry Burton and passenger Pat Cushnahan became the first Irish pair to win a TT sidecar race with victory in the first leg.

And in the second race, the 750cc Barton Phoenix engine, best known for its role in the film *Silver Dream Racer*, was powered to victory by Nigel Rollason and Donne Williams for another famous win.

Production Class C TT 1986
Padgett beats Wheeler by just one second

There was just something about the Production races in 1986 that seemed to tick all the boxes because, as well as Oxley's 100mph, the Production C was also a memorable battle as Gary Padgett beat Malcolm Wheeler by a single, solitary second.

And what the spectacle even more spectacular was the fact the pair had set off on the roads at the same time, setting up a truly memorable duel.

The Production C class, for 250cc-400cc two-strokes and 401cc-600cc four-strokes, was new to the TT that year and Padgett, on a previously unseen Suzuki RG400, started alongside veteran Malc Wheeler, who was riding a GPZ600 Kawasaki.

Padgett led the way early on, pulling a gap of 4.6 seconds by the end of the opening circuit but the pair would spend the next three laps tied together. Nothing, it seemed, could separate them.

After both pitting for fuel after the end of the first lap, Steve Linsdell temporarily took a 5.2-second advantage by the end of lap two.

However, as Linsdell had to slow to conserve fuel, Padgett and Wheeler made their moves and both had soon closed the gap, eventually moving ahead for the final lap.

And then the race really kicked into life as the pair continued to swap the lead, especially over the mountain descent. With fans and team nervously counting down the clock, it was Padgett who crossed the line first with Wheeler one second further back after 113.19 miles of tremendous road racing.

The Production A class had been more straightforward as Trevor Nation destroyed the field breaking lap and race records in the process. Lapping under 20 minutes on a production machine for the first time, he raised the speeds to 113.26mph, taking the win ahead of Kevin Wilson and Brian Morrison.

Phil Mellor put in a similarly dominant display in the Production Class B TT. He too broke the lap record, with an average lap speed of 110.69mph, which had not just raised the level, it had annihilated the previous best by 5mph.

Senior TT 1987

Joey does big bike double in treacherous conditions

An unstoppable Joey Dunlop made it five F1 wins in a row in 1987, despite his exhaust falling off, en route to claiming a big bike double on the island with a further victory in the Senior TT later that same week in more terrible conditions.

Phil Mellor had been touted as Joey's biggest rival for the win on his works Suzuki, having broken the lap record during practice. It seemed the lap record could fall once again, especially with Roger Marshall and Geoff Johnson also on the start line, not to mention Andy McGladdery, Trevor Nation and Klaus Klein.

McGladdery and Joey were towing each other along nicely during the early part of the race as they closed in on Klein and Johnson at Union Mills and heading into Ballacraine.

Mellor, as predicted, was Joey's closest rival with Marshall and Nick Jefferies already ahead of Brian Reid and Mark Johns.

Joey continued to pull away as he reached Ramsey on the opening lap, eventually enjoying a 22-second lead, with Marshall slotting into third behind Mellor in second.

Lap two saw more of the same, although Marshall had reduced Mellor's lead over him to 2.8 seconds while Johnson slotted into third.

But out front, Joey lapped at 117.55mph on lap two, which would be the fastest of the race as he extended his lead to 25 seconds, which increased by a further second as they completed lap three.

With the second pit stop approaching, Joey continued his superb speeds, despite knocking his exhaust out of place while changing gears. Behind him, Mellor and Johnson were lapping at the same pace, holding second and third respectively.

Despite pitting, Joey's team could not fix his exhaust in time so he set off with the problem still hampering him for lap five, but vitally with a 33-second lead on Mellor, who was aware of the bike problems facing the race leader.

However, by Kirk, Michael Joey had a lead of 40 seconds, which was increased still further by Quarry Bends, despite his exhaust issues.

With a 47-second lead heading into the final lap, the 35-year-old eventually crossed the line to take another commanding lead, followed by Mellor and Johnson, with Marshall in fourth.

With conditions again taking a turn for the worst, the Senior TT was reduced to four laps and moved to the Saturday.

But with mist on the mountain leaving the roads wet, and wet leaves beneath some of the trees, none of the riders were looking forward to racing.

And as they set off, spray could clearly be seen trailing the bikes as they nervously made their way around the 37.73-mile course for the opening lap, completely unaware of what lay ahead of them.

Slightly surprisingly, it was Nation who held a slender, early two-second lead at Ballacraine with Mellor in second, but not for long as Joey soon retook the lead – and he had the front tyre in the air as he screamed down Bray Hill for the start of lap two, with Mellor still holding second, some 25 seconds behind, with Nation in third.

As they came into the pits, Joey's lead had fallen to nine seconds, as Mellor continued to circulate for another lap, hoping to stretch his gap. And he was soon leading the race by half a minute, with Johnson now in third.

Marshall, with his visor no longer steaming up, was beginning to pick up the pace again while Johnson was also flying, putting in the quickest lap of the race.

And there was soon another huge shock as Mellor was suddenly leading on the roads and on corrected time as Joey had dropped back, with Marshall in fourth.

With conditions getting worse, Joey was soon back in the lead and then Mellor came off at The Nook while trying to clear his visor, injuring his shoulder and elbow while a broken clutch lever prevented him from bravely trying to continue with the race.

It left Joey to take the win from Johnson by more than a minute, marking one of the toughest TTs of his already illustrious Isle of Man career. Afterwards, he said the race should not have been run, despite his victory in the 80th year of racing at the TT.

Formula TT 1988

Joey's record sixth straight F1 win en route to another treble

More records would tumble for Joey during the 1988 TT as he matched Mike Hailwood by becoming only the second rider in the history of the TT to claim two hat-tricks on the island.

Beating the likes of rising stars Steve Hislop and Carl Fogarty, he would once again show why he was truly the King of the Mountain.

Aiming to start the week with a sixth straight victory in the F1 race, one of his main rivals was Yamaha's Geoff Johnson, who had enjoyed a solid practice and was pushing for first TT win.

Johnson set off first on the road with Nick Jefferies, followed by Joey ten seconds behind. Roger Burnett, who had won the 1986 Senior TT in stunning fashion, was also on form as was Roger Marshall, who was still looking for that elusive TT win. Sadly, his bad luck would continue as he broke down on the first lap at Ballacraine.

Meanwhile, Joey had already caught Jefferies and Johnson on the road, while Hislop was also looking very fast.

Mellor was forced to retire as Joey led on the roads and on corrected time, posting a 116.77mph opening lap from a standing start to lead by 14 seconds.

Hislop, with a lap of 118.44mph, was up to fourth by lap two with Jefferies in third, closely followed by Johnson.

Lap four and Joey's lead was 44 seconds, with Hislop now up to second and Johnson maintaining third. Foggy was in sixth while Burnett was back in the mix following a puncture on his rear tyre as lap five approached.

Following a leisurely pit stop, 23-year-old Hislop had cut the lead to 20 seconds while Johnson suffered bike problems during his battle with Jefferies, forcing him to retire.

And with Hislop also suffering an engine seizure, Joey's commanding lead increased even further as he became the first rider to win six TTs in a row, as well as taking second place on the all-time leaderboard.

Eddie Laycock had won the previous year's Junior TT but was recovering from a broken collarbone, while Brian Reid was racing with a broken toe and Joey had only posted the 11th fastest time in practice. It seemed an intriguing race lay ahead.

But it mattered not to Joey as he was soon leading the race by 12 seconds ahead of fellow Honda rider Reid, with Laycock in fourth.

Joey looked unstoppable, recording the first sub-20-minute lap in the class, but a terrible pit stop meant all his hard work had been temporarily undone as Reid stole the race lead.

They were soon circulating together on the roads at Sarah's Cottage but Joey proved to be too strong and extended his lead once more en route to his 12th TT win, setting yet more race and lap records, taking the win from Reid with Laycock battling to a superb third place.

Joey headed into the Senior feeling it was going to be his toughest of the week but he also believed the lap record was likely to tumble once more.

Jefferies was ahead of the road with Joey catching Johnson, despite the latter starting ten seconds ahead.

In perfect conditions, Joey was pushing to be leading on the road and he soon had his wish by the Bungalow as he shattered his own lap record from a standing start, posting a speed of 118.66mph, with Cull amazingly just five seconds behind by the end of the lap and Jefferies in third.

With Cull and now fourth-placed Hislop pushing hard, Joey knew he had a real race on his hands – and sure enough, by the end of lap two, Cull had cut the lead to just 1.4 seconds.

Somehow, Joey was able to respond once more, increasing his lead to four seconds by the middle of lap three. Cull's record-breaking efforts would take their toll on his Honda, pushing a hole in his exhaust, allowing Joey to increase his lead to 18 seconds, with Hislop in second place.

On the last lap, Joey's lead had increased to nearly a minute, as Cull's bike burst into flames, with Johnson now in third and Hislop taking second. It marked win number 13 for Joey, putting him just one behind the then record TT winner, Mike Hailwood.

Junior TT 1989

Rea claims an emotional first win as Hizzy crashes out

The year 1989 was filled with incredibly close battles that saw new TT winners crowned by winning margins of between one and three seconds in three of the races.

There were also plenty of high-speed crashes and tragedies that reminded the watching public why the TT was so dangerous and why all the riders were held in such high esteem.

The Junior TT that same year was also held over four laps, and was contested by the likes of Phil McCallen, Carl Fogarty, Johnny Rea and Steve Hislop.

Foggy found himself down to seventh during the early stages of the race, behind Steve Williams, who had slotted into sixth with Ian Newton also going well on the roads.

This would be McCallen's first TT but he arrived with confidence as a double Manx GP winner. However, leading the race by about five seconds was Hislop.

By the end of the opening lap, Eddie Laycock was leading on the road and third on corrected time, behind second-placed Rea and race leader Hislop, who posted an opening lap of 113.1mph to lead by six seconds, with Foggy in seventh on a brand-new bike.

Graham McGregor was also going well in fourth place but out front Hislop was closing in on Laycock and was primed to lead on the roads as well as corrected time early into lap two.

However, everything would soon change as Hislop would suffer a 130mph crash. Somehow, he had ended up unscathed and was even seen watching his rivals go by as a spectator soon after.

Williams was up to fourth place with reigning Junior Manx GP winner Steve Hazlett, in his first TT, in an impressive fifth.

Laycock had moved into second place but he was still 17 seconds off race leader Rea, with Foggy still in seventh, Newton in sixth and Hazlett in fifth at the end of lap two.

McGregor had moved into third with Williams in fourth during the penultimate lap but Rea still held a very commanding lead while also being reeled in on the roads by second-placed Laycock.

Bike problems for McGregor moved Hazlett into third while Foggy had moved into fourth and Ian Young in to fifth as the riders headed into the final lap.

Laycock seemed to be on record-lap speed and was pushing Rea, but he too was determined to claim his first TT win.

With Foggy, who had only had one practice lap on his bike before it was flown in for the TT, now flying and Hazlett on for a podium in his first TT, not to mention the battle raging at the front, the Junior TT of 1989 was set up for one of the classic finishes.

And as the riders headed to Hillberry, new lap record holder Laycock was unable to close the gap enough as he eventually lost the race to Northern Ireland's Rea by under three seconds.

It was an emotional first TT win for Rea, who was followed by Eddie Laycock in second, Steve Hazlett in third, Foggy in fourth, Ian Young fifth, Barry Woodland sixth, Derek Chatterton seventh, Richard Coates eighth and Richard Swallow ninth, with Robbie Boland rounding out the top ten of a truly wonderful, closely fought race.

The four-lap supersport race had been held in very different conditions, with light rain affecting pretty much all sections of the circuit.

Again, Hislop had very much been seen as the man to beat, having posted a new lap record of more than 121mph during the practice week.

Early in the first race, Leach had powered his way into second place behind the ferocious Hislop leading on the roads and the race.

On to the final lap, and the Flying Scotsman was well out in front, with Leach second on the roads, with Whitham and Mellor circulating together, despite Whitham having started ten seconds behind his team-mate.

Hislop would go on to win by 28 seconds, to give Honda their first win at the TT marking their 30th anniversary of racing around the island.

Production 1300 TT 1989

Close battle ends in two tragedies

Racing over four laps, three-time winner Phil Mellor and his Suzuki team-mate, Jamie Whitham, were donned in their Durex-sponsored livery and leathers on the start for what was about to be truly epic TT battle.

Dave Leach, going off at number seven, was the race favourite and had won a TT the year before, while Nick Jefferies was also seen as a guaranteed front runner.

Jefferies and Brian Morrison led the riders away, and it was indeed Jefferies who was leading on the roads early in the race, followed by Morrison and Steve Henshaw.

Leach was leading the race on corrected time, with Mellor and Whitham not far behind.

Jefferies found some serious air going over Ballaugh Bridge to show he was really on the pace. As a former

AJS rider Eric Williams is assisted by A J Stevens, left, one of the founding members of the motorcycle company, along with his brother Joseph Stevens Jr, right.

AJS rider Howard R Davies, on an AJS motorcycle, during the 1914 Isle of Man TT.

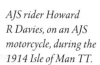

HOWARD R DAVIES A.J.S.

The AJS team prepares for the 1914 Isle of Man Junior TT races, probably at the Graiseley Hill site of the AJS factory.

John Surtees, the only man to win Formula One and motorcycle grand prix titles, was a TT great.

John Surtees was a master around the Isle of Man TT course.

Bill Doran was immortalised at the Isle of Man TT with a bend named in his honour – Doran's Bend – after he came a cropper there in 1950, riding for the AJS works team. He escaped with a broken leg. [**MNA media**]

Pip Harris and his racing partner, Ray Campbell, compete at the Isle of Man TT races during the early 1960s. [**MNA media**]

*Pip and Ray take a break from competing at the Isle of Man TT races. [**MNA media**]*

*Brian Meeson, left, and Tony O'Brian, of Walsall Wasp Racing, with their finished new sidecar outfit, which was prepared for the TT races during the late 1970s. [**MNA media**]*

*Barry Randle, of Wordsley, competed at the TT for more than a decade and had a best finish of second in 1971. [**MNA media**]*

Graham Cannell, Tony Rutter and Phil Mellor collect their rosettes.

Tony Rutter and Phil Mellor on the start line in the 1970s.

Tony Rutter, left, and Dennis Ireland, right, watch Mike Hailwood spray the champagne after the 1979 Senior TT.

Mike Hailwood, who lapped in 111.75mph, Tony Rutter (109.84), and Dennis Ireland (109.45) after the Senior TT in 1979.

Tony Rutter and Ray McCullough.

A young Michael Rutter celebrates one of dad Tony's Isle of Man TT wins with his mum, Pauline.

That's how you do it, son! Tony Rutter is smiles in front of Michael (bottom left) after another TT win.

Ron Haslam was involved in one of the most memorable TTs when he was stripped of the win in 1981.

Tony Rutter looking super smooth at Ballaugh Bridge.

Tony Rutter was a master on a Ducati during his illustrious racing career on the Isle of Man.

Tony Rutter on the Isle of Man in 1985 just prior to the accident that effectively ended his career, although he raced on the island until 1991.

*Mayor of Kidderminster, Mike Shellie, and his wife, Gloria, during their days as motorbike and sidecar racers at the Isle of Man TT race in 1993. [**MNA media**]*

Carl Fogarty was involved in one of the TT's greatest battles during the 1992 Senior. **[MNA media]**

Michael Rutter began his TT racing career very early. Here he is being interviewed in 1997.

Michael Rutter on the start line with Joey Dunlop, Ian Simpson and Phil McCallen.

Joey Dunlop talks Tony Rutter through his stunning wins in 2000, just prior to his tragic death.

Joey shocked the racing world when he claimed the Formula 1 TT in 2000, aged 48.

Passenger Kevin Morgan racing with his friend Cliff Pritchard during the 2002 TT races.
[MNA media]

David Jefferies and the TAS Suzuki team seemed a match made in heaven until tragedy struck on Friday, 30 May 2003.

Multiple TT winner Michael Rutter racing in 2006.

John McGuinness on his way to a memorable, record-breaking 130mph lap.
[ottpix@btinternet.com]

John McGuinness, at Glen Helen, en route to claiming the 2008 Senior TT win. He etched his name even further into the Isle of Man TT record books, taking his 14th Isle of Man TT victory and equalling the tally of the legendary Mike Hailwood.
[ottpix@btinternet.com]

Michael Rutter had switched to
Kawasakis for the 2009 TT races.

Conor Cummins, in the trademark
McAdoo Kawasaki Racing colours,
suffered an horrendous crash during the
Senior TT in 2010. [*John Cleator*]

Guy Martin heads down the Cronk y Voddy Straight during the 2011 Isle of Man TT.
[*John Cleator*]

Michael Dunlop,
heads over the
mountain section
in 2011.
[*John Cleator*]

Bruce Anstey heads down the Cronk y Voddy Straight during the 2011 Isle of Man TT. [**John Cleator**]

John McGuinness has clear road in front and behind during the 2011 TT races. [**John Cleator**]

William Dunlop leads Dean Harrison and Michael Rutter. [**John Cleator**]

*Michael Dunlop in action during the 2013 TT. [**John Cleator**]*

*Donald leads McGuinness as the fans watch on in 2013. [**John Cleator**]*

*Ben and Tom Birchall en route to victory during the second 2013 sidecar TT. [**John Cleator**]*

*Cummins in action during the 2013 TT. [**John Cleator**]*

Michael Dunlop leads Bruce Anstey and James Hillier through Sign Post Corner, Onchan, in 2014 [**John Cleator**]

Conor Cummins can see Michael Rutter hot on his heels at Sign Post Corner, Onchan, in 2014. [**John Cleator**]

Big wheelie from Michael Dunlop with Guy Martin in the distance, at Lazayre Church, 2014. [**John Cleator**]

Ian and Colin Bell through Kirk Michael in 2014. [**John Cleator**]

Michael Dunlop gets some serious air in the supersport race at Kirk Michael in 2014. [**John Cleator**]

Tim Reeves, left, and Patrick Farrance teamed up for the 2016 Isle of Man TT, coming third in the second sidecar race. [**MNA media**]

McGuinness gets a hug on the startline before the second supersport race in 2016. [**ottpix@btinternet. com**]

Dunlop heads down Ballacraine on his Suzuki during Wednesday evening's practice in 2017.
*[**Ellan Vannin Images**]*

Bruce Anstey during the 2017 TT Friday evening Superbike practice at Creg Ny Baa.
*[**Ellan Vannin Images**]*

Hutchy in action during the Friday evening practice at Creg ny Baa in 2017.
*[**Ellan Vannin Images**]*

Johnson during 2017 Senior TT practice at Ballacrye leap.
*[**Ellan Vannin Images**]*

motocross and trial bike rider, he was renowned for keeping such big leaps under great control.

But it was fellow Yorkshireman Leach who still led the race on corrected time, which was how it remained as he careered down to the bottom of Bray Hill to start lap two, with Whitham now promoted to third place. Leach had maintained his lead with an opening lap of more than 115mph.

The positions were still the same at Rhencullen, but then a tragic accident claimed the life of popular rider Steve Henshaw during the second lap, as well as Mellor, who came off at Doran's Bend. As the race continued, Leach was still lapping at 115mph and Jefferies, ahead on the road, was keeping the pace up front, but behind them Alan Batson had moved into third and Howard Selby into fourth.

With both Leach and Jefferies now lapping at more than 115mph into the third lap, Batson was holding third place.

Jefferies would endure quite a solitary race as Brian Morrison, who set off at the same time, had been forced to retire at the halfway point, while Leach continued to close the gap on the road, setting a lap of more than 113mph despite his pit stop as they headed into the final lap.

So it was Leach leading, Jefferies in second and Batson in third, despite having a bit of a moment at Glen Helen.

It was a case of so close and yet so far for Jefferies, who again had to settle for second, while Leach claimed his second TT win with a record-breaking lap of 115.61mph.

Batson, with his first TT podium, ensured it was a Yamaha one-two-three across the finish line.

Production 750 TT 1989

Foggy beats Leach by 1.8 seconds to claim first TT

When you have Steve Hislop, Carl Fogarty and Dave Leach all dicing for the lead, you know it's going to be a classic race, and it proved to be during the 1989 Production 750 race as victory was stolen by less than two seconds.

For four laps the racers changed the roads into a short circuit as they went toe-to-toe for four exhilarating laps.

Hislop, who had become the first man to break the 120mph barrier in the Formula 1 race earlier in the week, led to begin with on his RC30 Honda but he had to stop for fuel at the end of the first lap while Fogarty was able to stretch his machine for two laps.

After the last round of pit stops, all three were together on the road once more and it eventually ended in what all the fans had craved – a last-lap dash to be crowned TT winner.

And Foggy's gamble of taking a later pit stop had paid off as he etched out a 1.8-second advantage.

When his Honda team-mate Hislop realised he was unlikely to be able to close the gap, it meant the three-way battle had turned into a straight duel between Foggy and Yamaha-mounted Leach.

Reigning TT Formula 1 world champion Fogarty and Leach swapped the lead repeatedly but as Leach's exhaust began to work its way loose, it allowed Fogarty to dive ahead at Brandish and he pulled away for his maiden TT win.

Robert Dunlop, Joey's younger brother, upheld the family name by winning the first 125cc race on the Mountain Course for 15 years, with Ian Lougher in second and Foggy in third.

And in the Senior, Hislop was simply unstoppable as he took the win on his 750 Honda, taking the win ahead of Nick Jefferies and Graeme McGregor in third.

CARL FOGARTY

It is highly unlikely the achievements of Carl Fogarty will ever be repeated and the master revealed all about his love for the TT and his illustrious career during an article in the Express & Star *newspaper:*

The four-time World Superbike champion dominated the series when it was at its absolute peak, with riders cheered on by more than 120,000 raucous fans when they sped around the British tracks. But what really made 'Foggy' unique was how he was able to conquer the road racing scene while also holding a world title at the same time – all before his WSBK career even began.

'I was the last racer to win a TT and then a world championship in the same year,' he said. 'Nobody will ever win both again, in my opinion – those years are long gone. The TT is dominated by British riders but racers tend to enter the TT just because they want to.

'But it is still the one race I don't want to miss every year and I have a lot of special memories of that place, which includes going there with my dad when I was younger.'

Foggy, aged 51, from Blackburn, first broke on to the international scene racing on the roads rather than the circuits, following in his father's footsteps. He first became Formula 1 TT world champion at the age of 23, in 1988, and then defended his title the following year.

The series then lost world championship status from the FIM – mainly due to the dangerous nature of racing on public roads – but Foggy remained and the world really took notice of his incredible talents when he completed a double race win at the TT during 1990, claiming the Senior and F1 trophies, as well as being named FIM F1 World Cup Champion.

His domination at the turn of the decade would see him given his first WSBK ride and, despite going on to reign supreme, he admits he should perhaps have left the road racing scene behind him at the same time.

If he had, however, he would never have battled with the late Steve Hislop during the 1992 Senior TT race, which has since been voted the greatest race to have ever taken place on the island, numerous times.

'The race was annoying for me really because no one could've raced that bike harder than I did that day,' said Foggy, who eventually settled for second despite breaking the lap record. 'Yamaha did not have a very strong package that year and my top speed was never in the top eight.

'It was still a great bike to ride though and looking back at how hard I rode round there I'm lucky to still be here really.

'I pushed very hard and I was trying to beat a very special rider, the greatest to ride round there in my opinion.

'The lap record I set was 122mph and that stood for seven years, which is quite rare.'

Average lap speeds around the 37.73-mile island course are now just shy of 134mph but Foggy is confident, if he was racing today's modern bikes in his prime, he would still be the best.

'I think I would still be going faster than those boys today if I was still racing,' he said. 'Everything gets faster each year in all forms of racing.

'The TT has got really big and popular now. It's become much more famous because of the TV money and interest. Personally, my favourite memory was winning the Senior TT in 1990.

'I probably should've stopped racing around there after that because that was the one thing I wanted to achieve before focussing on the short circuit racing.'

When Foggy did start shifting his focus to the tracks, he made his WSBK debut in 1991, finishing seventh.

The following year would prove to be one of his busiest as he lifted a first World Endurance title while also finishing ninth in WSBK. Foggy, who is married and has two daughters, secured a first factory ride in WSBK with Raymond Roche's Ducati team in 1993.

Despite winning 11 races, a number of crashes forced him into second place – but what followed after that was four titles in six years, with his aggressive and passionate riding style drawing in record-breaking crowds to the British circuits, particularly his favourite, Donington Park.

After winning his first title in 1994, he retained it in 1995. A move to Honda in 1996 proved unfruitful but he was right back on the pace with Ducati in 1997, settling for second, before dominating the series once again in 1998 and 1999.

'MotoGP is so big now and replaced what World Superbikes used to be,' said Foggy. 'It has struggled to match the funds since 2003 but it was huge when I was racing and we were the biggest four-stroke championship in the world.

'We had 121,000 fans at Donington Park, which I think is still the largest crowd for any sporting event ever held in the UK – quite an achievement.

'There were people climbing over the fences to get in and every section of the circuit was filled, which was something I had never seen before.

'Donington was also my favourite circuit because, from turn one, there were six or seven fast-flowing corners in a row, and that really suited my racing style.

'Racing abroad, the old TT circuit in Assen, Holland, was my favourite. It's changed a lot since then though.'

Foggy was at the pinnacle of his powers when a freak accident during the second race of the 2000 season, at Phillip Island, Australia, shattered his shoulder and forced him into early retirement, leaving him with WSBK career statistics of four titles, 21 superpoles, 59 wins, 108 podiums and 16 double race wins.

But rather than being bitter, he remains philosophical about what happened.

'Even if I hadn't got injured, I don't think I would've carried on much longer – because I had to win,' he said.

'I couldn't see myself going much beyond 2003 so it probably cut my career short by about three years.'

The retirement years have seen Foggy keep just as busy thanks to his enduring popularity and a love for motorbikes that will never end.

He became team owner of Foggy Petronas Racing in 2001 before escalating financial costs saw the team wound up five years later.

Nowadays he spends most of his time making personal appearances – especially after winning ITV's *I'm a Celebrity... Get Me Out of Here* in 2014 – as well as working with iconic British motorbike brand, Triumph, and undertaking plenty of charity work.

'Appearances have increased since I won the jungle really,' said Foggy.

'I work with Triumph motorcycles so that's my main involvement with the bikes. It's great working with Triumph, especially as they're a British manufacturer.

'It's mainly to promote modern road bikes but I also race a few of their classic bikes and I actually won one in Germany, so it was good to know I could still do it after all these years.

'I also do some charity work with the NSPCC, which included walking across Iceland this year, and I'm happy to be back leading out Bike4Life, from Meole Brace in Shrewsbury to RAF Cosford.

'It's a really good event and the charity it raises money for, Midland Air Ambulance, has a real connection with bikers – I've had to use them a few times in my career too.'

It is clear, despite retiring nearly 17 years ago, Fogarty's passion for motorbikes burns as brightly as ever – and he has some simple advice for any of today's riders looking to emulate the man who remains one of the world's most successful and iconic racers to have ever graced the sport.

'My advice to up-and-coming riders would be to enjoy it, first and foremost,' he explains.

'Work hard and if you're getting beaten work out why – brake later and work on increasing speed around the corners.

'It's not rocket science but it always goes a long way towards winning.'

Sidecar TT 1989

Dave Molyneux beats Kenny Howles by just 1.2 seconds to win first TT

Another 1989 TT and another win by less than two seconds – this time for future TT legend Dave Molyneux who was passengered by Colin Hardman. Moly took full advantage of a couple of high-profile breakdowns to pounce and claim victory in the opening sidecar race.

Pre-race favourites Mick Boddice and Chas Birks had been forced to stop with a split fuel line two miles in, which immediately blew the field wide open.

The first to pounce were Kenny Howles and Steve Pointer, who had opened their own 20-second lead after the opening lap, despite losing the clutch halfway round.

However, poor boards and timing signals throughout the race eventually cost them dearly as it allowed Moly and Hardman to close the gap as they pushed hard for the win.

It was a five-second error that cost them dear as Howles and the rest of his team believed he had actually won the race, but joy soon turned to despair as it emerged Moly had been closer than they had realised.

It meant by the end of the three laps Howles and Pointer were placed second handing the win to Moly and Hardman by just 1.2 seconds.

The victory was also all the sweeter for the island's diehard fans as Moly's win was the first Manx success in the sidecar class for more than 20 years.

It also marked the final time Open racing machines would be allowed in the class, as they switched from 1000cc engines to a smaller 600cc capacity.

Boddice and Birks, however, were able to gain revenge in the final sidecar race of the week as the Kidderminster rider smashed Jock Taylor's eight-year-old sidecar lap record from a standing start.

Lapping at an incredible 108.31mph, he was simply too hot to handle as he took a comfortable seventh win over Dennis Brown and Bill Nelson, which saw him become the second most successful TT sidecar racer of all time.

DAVE MOLYNEUX

HOWEVER, THE person who would go on to become the most successful sidecar racer on the island of time would be Manxman Dave Molyneux who currently sits on 17 TT wins.

After making his debut in 1985, aged 20, he impressed straight away and a year later was lapping regularly above 100mph.

After taking his first win in 1989, he then had to deal with a rule change, which saw the 1000cc machines change to FII specifications for the 1990 TT.

Most people believed the switch would prove to be a mistake and might even kill the sidecar class off but over the years the lure of racing 600cc machines would see a mini-explosion in the motorsport.

With solo bikes moving from two-stroke towards four-stroke, it seemed more power was the way forward, but instead, moving to smaller engines worked well because they were easier to handle around the tough TT course.

Behind the scenes, Moly had also begun manufacturing his own machines and, once he got to grips with the new F2 class, he became the man to beat on the island.

Just three years after the engine changes had been introduced, Moly claimed a double victory in 1993 before adding three runner-up spots in the next couple of years.

However, it was in 1996 when he really made history as he became the first sidecar driver to break the 110mph barrier as well as adding another double victory.

Molyneux had also begun racing in the world championship but it was the TT where he continued to shine and what his entire year was based around.

He continued to break his own lap records racing sidecars he designed himself, including the chassis. And such was his skill he was able to win on Yamahas, Suzukis, Hondas and Kawasakis.

Such was his skills in building race-winning machines, he would go on to supply sidecars for the likes of ten-time winner Rob Fisher, 2006 double winner Nick Crowe and six-time world champion Tim Reeves.

Competing in a maximum of two races a year, Moly was able to claim 17 wins – the fourth-highest total ever – as well as securing 30 podiums.

His win ratio may have been a little leaner in the last few years, thanks in part to the rise of the Birchall brothers and a succession of mechanical problems, but he remains an outstanding competitor, who had taken the brave decision to race despite being struck by a tragedy during his teenage years.

Aside from his father, Moly's other racing heroes included the likes of George O'Dell, who became the first sidecar rider to break the 100mph barrier.

Inspired to race by family and heroes, both as a fan and a fearsome competitor, Moly would go on to enjoy remarkable success, which included his first double during the 1993 TT, becoming the first sidecar driver to break the 110mph barrier when he hit 111.9mph during the 1999 TT and then became the first sidecar racer to lap in under 20 minutes in 2005 during the Sidecar B TT.

A year later he crashed along with passenger Craig Hallam during Thursday afternoon practice at Rhencullen and was unable to compete in the actual races due to injury.

But he made a comeback in 2007, taking another double victory, raising his tally to 13 wins.

Victory number 14 followed in 2009, when he also became the first winner of a TT sidecar race on a Suzuki-powered machine, and he broke the race record too.

Having decided to miss the 2011 race meeting, he again returned successfully a year later, this time on Kawasaki-powered machines, winning both races – it meant he won on all four Japanese machines too.

He looked on course for his 17th win during the opening race of the 2014 TT but, while holding a 20-second lead, an engine misfire caused him to stop on the final lap.

But he would recover, as he had on so many occasions, to take what is currently his last TT win to date in the second sidecar race that same year, but he remains a solid competitor and will be known as a true legend of the sport and the TT.

Junior TT 1990

Lougher announces himself in stunning fashion

Setting a lap record around the 37.73-mile TT course on any bike, in any class, is a phenomenal achievement. Those who have done so can say, for a time, no one has ever lapped the toughest, hardest and most unforgiving circuit in the world faster than them.

But when you manage to knock 38 seconds off the previous best, it really does take everyone's breath away.

And that's exactly what happened when Welshman Ian Lougher came up against the late, great Steve Hislop to steal the Junior TT win by just 1.8 seconds in 1990.

Lorry driver Lougher was 26 years old at the time when he set a new lap record of 117.8mph on the final lap of the race.

And it could have been even quicker too as he had been forced to run wide at Ramsey Hairpin to avoid a diesel spill, not to mention suffering a big slide too while going into Guthrie's.

Even still, his stunning lap was a record and also brought him his first of ten TT wins.

Having finished second in the 125cc class at the 1989 TT, Lougher had already announced himself to the paddock as a serious competitor but really made people sit up and listen in spectacular fashion a year later.

He capitalised on a poor pit stop by Hislop and his crew to steal the lead on lap three, a position he maintained until the chequered flag.

It was clear Lougher was fast. As far back as 1983, he had finished third behind Robert Dunlop and Hislop at the Manx GP in the newcomers class, which was no mean feat by any stretch of the imagination.

But he was still a relatively unknown quantity coming into the 1990 TT, despite showing real early promise by breaking the lap record with a time of 115.83mph during practice week.

Facing strong winds on Junior TT race day, Hislop and Lougher were only separated by a few second, after two laps.

But when Hislop and his team struggled to get the fuel cap back down on his bike during the pit stop, Lougher made his race-winning move.

He led Hislop by two seconds at Ballacraine and then Hislop's bike began cutting out every time he hit a bump in the road.

And yet, such was the Scotman's unbelievable skill on a motorbike, particularly around the TT course, he had managed to retake the lead and pull out a 2.4-second advantage as he began climbing up the mountain for the final time.

Lougher responded in stunning fashion to open a 2.2-second lead himself. Hislop crossed the finish line first on the road, and then a nervous wait to see what time Lougher had managed to pull off. It ended up being heartache for Hislop as Lougher's record-breaking response was enough to claim his first TT win.

Senior TT 1990

Foggy double as Norton-mounted Nation falls just short

There was so much going on with the 1990 Senior TT that it was hard to keep track with events during the race. Foggy had also won the Formula 1 TT earlier that week.

Steve Hislop, riding a 750 Honda, broke the record, lapping in 18 minutes and 27.6 seconds, at 122.63mph.

Having been snapped up by the Japanese factory a year earlier, he had spearheaded the team's programme in 1989 becoming the third man to win three races in a week.

He also entered the history books by becoming the first rider to break the 120mph barrier.

Honda had begun to dominate the timesheets with Hislop taking the record into the 1990s, an era that saw the beginning of another great Isle of Man rivalry, with Hizzy taking on Carl Fogarty. But there was so much more going on behind the scenes too as Norton was also hoping to make its own headlines with its work on what would become one of the most iconic bikes ever built – the Norton Rotary.

Back in 1967, Norton had produced a vibration-free version of the Dominator – the Commando. It was a quick success and won MCN's best bike of the year award from 1968 until 1972.

A total of 55,000 were sold, making it easily Norton's biggest seller, but still the British firm could not compete with its Japanese rivals abroad.

The bikes were cheaper, faster and more reliable. The British manufacturers had no answer to the Japanese superbikes. After the last Commando was built in 1978, it looked like the game might be up for Norton but, in the mid-1980s, the brand was relaunched on the back of some ground-breaking technology.

It looked like the game might be up for Norton but, in the mid-1980s, the brand was relaunched on the back of some ground-breaking technology.

The rotary engine had been written off by pretty much every other manufacturer but Norton had decided to take a punt. The piston-free engine had in fact been designed by a German engineer in the 1950s.

Several experimented, but Norton saw an opportunity, thanks to Brian Crighton who still runs an engine-building company today.

Rotary bikes were being trialled with the police but Crighton realised their future laid in race bikes.

At the time, race bikes were producing around 85bhp but he was convinced he could get 120bhp out of the rotary engine.

When it took third in its club race debut at Darley Moor, the factory decided to get involved.

The prototype race bike was entered into the British Superbikes series for the first time at Brands Hatch in 1988, ridden by Steve Spray. He went out and won the two main races. The victories persuaded cigarette manufacturer John Player to sponsor Norton, which eventually led to the Norton Rotarys appearing in their famous black, silver and gold liveries.

Spray's team-mate Trevor Nation also began winning races pretty much straight away in the British championship.

Suddenly, Britain had a world-leading race bike again for the first time since the 1950s. And with Nation as the pilot, the success soon began to return to Norton.

In 1990, Nation and Norton came agonisingly close to claiming a memorable Senior TT.

Nation had broken his ribs and sternum just before heading out for the TT. The Senior, however, had been declared a damp race and was reduced to four laps.

Nation made the right tyre choice but still just missed out on the win – despite having won on the same bike at the North West 200 week earlier.

The team, however, had still enjoyed plenty of other success in 1990, with Nation winning the MCN Superbike series and Robert Dunlop taking third place in the Formula 1 TT on the Isle of Man. Dunlop also won both Superbike races at that year's North West 200.

Paul Simpson would also win a British Superbike Championship on a Rotary Norton in 1994. But of course the climax of Norton's Rotary adventure came in 1992 when Steve Hislop won the Senior TT on a bike nicknamed the 'White Charger'.

1991 Formula 1 TT

Hizzy and Foggy part one

With Carl Fogarty and Steve Hislop both mounted on Honda RVF750s, this race was always going to be a belter.

The Honda bosses had been worried fairly early in the TT fortnight that Foggy's ultra-competitive spirit may been forcing him to push too hard trying to keep up with Hizzy, who had already beaten his own lap record by 7.6 seconds.

The rivals had already made a pact – ride as hard as possible for the first two laps and then whoever was leading could enjoy an easier ride to victory.

Hissy was already nine seconds up after the opening lap and had 30 seconds on Foggy by lap two. It meant the two rivals were able to ride together, side-by-side, until the second pit stop.

After Trevor Nelson was disqualified for an over-sized tank, Brian Morrison was able to bring his Yamaha home in third.

Hizzy's win also marked the tenth successive victory for Honda in the F1 race during the same year Yamaha had been celebrating its 30th year of racing on the island.

He did it in style, too, raising the lap record to 123.48mph.

STEVE HISLOP

A 250CC champion and double British Superbike title holder, on his day Steve Hislop could beat anyone in the world on any track. Remembered so fondly on the island for his heroic exploits, his racing prowess became a thing of legend. And, rightly or wrongly, his road racing career somewhat overshadowed his talents on the circuits.

During a career blighted by injuries, bike problems and team fall-outs, most of his success came when his was with a small team and when his back was against the wall. It was the sort of situation he simply thrived on.

But as his career flourished and the success flowed, it became more and more difficult for Hizzy to be considered an underdog – and yet, that was where he always performed at his best.

Give him a bike even remotely capable of winning a race, and he would simply be unstoppable.

Rob McElnea, who was his team boss at Yamaha, said the Scotsman was the fastest man to ever sit on a motorcycle. High praise, indeed.

Hizzy just had a feeling for riding a motorbike, something that could not be taught, and it was that raw talent that set him apart from everyone else.

Despite all that talent, however, he was still plagued by a lack of confidence for much of his career.

And yet he was still able to keep picking up wins on the island and looked destined to compete on the world stage on the circuits too.

Sadly, in the end, it was not to be, so he instead returned to the British championship where he was able to pick up more silverware, although his talent looked capable of so much more. Honda still stuck by him, both on the roads and in the BSB, and it really was a match made in heaven when everything clicked.

Hizzy would later admit that despite enjoying every single one of his 11 TT victories, putting so much effort into winning on the island had, in hindsight, scuppered his chances of competing on the world stage.

But he just took to the roads so naturally, which began with winning the Junior Manx GP in 1985, breaking the 100mph barrier in the process.

Four years later he picked up his first TT win, riding a Yamaha TZ 350 in the Formula 2 race.

By 1989, Carl Fogarty had joined him as a team-mate at Honda in the World TT F1 series.

Despite winning another three TTs that year, along with another two races abroad, a bike issue meant Foggy would eventually pip him to the world title.

His TT victories had come in the Formula 1, Senior and Supersport classes, while he also became the first rider to break through the 120mph barrier.

Two years later, he claimed another three TT victories with Honda in the same classes, but eventually he would switch to Norton, which in turn would set up one of the most memorable TT wins in history, over his former team-mate Foggy. However, before the classic 1992 Senior TT victory, he had remained team-mates with Foggy and Terry Rymer – and the team would go on to win the Bol d'Or in 1992.

Hizzy's career was never a straight path, being littered with silverware and sackings right up until his untimely and tragic death.

And yet, despite all the turmoil, he was still able to claim the BSB title in 1995 and also claim two TTs in 1994.

Hizzy also won a second BSB title with Ducati just before his death, having previously been let go by Yamaha and Kawasaki, such was his talent.

The Scotsman was always able to bounce back and, right up until his helicopter crash in 2002, he had been dicing with the best in the business, and beating them.

He had planned a return to the BSB in 2003 to defend his crown with the same bike and few would have bet against him retaining his title.

Sadly, it was not to be but he still left this world as an 11-time TT winner and a three-time British champion – and very few riders have been able to match that record.

He had also claimed all of his TT wins in just seven years, with all his victories coming between the years of 1987 and 1994. He also claimed nine Ulster GP wins, three Macau GP wins and a victory at the North West 200.

ISLE OF MAN TT MEMORIES

Wayne Martin, from Telford, in Shropshire, is a regular competitor at the Manx GP, Southern 100 and Irish road race scene. He is also the nephew of Geoff Martin, who had a career-best finish of third at the Classic TT:

One of the most memorable would have to be the 1978 Formula 1 TT, when Mike Hailwood made his winning return to the Isle of Man after 11 years of not racing there.

The 2000 Formula 1 TT, when Joey Dunlop won the main race at 48 years old, was truly special too.

Everyone thought he was too old to win it but he also won the 125 and 250 races that week too, taking his total wins to

26, which is still the most to date. And it all happened just weeks before his tragic death.

But the one that really stands out is the 1992 125 TT, when Joey equalled Hailwood's race wins, reaching 14 in total.

I suppose it was mainly the fact he was worried that if he equalled the record the fans would turn against him.

He didn't want to upset them but then the year after he beat the record. But he was never big-headed about it, stayed quiet and just got on with his business. He was just the normal Joey, I suppose.

Hailwood's wife was there to congratulate him as well but I can't remember if that was when he equalled or beat it. Either way, it showed how humble he was and how well respected he was by everyone.

Ultra-Lightweight TT 1992

Joey beats Robert to equal Hailwood's record

Serious injuries meant that Joey would have to wait another four years before he was able to match Mike Hailwood's record of 14 TT wins, as he struggled on the bigger bikes.

However, he managed to become a master of the smaller machines during the 1992 TT – but it was not just the course he was battling against, it was his younger brother, Robert, too.

At that time, the Ultra-Lightweight TT was run along the Supersport 400 TT, which made for a packed grid.

Brian Reid had set off as one of the favourites in the supersport class, along with the likes of Phil McCallen, Steve Hislop, Nick Jefferies and Carl Fogarty, but all eyes were on the Dunlop brothers in the other.

Robert had claimed victory in the race the year before, beating Joey into second – but the older sibling was aware victory would see him enter the record books.

Robert was first off the line and first over Ballaugh Bridge, where he suffered a small wobble, closely followed by Joey who was trying to catch his brother. The mountain was covered in mist – and that was with a delay too – and it was impossible to tell which riders were making their way towards the end of the first lap.

As it was, Joey had taken a three-second lead over Robert as they began their second lap, with Mick Lofthouse in third but well back on time.

Meanwhile, Foggy had been forced to retire for the second time that week, but it was all action in the 125cc race as Robert had reduced his brother's lead to just 0.2 seconds by the end of the second lap.

The mist had still not cleared on the mountain as the riders approached the final lap, which had seen Reid take a huge 50-second lead over McCallen, who in turn had an advantage of more than a minute and a half over Steven Linsdell in third.

Back to the 125cc, and Joey had pulled out a 7.6-second advantage over Robert with Lofthouse now a further minute-and-a-half behind in third place too.

It seemed Joey was well on course to equal Hailwood's 14 TT wins as he continued to push on, head tucked in and 125cc engine screaming.

First to be sorted out was the Supersport 400 TT, which saw Reid take his fifth TT nearly a minute ahead of McCallen with Linsdell in third.

The fans waited eagerly for the result of the smaller bike race as Robert was the first to see the chequered flag on the roads. It was then a waiting game, to see how quickly his brother would appear behind him and, as Joey's yellow helmet appeared, it was confirmed he had taken the win by 8.4 seconds, with Lofthouse more than two minutes behind Robert in third place. Joey said after the race he was pleased to have equalled the record, and even more pleased the record would finally stop being mentioned, while at the same time saying he no intention of trying to break Hailwood's 14 wins.

However, the following year, Joey did indeed become the most successful racer in the history of the Isle of Man when he again claimed the 125cc TT – again beating his brother into second place.

Robert had bruised some of his ribs during an incident in the Formula 1 race but he, along with Lofthouse, were again the two riders who had any chance of stopping Joey taking his 15th win.

Although he hated racing against, and trying to beat, his idol – his older brother – as professionals they knew it was what they had to do.

First again, however, were the supersport 400 riders with Jim Moodie this time the firm favourite, along with Reid.

Robert was flat out from the start, and once again the brothers could not be separated early in the race, but Joey had stretched his lead to five seconds by the Gooseneck.

With Moodie running away with the supersport race – having already done the double at the North West 200 – all eyes were again on the 125cc class, which was by now being led by Joey by 14 seconds.

There was a nervy few seconds as Joey's bike refused to start up, but once he got going his lead was still at 12 seconds. Again, Robert was first over the finish line but it was Joey who became the first rider in TT history to win 15 races around the island.

Moodie took the supersport race by exactly a minute ahead of Iain Duffus, with Steve Linsdell third, a further 45 seconds behind. Reid was fourth.

JOEY DUNLOP

IN THE 1970s, the TT was the most lethal race in the world and came close to being banned – but Joey came to the island and dominated the race, winning a record-breaking 26 times.

Of course road racing is more popular than football in NI – but the TT was still the most prestigious race on the calendar, the ultimate test of nerves and skills. Exciting but deadly.

In 1972, 125cc championship contender Gilberto Parlotti was the tenth rider in three years to be killed. Agostini became furious that riders were forced to ride the TT as part of the championship.

A boycott followed and the TT lost its world championship status – but it proved to be a golden opportunity for Joey.

He grew up with three brothers and four sisters in Ballymoney and began working life on the dole. But when his sister's boyfriend, Merv Robinson, introduced him to road racing, his life would change forever.

They would eventually become close rivals on the track, joined by another friend, Frank Kennedy.

After a few years' practice and a bit of sponsorship, he was eventually able to beat his long-time hero Ray McCullough and was on his way to becoming famous. The adrenaline, the buzz, the thrill of getting the best out of the bike, the circuit, all while sometimes topping 200mph, there was nothing quite liked it. Like a drug, is how all road racers describe it – or, at least, an addiction.

After seven years of competing in some of the toughest road races in the world in his home country of NI, it was time to head over to the TT.

Arriving with his bikes on board a fishing boat in 1976, Joey failed to finish two races and then finished 16th in the Junior TT on his Yamsel, a Yamaha in the frame made for a Suzuki.

He returned a year later aware of what was needed, and working on his bikes as he always did – checking every nut and bolt – he would also study the track late at night, when the roads were quiet.

And it worked too, as in just his second year of racing on the island, he won the Jubilee TT race to truly make his mark.

Despite his scruffy nature, he knew his bikes and posted a 115mph lap, which at the time was very special – and he picked up a cheque for £1,000 for good measure.

Of course during the 'golden era' of road racing during the late 1970s and early 1980s, health and safety remained a moot point and a time when fans could mix even more easily with the top racers.

Joey gave every race 100 per cent effort as soon as the flag dropped and continued to prepare his own machines, adding that 'extra bit'. It gave him faith his bike was better than the next rider's, which helped him to win.

The combination of no fear and the talent made for an awesome package, but he also had to know where the absolute limit was.

Working with his mechanic Sam Graham and brother Jim, they would test regularly – and illegally – near their home, with fans and neighbours stopping the traffic for them and watching out for police as they tested their home-made machines.

Joey liked to stay busy, which helped take away the nerves of racing. Also, because he had built the bike himself, it also gave him that extra confidence that what he had was right and would not let him down.

But just when his career was really starting to take off, the death of his close friends, Tom Herron and Frank Kennedy, almost convinced him to hang up his leathers for good.

It made it clear to him that if riders as talented as them could lose their lives, anyone could.

Things would get even worse too, when his brother-in-law Robinson died at the 1980 North West 200. It made him consider quitting even more.

And yet, instead, he continued and, despite the deaths of three close friends, he went on to win that year's Classic TT, beating superb riders Mick Grant and Ron Haslam, all while riding with a broken tank.

Joey was charismatic, talked with his eyes without actually saying anything, and did everything on his own terms. He raced because he loved it, and the winning came second.

He was a fussy eater and everything had to be done his way. You never knew what you were getting from him, but everyone who was close to him knew him as a great character and wonderful person.

In 1981, having won two TTs, Honda made their move to sign him up from under the nose of Suzuki.

Honda was more reliable at the time than any other motorcycle but it was also the biggest team in the world – and no one could be sure how the two would gel.

Honda had a highly polished corporate image and could not understand why Joey would still want to work on the bikes, as they classed themselves as the best.

When he first started riding in the UK, it was not working, but he was soon given two bikes of his own to work on and then everything began falling into place.

Joey also had to work with the media, clean-shaven, but he knew it was important for sponsors. Clearly so uncomfortable, the team eventually let Joey live how he wanted to live – and he was backed by superb results, soon allowed to return to his old ways.

Missing meetings and missing out on potentially millions of pounds, Joey was just happy to race, without signing autographs, posing for pictures or any kind of PR.

He would simply work on the bikes with his friends until the early hours, but the package was one of the greatest ever assembled and, more importantly, both Joey and the Honda team wanted to win the TT more than anything else.

Soichiro Honda, the founder of the Honda motor company, had fallen in love with the TT on his visit to the island in 1957. Honda had returned every year since.

Joey was a brilliant engineer and mechanic but there was still some tension with the team as to who would work on the bikes and when.

He had become part of a racing dynasty, but Japanese ways of working were very different to the Northern Irish way. Honda, however, learned to do it the Joey way and the success was superb.

Having asked to bring the bikes home to work on them himself, he would be trained to look after the machines, lived and worked with the mechanics, and then could also race the F1 bikes – which he could not take home – with more confidence.

He refused to discuss the bikes with team-mates and kept his card close to his chest. If he found something that worked better, he would not give it away.

And yet he would let the other riders follow him through certain sections so they could improve themselves.

By 1983, Haslam was Joey's only match and yet the Northern Irishman went on to win five F1 championships back-to-back, beating his team-mate.

Along the way he clocked F1 TT wins in 1983, 1984, 1985, 1986, 1987 and 1988. He was awarded an MBE for services to motor racing.

He had made the TT his own and became one of the most famous motorcycle racers in the world – but he continued to ride with the mentality of a club racer.

En route to the 1985 TT, his continuing tradition of bringing his bikes over to the island on board a fishing boat nearly ended in disaster.

The boat sank, everyone on board almost died and seven bikes were temporarily lost to the ocean, 100 feet under water.

Frightened and shaken, he still went on to win three times at the 1985 TT in the Junior, Senior and F1 classes, the first of his TT hat-tricks. His legend had really started to flourish and civic ceremony in his home town grew.

Becoming one of the most known NI sports stars, he started attracting hundreds of fans and yet he waited in the queue of the MCN motorcycle show to pay to get in, despite being the star of the show. And he remained invincible on the roads.

On Good Friday 1989, Joey was at Brands Hatch in Kent at the peak of his powers but had a huge accident.

He badly injured his thigh, collarbone and wrist at Paddocks Bend. He was given two months before being able to walk properly again and his outlook for riding again – let alone racing the TT – looked slim.

Yet he still tried to enter the TT that same year, only for the course doctor to turn him away. He was written off by quite a few, but over time his body began to heal and he returned arguably better than he had been before. Returning on 125cc and 250cc machines, which were lighter than the superbikes, Joey was still in a bad condition following his crash.

But instead of sulking and shying away, he instead turned to Phil McCallen and gave him the chance to ride his bikes.

It was such a huge opportunity for his fellow Irishman, to work with the factory Honda team. So Joey gave McCallen his bikes and the younger rider would go on to win 11 TTs, while they remained team-mates for the next nine years.

Meanwhile, Dunlop continued his slow journey back to health with Mike Hailwood's 14 TT record wins in front of him. He also happened to be one of his heroes.

In 1992, Joey won another TT on his 125cc, matching Hailwood's record. He gave up drinking and smoking, focussing on his fitness, concentrating on racing the smaller bikes while he continued to build up his body.

Delicate and difficult to ride, Dunlop managed to get speed and power out of them, keeping the momentum up and dominating the class despite his slightly advancing years.

His knowledge of bikes in all shapes and sizes was once again coming to the fore. So much so, he went on to win at least one TT every year from 1992 to 1997 on smaller bikes.

But, at the Tandragee 100 race in 1998, he suffered another horror crash. This time it was to his hand and pelvis that he suffered career-threatening injuries.

Yet he could not stop road racing. He didn't want to stop on an injury like so many racers.

He went on to win another TT just two weeks later while racing in the wet. The determination was just unimaginable.

Joey was also serious about getting back on a superbike and Honda gave him some of the finest machinery they had, to give him every chance of achieving his goal at the 2000 TT. Joey was fitter and more determined than ever before and he would go on to win the F1 TT, beating Michael Rutter and John McGuinness, at the age of 48. But still not content, he would win two more races that week, on his 125cc and 250cc.

A hat-trick while nearing the age of 50 – 12 years after his last treble – was such an incredible feat and it meant he had now won 26 TTs.

Not only was he able to throw around his superbike and ride it to victory, he was also able to beat the up-and-coming racers on the smaller bikes too.

It seemed like the perfect time to hang up his racing boots, but Joey was his own man. And, especially having won three TTs aged 48, it made retirement even harder to contemplate. He saw no reason why he should stop doing something he loved so much, despite the respect, awards and family he had behind him.

Andy McMenemy, a long-time friend and sponsor, took his own life. To escape the public glare, Joey went to Estonia – drove the 2,000 miles in a beat-up old van, with his bikes in the back – to take part in a road race.

He was going to make his mind up whether to continue racing or not. When he arrived, the rain was pouring down but Dunlop decided to race as normal.

After winning the first two races on the bigger bikes, he went out on his 125cc – and crashed into the trees.

Four weeks after his incredible comeback, Joey Dunlop had died. Fifty-thousand people attended his funeral.

Simply put, he did what he wanted to do and raised the bar higher than anyone else. He was special to everyone who knew him.

Simply put, a fine human being.

Senior TT 1992

Foggy vs Hizzy, Yamaha vs Norton

A year before, Carl Fogarty and Steve Hislop, who were then Honda team-mates, had provided a week-long battle on the island.

It meant the writing had been on the wall all year that the 1992 TT may be another memorable meeting between the rival racers, who had so much respect for one another on and off the track.

And once again the Senior TT would provide the platform for one of the greatest-ever races the world had ever seen, although plenty had gone on behind the scenes before the big race.

By 1992, Foggy was back on a Yamaha, a bike he had high hopes of ending his TT career on with a race win, while Hizzy was aiming to give Norton its first TT victory since Mike Hailwood in 1961.

Neil Tuxworth had been in charge of Honda during that era, when Hizzy had claimed a double on the big bikes in 1991, but said both had left the team for various reasons.

Foggy had entered the world championships with his own bike, which had cost more money to run than he had bargained for, so when the opportunity suddenly came up to race the Loctite Yamaha, he decided to go for it.

Strangely, the bike he would compete on had actually been offered to Hizzy in the first instance but because the Scotsman had not gelled with the Yamaha team he had instead run a Kawasaki at the British Championship and then turned his head to ride a Norton at the TT.

Meanwhile, Foggy had decided to use the money he would earn from riding the Yamaha to plough back into his world championship push. It pretty much funded an entire year of racing for the Blackman rider.

The Norton, however, had a very fragile engine that was producing too much heat – and after some poor testing sessions it had looked like Hizzy might walk away, but thankfully the team and the rider decided to persevere.

Foggy had left it late too, only really gelling with his bike by the Friday morning of the practice session but that was enough and, by the time the first big bike race of the week had rolled around, he was dominating the Formula 1 field, leading the race by about 35 seconds on the fifth lap only for the gearbox to go, blowing his chances of stopping Honda winning the race for a tenth year in a row.

With Hizzy also struggling, the victory went to Honda's Phil McCallen. By the time the Senior arrived, neither of the former Honda team-mates had won a race.

Nick Jefferies believed the VFRs they had raced the year before were the most perfect bikes to have ever graced the island, and yet here they were, ready to do battle against one another on a pair of extremely unreliable bikes.

Foggy admitted, despite having a lot of respect for his fellow riders, he did not fear McCallen or Joey Dunlop, and it was all about whether Hizzy and the ultra-fast Norton could stay in one piece.

And sure enough, the temperature stayed down, which meant immediately Hizzy could use all of the Norton's power as his confidence in the machine continued to grow.

The battle royale eventually would rage for the entire, nerve-wracking, spine-tingling 226-mile race, which would eventually see Hizzy claim the win by just four seconds.

McCallen knew early on his race would be over as his own Honda began to overheat while the Norton seemed to be riding very sweetly.

Further at the front, race leader Foggy soon feared the worst too, but for different reasons.

Despite putting the hammer down early on, he had been unable to break away in any way, shape or form, as he had in the Formula 1 race, even over the mountain section where he often opened up a sizeable gap on some of the more pure road racers as his short circuit skills came to the fore.

Of course, Foggy was smart enough to realise what was going on – he was being chased hard by Hizzy and his Norton.

He knew he would be in for a hell of a race, and so it proved, especially when competing against a bike with an extra 15mph top speed, as well as a rider he saw as one of the best ever to take on the TT course.

Foggy was able to hold on with a one-second lead but, with the mountain section approaching, it was there that the Norton really shone, with Robert Dunlop also pushing for the final podium spot on another Norton throughout the race.

Joey was soon forced to retire, as was McCallen, which meant even more eyes were now on the Hizzy's Norton and Foggy's Yamaha as they screeched around the course during lap three.

By the start of lap four, Foggy had realised Hizzy was in fact pulling time on him over the mountain section, which never happened, and showed again the Norton's formidable power as it roared into the lead on corrected time, which had reached eight seconds by the second pit stop.

Foggy, with a shorter pit stop, had managed to pull some time back which had galvanised him and swung the race back in Yamaha's favour as he gained a three-second lead.

Alas, Hizzy was far from done, and again he retook the lead, managing to pull seven seconds on his nearest rival as he closed in on Robert Dunlop on the road.

And then the bike problems began to kick in. The clock had bounced out of Foggy's Yamaha, the screen was broken, there was fluid everywhere and then the exhaust blew up, but he ploughed on regardless.

It meant everything went into a last lap decider, which happened quite rarely in the Senior TT. It was unusual to see two riders pushing so hard on the sixth lap as they both continued to break lap records.

Over the mountain, Foggy found himself nine seconds down, but he had reduced that to four despite the bike falling apart around him.

As Foggy crossed the finish line smashing the lap record again by three seconds, all the other riders, teams and fans waited with bated breath for around two minutes for Hizzy to appear.

With the countdown continuing, it eventually became clear Hizzy had done it. He had given Norton and himself one of the most memorable victories in the history of any race on the island.

And he had done it with a new team, new chassis and pretty much a brand-new bike, at a time when Norton had been in severe financial difficulties.

Foggy, of course, had the satisfaction of knowing he had broken the lap record – a record that would last for seven years – as well as finishing second to one of the greatest-ever TT racers.

All while winning a world championship race at the same time – and it was highly unlikely a TT racer would ever win a world title at the same time ever again.

Fogarty remains proud of his stunning lap time of 123.61mph on his 750 Yamaha, which saw him complete his final circuit during the Senior in 17 minutes and 18.8 seconds.

It's the race everyone talks about when he meets fans. Foggy had not really had any intention of returning to the TT but after arriving in red-hot weather in 1992 he would go on to break the lap record in a race still consistently voted the best of all time by fans.

The bike may have been falling apart all around him and the Norton may have been faster but somehow he managed to pull four or five seconds back over the mountain, which had always been his favourite part of the circuit, with this bike blowing its head off and the exhaust pipe completely gone on the final lap.

Because Foggy had set off number four and Hizzy had been given the number 19 slot, it created an agonisingly long wait for the announcement to be made, but in the end Hislop had done it by four seconds.

Foggy was left gutted but, once the fastest lap of the race and new lap record had been announced, he looked across and saw Hizzy's face drop because the record had meant a lot to the Scotsman – and it meant a lot to Foggy to be the fastest racer around the island.

Foggy even went as far to say that, after all his World Superbike titles, winning the TT and holding the lap record for several years were probably the proudest moments of his racing career. And that says everything that needs to be known about what the TT means to all the riders.

Another memorable race during the 1992 TT came in the Sidecar A event when George O'Dell and Keith Cornbill broke the 100mph barrier for the first time on three wheels, hitting 102.54mph on their second lap.

The pair went on to win by 35.2 seconds from Eddy Wright and Pete Hill after Dave Saville and Nick Roche retired, with Mick Boddice and Dave Wells third.

Bell and Cornbill went on to complete a sidecar double with a start to finish victory in race B, lapping just 0.6 seconds slower than before, beating Boddice by 33 seconds, with the Manx crew of Dave Molyneux and Karl Ellison coming third. A year later, Moly would get his revenge by taking his own double in the sidecar class.

ISLE OF MAN TT MEMORIES

John Dickenson, of Laxey, on the Isle of Man, adds another of his favourite memories, this time as part of the pit crew:

My best-remembered TT meeting with some personal involvement was in 1994, when acting as mechanic/pit crew for my friend Gary 'Radish' Radcliffe.

Gary had his own Honda RC30 on which he had raced in the TT from 1988 onwards.

For 1994, he had secured sponsorship from Martin Bullock for the RC30 and also had a 250 Spondon Yamaha and 680 Spondon Yamaha Single from Dennis Trollope Racing.

In the Formula One race, he finished fourth behind the three works Hondas of Steve Hislop, Philip McCallen and Joey Dunlop, fourth in the Singles race, 11th in the Junior and sixth in the Senior.

As well as riding the three different bikes, Gary was involved in all the machine preparations assisted by myself and his father, Alan.

It was very satisfying to Alan and I to see Gary do so well in each race and to be competitive against the larger and better supported teams.

I remember Gary telling me after the races it was the only time he had made a profit out of riding in the TT despite being a consistent leaderboard finisher over a number of years.

Senior TT 1996

McCallen makes history with four wins in a week

Northern Irish road racing ace Phil McCallen had begun turning heads as early as 1988, when he incredibly became the first rider to win a newcomers race and a Manx race in the same year at the Manx GP.

It showed what he was capable of and eight years later he was back at it again, this time competing against the best road racers in the world en route to scooping an unprecedented four TT wins in a single week.

It all began with the Formula 1 TT. McCallen was the reigning champion and had started off as favourite.

By the end of lap one, he led by 6.9 seconds, again from Iain Duffus in second, while Nick Jefferies round out the top three.

Pit stops made a difference during the F1 race because although McCallen still led, Lee Pullan had taken second with Jefferies retaining third.

Duffus had dropped to tenth but by the time the second round of pit stops had taken place he was up to sixth.

This time it was Pullan who was forced to suffer, as changing his rear tyre saw him begin lap five way back in 14th.

With all the commotion behind him, McCallen now comfortably led Jefferies by 52.3 seconds, followed by a young Michael Rutter and Duffus, which was how they stayed at the flag to give McCallen his second win of the week.

The Junior TT was affected by the weather and reduced to three laps. Yet another battle raged between McCallen and Duffus on their Hondas – and McCallen, who led early on by 14 seconds at the end of the opening lap, was followed by Duffus and Ian Simpson.

Duffus pitted for fuel at the end of the first lap but McCallen still led, with Simpson second. A lap later as the Ulsterman took his second win of the week at record speed, Iain Duffus was back in second and Ian Simpson in third.

The Production race, which had been relaunched over three laps of the Mountain Course in 1996, attracted a lot of interest from manufacturers, riders and fans.

Duffus was the early leader with McCallen 3.6 seconds behind and Nigel Davies, on a Yamaha rather than a Honda like the others, in third.

McCallen upped the pace on lap two and etched out 3.1 seconds from Duffus, as Pullan moved up to third ahead of Davies.

He proved too strong, eventually taking the chequered flag by 5.9 seconds from Duffus and Davies, who had regained third spot from Pullan.

No rider had ever won four races in a week in the history of the TT and it came down to whether McCallen could steer his mighty Honda RC45 to victory in the final race of the week – the Senior TT.

He opened with a lap of 121.69mph to lead Kawasaki's Moodie by 7.2 seconds while Jefferies again slotted into third.

McCallen had almost doubled his lead after two laps as he looked destined to rewrite the record books.

And when Moodie was forced to retire in the pits, McCallen led Jefferies and Joey, who had moved into third, with one lap to go.

McCallen eased to victory by more than a minute to take his fourth TT win of the week, ahead of Joey, who pipped Jefferies to second by just over two seconds, making it another one-two-three for Honda.

It rounded off a truly remarkable week for McCallen, who had claimed the first of his 11 TT wins in the Formula 1 race of 1992, the year he did the double by also claiming the Supersport 600 race.

He followed that up with four more wins in 1996, which could even have been five had he stayed in front during the Lightweight TT.

The Ulsterman had previously come so close to winning the Lightweight class but had always been the bridesmaid.

All the planets were aligning for him in 1996 and it seemed a Lightweight win could finally be on the cards as he prepared to launch himself down Bray Hill.

But leading Joey and Moodie, he suddenly began experiencing exhaust problems. Joey took the lead at the end of the third lap, with Moodie in second while McCallen had slipped to third place.

Eventually, he was unable to secure the final podium spot as Jason Griffiths took third behind Moodie and Joey.

However, it was a small dent in a week of glory for McCallen who followed up his four wins with a hat-trick of TTs a year later. On his day during the peak of his career he was unbeatable and had even gone one better at the North West 200, winning five races from six starts in a week during the 1992 meeting, as well as five wins in a day at the Ulster GP – the same year he had claimed four TTs.

The year 1996 also saw Dave Molyneux take record-breaking victories in both Sidecar TT races

He shattered all records, setting a new lap record of 111.02mph in the second. Even the great Rob Fisher proved no match for the Manxman.

The Singles TT, which was reduced to two laps from four due to the weather – meaning no pit stops – was won by Moodie, while Joey claimed win number 21 in the Ultra-Lightweight TT.

Behind the scenes, another rider was making his road racing debut – and that man was John McGuinness.

All he had was a bike but he had still managed to run at the front end at the North West 200 earlier in the year, competing with the likes of Joey, Woolsey Colter, Owen McNally, John Creith and other top 250cc riders.

McGuinness was already living the dream and even took Joey's bike, which had a dent in the tank following an accident at Tandragee, with him in his van as a favour to the Isle of Man.

Riding around for his first practice session, he said it immediately felt like home to him. He was aged 24 at the time. The first time he had been sat at the bottom of Bray Hill as a fan had been back in 1982.

Practice week had not turned out great for any of the riders, with bad weather leading to cancellations, but he was still enjoying himself. Then, on the final practice session, Mick Lofthouse – the man he had been sharing a room with on the island and who had been giving him some tips and advice – was killed. Robert Holden also died.

McGuinness had considered, there and then, leaving the island before he had even completed a race but Arthur, Mick's father, convinced him to at least try the first race.

Come race day and beautiful weather greeted the riders. The 250cc race was eventually won by Joey with Jim Moodie second and Jason Griffiths third. McGuinness had finished 15th but it was the start of something truly special.

And as well as McGuinness, the 1996 TT also heralded the arrivals of Dave Jefferies and Bruce Anstey, who were also making their debuts.

DJ just took to the TT like he had the North West, Scarborough and Macau before that. It proved to be a great week for the close friends as McGuinness was crowned best newcomer during race week.

McGuinness then won his first 250cc race for Paul Bird at Cadwell Park as he continued to start really making a name for himself, as well as taking third at Scarborough for good measure having been loaned a new clutch pack from his hero Joey to compete.

A year later and Paul Bird had supplied him with a new Aprilla 250 for the campaign and he entered the

BSB, Scarborough, North West, TT and even Daytona. McGuinness achieved his first TT podium on the Aprilla in 1997, despite the bike not behaving itself during practice.

He had also entered the Ultra-Lightweight 125cc class and had found himself in the top six before the bike started misfiring. Stopping to change the battery pack, he still brought it home in 15th, earning a bronze replica.

Starting the 250cc Lightweight race in 26th, he finished third after banging in the fastest lap of the race on the final lap.

After Gary Dykes broke down, he secured the final podium spot behind the winner Joey and second-placed Ian Lougher.

Despite his success on the smaller machines, the bigger four-stroke bikes did not come to McGuinness as easy.

The likes of Michael Rutter, Chris Walker and DJ had all stuck with them and were coming on leaps and bounds, but McGuinness just did not feel comfortable on them.

He eventually finished 24th in the Junior TT on a 600cc Honda but of course his domination on the big bikes would follow in later years. Back on his 250cc, he won his first BSB race at Knockhill and went on to claim five podiums that year too, finishing fifth in the championship.

He even entered the British MotoGP as a wildcard, coming 14th, won at Scarborough and came fifth at Daytona. His future was beginning to look very bright indeed.

Ultra-Lightweight TT 1998
Robert's stunning comeback is complete

Joey Dunlop's rise to becoming an international star during the 1970s, 80s and 90s would continue to have a huge influence on all those back home in his native Northern Ireland – and none more so than his younger brother.

Robert had eventually decided to take his first steps in the sport after being inspired by his big brother. Watching Joey prepare his own motorbikes, one day he notice d he was preparing one for Robert too. It was a wonderful shock, especially when Joey also announced to those around him at the time that little brother was going to become a top racer.

Robert was different because he enjoyed the limelight more, as a bit of a Jack the Lad, who first started racing for fun and did not really look too much further ahead.

Behind the scenes, he lacked some self-belief, especially having a brother like Joey to try and emulate, so he groomed himself into something different from his brother, refocused and soon began to win plenty of races.

Despite the pressures, he enjoyed great success, becoming a professional racer. And he was equally as good on the circuits as he was the roads, becoming a British champion.

For a road racer, success and tragedy are never far away, so Robert would think more about god before a road race. He would not be as edgy on the circuits, or as nervous, which was just a natural reaction.

Robert knew the TT was the most dangerous circuit of all but the thrill of racing the 37.73-miles and getting home safely again outweighed the fear, especially when there was silverware at the end of it.

In May 1994, he returned to the TT. He was one of the favourites to win, but as he set off on his first race of the week disaster struck.

He crashed in a bad way and it was immediately clear the accident was a serious one. He was taken to the trauma room where the doctors explained to his family and friends that Robert was seriously ill and the following 48 hours would be touch and go.

After regaining consciousness, he told those close to him how his rear wheel had flown off, which had set him straight into a stone wall. Robert was left with a severely damaged right-hand side and it was believed he would never race a motorbike again.

A racer's trust in his machine must be unbreakable but for Robert that trust had been betrayed. Escaping with his life, he was left badly injured, and it seemed his road racing days had come to an end.

With his leg badly damaged and in a cage, he had no movement in his right arm either, which meant he could not walk properly or pick anything up.

His injuries were horrendous and his chances of earning money for his family had ended, albeit temporarily. His son, Michael, would recall how he went two months without seeing him after crashing at Ballaugh Bridge. He was eventually moved to Royal Belfast Hospital. Carl Fogarty said the accident had robbed the world of great riding talent because Robert had been hoping to get into World Superbikes at the time. Foggy and Dunlop were good friends.

The race itself was eventually won by Joey Dunlop, who completed a hat-trick of wins in the 125cc class.

Before the race, he admitted to being the most nervous he had ever been, following the incident with his brother, but he was able to let his riding skills take over to claim a 16th TT win with an average speed of 105.74mph ahead of second-placed Dennis McCullough who was more than a minute behind in second. Chris Fargher came third.

Victory number 17 followed for Joey later that week in the Junior TT as he battled back from third place early in lap one to take the win after Phil McCallen had run out of petrol.

Joey then claimed his first Senior TT in seven years in 1995, as well as taking victory in the Lightweight TT, for wins number 18 and 19, having been forced to retire from the Ultra-Lightweight TT earlier that same week.

And he showed no signs of slowing down either as he took yet another double on the island a year later, with wins in the Ultra-Lightweight TT and Lightweight TT, which moved him up to 21 wins.

The wins have kept flowing for Joey, but Robert appeared to finally be on the road to recovery. And despite all the odds stacked against him following his bad crash, he did indeed make his comeback on 20 April 1996, at the Cookstown 100 and finished ninth.

But he was not allowed to race at the North West 200 in 1997 after the clerk saw him eating with one hand and concluded he was in no fit state to race.

The Lightweight class at the TT was nothing above a 250cc, nothing like the 650cc four-stroke twin-cylinders used today.

There was also the Ultra-Lightweight class for 125cc machines, which was scrapped in 2004. However, Robert saw it as the perfect class for his comeback. Stunningly, after four laps of racing, he had finished in third, with Joey back in tenth.

He was determined his injuries would not end his career, and finally, in 1998, he was back out racing at the North West 200.

However, things went badly wrong as he was clipped by another rider and sent straight into a lamp post. It was a horrible crash, which left Robert with a broken collarbone and concussion.

It was only the metal pin that was already in his leg from the 1994 crash that had stopped his leg from breaking too.

And yet, just two weeks later, despite all of those injuries, he was back at the Isle of Man TT. And he went on to win the 125cc TT race too, the very same race that nearly killed him.

He was one of the toughest, hardest men to ever grace the TT circuit, and his incredible performance touched everyone who had witnessed it.

Lightweight TT 1998

Joey battles through injury for win number 23

Robert was not the only Dunlop to take an emotional win either as Joey also claimed a memorable TT victory that same year.

Despite losing part of his finger, as well as breaking his hand and cracking his pelvis, Joey was still able to retain his rightful place at the top of the TT podium in 1998.

He had won his fourth straight Lightweight class the year before, which had given him his 22nd TT victory.

But he then badly injured himself and damaged his 125cc bike while racing the Tandragee 100 in the May of 1998. However, brave to the end, he still decided to enter the TT a month later despite his arm being in a support.

After notching the 15th fastest time on his 125cc during practice week, he eventually dropped to 40th on the timesheets out of 49 riders. The reason? He was struggling to twist the throttle after his arm and wrist had begun to swell up.

Despite the pain, he soldiered on, and when the weather began to turn and rain started to fall, a plan of action formed in his head.

Knowing the race would almost certainly be cut short, he decided to try and finish the race without stopping while all the others pitted to refuel.

It worked a treat but such was his performance he would still have won the race had he decided to pit anyway. His lead had been that commanding.

He even banged in the fastest lap of the race, with a 100.50mph effort for good measure.

But Dunlop admitted to being left disappointed at not being fit enough to race on the big bikes.

He had put himself through a gruelling training regime during the winter months to try and get himself back to winning ways on his superbike.

The year 1998 was a special year for his team too as Honda was celebrating its 50th year racing at the TT.

To mark the occasion, Dunlop had been given a brand-new Honda RC45, with full factory backing, but in the end he had to pass up the bike and let British Superbike rider Ian Simpson ride it instead, while Ian Lougher rode his NSR V-twin in the Senior TT.

Dunlop had completely dominated the Formula TT class during the 1980s, taking wins every year between 1983 and 1988 – but that 1988 victory had marked his last win in that particular class around the island in ten years.

He had won a Senior TT in 1995 but all the other victories had been on the smaller bikes. Of course, in two years' time, all that would change in truly magnificent style.

Simpson, however, repaid his faith taking victory in both big bike races, ahead of Michael Rutter and Bob Jackson in the Senior. James Courtney came third in both.

The results were reversed in the Junior TT as Rutter – who also finished third in the Production class behind race winner Jim Moodie and Nigel Davies – claimed his maiden win ahead of Simpson

John McGuinness had also quietly been making progress during the 1998 campaign, finishing third on his Vimto-sponsored RS250, with a TSR chassis, behind Joey and Bob Jackson in the Lightweight TT. He also came fourth in the British championship and entered the British GP as wildcard where he diced with the likes of Mick Doohan, Max Biaggi and Simon Crafar, who won the race at Donington Park, with McGuinness finishing in the points in 12th, again showing he was more than just a top road racer.

The year also marked his first foray to Macau. Because 1998 was the year the Portuguese were handing it back to China, many thought the road race would be coming to an end.

Senior TT 1998

Privateer Jackson so close to causing huge upset

Privateers very rarely manage to beat factory teams – unless they happen to be Michael Dunlop – but in 1988 Bob Jackson almost pulled off one of the greatest-ever TT upsets.

Jackson was riding a Kawasaki ZX-7R at the time but he was up against a formidable line-up, while Honda was also celebrating 40 years racing at the TT and was even more eager than usual.

Jim Moodie had already claimed the Production TT on a Sanyo Fireblade, which also marked Honda's 100th win around the Mountain Course.

Ian Simpson had also won the Formula 1 race and he was teamed with Michael Rutter, who were both on RC45s.

The only bonus, perhaps, was the fact the likes of Joey Dunlop and Phil McCallen were not racing as they were still injured, but David Jefferies was there on a Yamaha along with a very young, Honda-mounted John McGuinness.

Jackson, 43, was in the McAdoo paddock but had not even raced in the Formula 1 TT because of team owner Winston McAdoo's strong religious beliefs. The Northern Irishman refused to let his riders race on a Sunday.

The plan for the Senior was simple, but genius. Use an oversized tank and make one pit stop instead of two for the six-lap race.

Using a 32-litre engine, the biggest legally allowed for the TT, Jackson was confident one stop would get the bike round the circuit six times.

Jackson even used a normal-sized tank during the practice sessions to throw his rivals off the scent and did not even add a quick release can for tyre changes.

That was simply because he would be racing the entire six laps on the same tyres.

Setting off fifth, Moodie had established a 20-second lead but ahead of him was Rutter and Simpson. Jackson was 35 seconds behind the leader.

But when they all pulled into the pits at the end of the second lap, Jackson flew through and suddenly everyone realised what was going on – but it was too late.

By Glen Helen, Jackson now had a 28-second lead and then a puncture forced Rutter to retire. Jackson still had a three-second lead over Simpson when he came in to pit – but then disaster struck.

Just when it appeared the win was on the cards, the lock cap would not go back on the full tank of petrol.

The problem, it turned out, was it had been overfilled with fuel. A rag was used to remove the excess and finally Jackson was able to set off again for his final three laps while McAdoo's team watching in the stands stopped pulling their hair out.

The bike even cut out but Jackson managed to fire it up again. Simpson was now leading Moodie but just by one second with Jackson back in sixth, 52 seconds behind at Glen Helen on lap four, but vitally not needing to pit again.

When Simpson came in, his lead had been reduced over Jackson to 4.4 seconds, which was soon down to three seconds and finally 0.4 seconds.

Alas, Jackson's efforts would come up just short as Simpson pushed hard over the mountain section, clocking the fastest lap of the race at 122.57mph.

Jackson also posted a 122.65mph but came home in second, just 3.7 seconds behind. When considering the pit stop added 45 seconds to his time, it was a bitter pill to swallow for the team.

Formula 1 TT 1999

DJ and his Yamaha shock dominant Honda

Tyre changes, red flags, crashes, Yamaha finally breaking the Honda stranglehold on the F1 race and Dave Jefferies announcing himself to the TT fraternity.

It is fair to say the 1999 Formula 1 TT had pretty much everything, including the weather playing havoc with the race, which was stopped, restarted over a shorter distance and then won by the future star of the Mountain Course.

When the weather suddenly changed before the start of the race, it had forced the riders to gamble with what tyres to choose.

Once that decision had been made the riders set off, and early there was drama as Jim Moodie, who had posted the fastest lap during practice, was forced to pull up.

Despite running back to the pits to try and sort the problem and get back out there, he was forced to sit the race out.

It would be a week to forget for Moodie on the big bike because, although Honda agreed to fly in a new RC45 for him to race in the Senior, he would register another DNF despite breaking the lap record.

If that wasn't enough drama, the race was red-flagged for the first time since 1954 when Paul Orritt crashed at the bottom of Bray Hill. Thankfully, he was okay and only required ankle surgery.

The race scheduled to restart with a reduced four laps but the changes made for a very dramatic race.

Honda had won the last 18 F1 races, so not many fans would have bet against a Honda rider again picking up the Silver Lady.

Joey Dunlop had also been supplied with the best bike by the manufacturer, and he was hoping for win number 19 on the island.

Dave Jefferies, however, had other ideas. Armed with a £20,000 Yamaha and having only raced at the TT three times before, he came within a whisker of breaking the lap record en route to a stunning victory.

His three wins at the North West 200 prior to the TT had already given his rivals fair warning of his huge potential on the machine, but even the great man himself admitted to being surprised with how well the package had all come together at the end of the race.

Dunlop had done everything in his power to try and grab the win himself, even clocking a 123.26mph to also nearly beat Carl Fogarty's long-standing lap record, but it still wasn't enough.

Jefferies, who still felt he had been out of shape around much of the course, had managed to put the RC45s – the same bikes used by the likes of Colin Edwards in World Superbikes – well and truly in their place.

Jack Valentine had managed to find, and work on, an R1 that was capable of beating them all, under their V&M banner.

Moodie had managed to beat his Yamaha rival into second to claim the Junior TT but Jefferies seemed unstoppable on the big bike, claiming the Production TT, which set up a mouth-watering finale in the Senior.

It proved to be a tale of two riders as Moodie rewrote the record books, finally beating Carl Fogarty's seven-year record with a lap of 124.46mph.

Moodie said Fogarty had given the lap record real credibility.

The fact it had not been broken for so long – and a lot of very good people on good bikes had tried – and he managed to do it on his first attempt on an RC45, and raising the bar considerably, gave him a lot of satisfaction.

Moodie, however, would again be forced to retire paving the way for DJ to take his third TT in the week.

Such were the repercussions following DJ's stunning three wins, Honda withdrew the RC45 from racing and returned in 2000 to race a modified version of its road bike the SP1, on which Joey would create yet more history.

Valentine had given up racing in 1990 to concentrate on running V&M Racing – and there was more to the rivalry too as he had been sacked by Honda at the end of the 1998 season.

The team took the new Yamaha R1 road bike and modified it into a truly competitive superbike.

After David Jefferies won both North West 200 superbike races and set a new lap record of 122.26mph, he arrived at the TT full of confidence.

He then went on to win both premier races at that year's Isle of Man TT, the TT Formula One race and also the Senior TT.

The Yamaha V&M story was far from over too as Jefferies put the bike on pole position as a newcomer winning the superbike race and then narrowly lost to Joey in the second.

And to top off a truly memorable year and partnership, he won the 1999 Macau Grand Prix for good measure too.

Having won the treble at the TT in 1999, DJ was hungry for more, and he would not have to wait long before he returned to the top step on the Isle of Man.

JOHN McGUINNESS

Sitting on the grass banks as a youngster watching his heroes fly by on the Isle of Man, John McGuinness always knew he would be a TT racer, as the great man explained during an interview in the Express & Star *newspaper:*

HE HAD no idea how, he just knew it would happen – and after winning 23 TTs, placing him behind only the late, great Joey Dunlop, he went on to establish himself as arguably the greatest road racer of the modern era.

'I wanted to be a mechanic but my dad told me to go and get a trade,' said McGuinness. 'When I finished being an apprentice bricklayer I came out of college with a trowel in my hand then we hit a recession so there was no work.

'I started working as a mussel picker but all I ever wanted to be was a professional racer.'

McGuinness, aged 45, from Morecambe, would regularly jump on the ferry from Heysham and travel to the Isle of Man for free, hiding in between the vans, cars and motorbikes.

Having grown up around bikes, as his father was a mechanic, he eventually began circuit racing and won the British 250cc Championship in 1999.

But road racing was always in the back of his mind and he eventually took the plunge in 1996, entering the Lightweight class – with not a spare penny in his pocket.

'I first rode a bike around the TT course in 1982 in between watching the likes of Dunlop and Ron Haslam.

'I'd watch the practice week and then have to be dragged kicking and screaming back to school when the holidays ended.

'All I wanted to be was a TT racer – I had no idea how I would do it though.

'I started racing properly in 1990 and eventually won a British Championship but I wanted to race the TT.

'It took a while to get everything together and a lot of hard work.

'Paul Bird gave me my first break. I lied that I could raise the £10,000 needed but could only muster £2,000, so I ended up delivering chickens for him, working on the bikes, anything really to ride the TT.

'My first TT was in 1996 – the same year as Dave Jefferies and Bruce Anstey.

'I was sharing a room with a biker called Mick Lofthouse who died during practice so it was bit of a baptism of fire.'

McGuinness's dream would come true in 1999 when he won his first TT, which led to another dream move – when he became team-mates with his idol, Northern Irishman Joey Dunlop, at Honda.

'Joey could ride any bike and was such a special rider,' he said. 'I got his autograph in 1986 and told him I would be on the podium with him one day. He muttered something back then – but then it happened.

'Joey was a hardman and to see him win three TTs in 2000 was something special.

'For him to die in Estonia at a little road race a few weeks later after all those years racing was hard to take.

'I remember I knocked into him during practice in 2000 on my 250cc, which roughed him up a bit and even gave him an elbow on the way past. I regretted straight away and it really fired him up – I knew I shouldn't have done it.

'I went into the race as the British champion and lap record holder but I didn't see him again after he left the start line.'

After Dunlop's tragic death racing in Estonia in 2000, aged 48, and later his friend, Dave Jefferies in 2003, aged 30, McGuinness would go on to become the best of his generation.

Dominating the superbike class, he posted the first ever 130mph average speed lap around the 37.73-mile Mountain Course during the TT's 100th anniversary year in 2007 and would go on to win 23 in total.

Such was his success, he now has his favourite corner around the TT circuit named after him, which is now simply known as 'McGuinness's'.

However, ask him which of those 23 stands out and it's his memorable 2015 Senior win.

'Winning that race was probably my best moment, doing the 132.7mph lap – it's something I'll take to my grave.

'I was given odds of 18/1 to win and I thought, "I'm not having that."

'I used all my 19 years of experience at the time. I felt strong from the start and we've always been pretty good in the pits. People think there's a secret to it but there isn't, the Honda also uses less fuel than the BMWs so it actually takes less time to fill them up and get going.

'When you are on the bike and everything's working well, all you're thinking about is what's coming up next on the track, when's my next pit board, the next apex, the next pit stop.

'Little things like that can lose you half a second here and there if you don't get them right.

'You're trying to conserve energy where you can too in case there's a scrap at the end.

'I can't really remember much about the 2015 Senior race but the third lap was incredible because I could see the fans waving programmes at me as I'd just broken the lap record.

'The last lap was just about keeping concentration and when I won I'd equalled Mike Hailwood's record of seven Senior TT wins.

'It was very emotional and it was great to get the job finished and get in the bar.'

Last year's TT saw McGuinness surprisingly off the pace but he had renewed hope heading into 2017 after Honda unveiled a new Fireblade – and a new team-mate in Guy Martin.

But that hope soon turned to despair as McGuinness – renowned for his smooth riding style and years of racing without a major accident – suffered a horror crash racing at the North West 200 in May, which could potentially bring his glorious career to a premature end.

Martin also suffered a high-speed crash at the TT but escaped serious injury and both riders have blamed a fault with the bike for their crashes.

Investigations have taken place but neither rider has been pleased with the outcome – with McGuinness still seething about his treatment.

'I had a crash at Castle Combe in about second or third gear and went down really hard, dislocating my thumb which had to be put back in place,' he said. 'That's where the problems all started really and I was definitely not prepared for all that.

'At the North West, the throttle started sticking just before a turn so I grabbed the clutch but when that failed there was nothing I could do.

'I was heading toward the barrier so I just decided to jump off. The whole world slowed down and I was just thinking 'I should never have ridden this bike'.

'After 20 years' experience in racing, I should not have been on it.

'I hit the fence, landed about ten or 12 feet beyond it, and ended up in a golf course which was even worse – because I hate golf.

'I didn't realise I had injured my leg at first but when I looked down I just thought, "Oh dear."'

McGuinness is now having to endure painful rehabilitation on his leg, which includes lengthening it by 40–50mm using screws and bolts – about 1mm per day.

'My aim is get back walking again and then I'll decide if I'm going to carry on,' he said.

'All I've ever done is racing and it's all I've ever known.

'When I'm having a craic with people everything's okay, but it's when I'm lying in bed alone and the pain kicks in it gets hard. I don't know if coming back is achievable so I don't want to say too much.

'I don't want to see my wife crying again but when the pain goes away I might want to get back on a bike.

'I could even come back and just race the lightweight or electric bikes. But I never thought I'd be sat here with 23 TT wins and I'm not bothered about beating Joey's record.

McGuinness says, if he does retire, there are lots of ideas floating around in his head, including opening a museum in Morecambe.

'I've got 47 bikes at the moment, all the stuff I've collected and I think people would enjoy seeing it all,' he said.

'I like the classic bikes and all that stuff so maybe we'd get a good turnout – and I can tell everybody how good I used to be.'

Lightweight 250cc TT 1999
McGuinness opens his TT account

John McGuinness launched his illustrious TT career properly when he claimed the Lightweight TT first win in 1999, which included a lap record for good measure at midway point in the race, taking it from Ian Lougher.

It meant he was not only leading the race but he was also the fastest man to ever lap the course on a 250cc machine, a bike he simply gelled so well with during the earlier stages of his career before he finally got to grips with the bigger bikes, going on to dominate the superbike class for years to come.

The year 1999 was a truly stellar 12 months as he also claimed the British championship after securing 12 podiums, five poles and two wins during the season.

He also won at Scarborough, Daytona and Stars at Darley, the latter being a race around the iconic Darley Moor race track in Derbyshire.

And he also won the 250cc TT, crossing the line ahead of Jason Griffiths and Gavin Lee, who came second and third respectively.

He had gone from 19th in 1996, to third in 1997 and 1998, before finally standing on the top spot in 1999.

It was the first time McGuinness had decided to push as hard as possible on the opening lap to try and put a dent into the other riders.

It would be a tactic that he would employ throughout his hugely successful career – and the majority of the time it worked because his rivals had no response. Having only made his debut three years earlier, his performance in the 1999 250cc TT race really made all the competitors, fans and commentators stand up and take notice of this man, who was destined to become one of the greatest.

His stunning lead of 21 seconds during the race left many speechless as, rather than slowing down and beginning to feel the effects of the extremely tough course, or perhaps letting some novice nerves seep in, instead he continued to increase the gap to second by the end of lap two.

Joey Dunlop had set off number three, with McGuinness behind in fourth. It meant that as well as overtaking his hero, he also broke Lougher's long-standing lap record too during the same year his close friend and road racing rival Dave Jefferies also chalked up his first Formula One win on his V&M R1.

Griffiths had tried to mount some kind of a challenge but it seemed that instead of pushing for the win he might start trying to consolidate second, such was the gap to the race leader McGuinness.

And as the riders started their final lap, Honda-mounted McGuinness was able to start relaxing and to enjoy what was approaching him, his debut win, with Yamaha's Griffiths keeping hold of second, fellow Yamaha rider Gavin Lee third, and Honda's Dennis McCullough in fourth.

It marked the continuation of something truly special and the start of a new dynasty of TT heroes, with Vimto-cladded McPint – who would win the race by 33 seconds, in a race time of one hour, 17 minutes and 31.7 seconds – following in the footsteps of his great friend, Jefferies.

McGuinness, in his end of race debrief, explained how he had decided to push as hard as possible from the first lap and if he got a good board he would just go for it. Simple as that.

There was also a notable race in the Sidecar A TT in 1999 as Dave Molyneux and Craig Hallam became the first pair to break the 110mph lap barrier, raising the record to 111.9mph.

However, a year later, the history books would be rewritten once more as Joey Dunlop once again showed the world why he was still the King of the Mountain.

ISLE OF MAN TT MEMORIES

Michael Rutter, from Bridgnorth, Shropshire, is a seven-time TT winner, record-breaking eight-time Macau GP winner and 14-time North West 200 winner:

I suppose my most special memory would have to be finishing second behind Joey in 2000 in the Formula 1 TT.

I remember seeing him in that race basically just clear off and no one could catch him. He had caught up with me and we ended up circling together for about four laps.

After the race he told me how much he had enjoyed it and even bought me a pint, which was really special and very rarely happened.

Of course he died a few weeks later in Estonia but to have the chance to race with someone like that – someone who had raced against my dad too, when he was a lot younger – someone as good as him, is something I will also remember and always treasure.

Formula 1 TT 2000

Joey wins on a big bike to claim another treble

Dave Jefferies had looked invincible the year before and few felt results in 2000 would be any different.

But Joey Dunlop, a then sprightly 48-year-old, had other ideas.

He'd had a year to contemplate what had happened in 1999 and it seemed to spur him on to achieve newer, and arguably, greater heights.

With 23 TT wins already under his belt, he was already, unquestionably, King of the Mountain. Yet with the likes of Jefferies, Michael Rutter and Bruce Anstey snapping at his heels, it had looked for a brief moment like his reign might be coming to an end.

If anything, the opposite occurred as he dominated the 2000 TT race week, picking up another three TT victories – his third triple – with the highlight being his return to the top step on a superbike.

Despite his 23 wins and riding a factory Honda once again, Dunlop was still very much an underdog going into the race week, such was Jefferies's phenomenal pace and talent.

Jefferies had ended Honda's domination of the big bike class the year before and, to make matters worse, Rutter had also beaten the VTR SP-1 at the North West 200 the month before the TT.

The omens did not look good for Dunlop and he admitted before the first race he did not think he had a chance of winning on a big bike.

But behind the scenes work was in motion to try and close the gap, which saw the manufacturer agree to fly in a World Superbike-spec engine especially for the TT.

And another factor that swung the race in Dunlop's favour was the weather.

After rain had shortened the number of practice laps any of the riders were able to get before the opening race, the Northern Irishman's experience would again prove to be invaluable.

Aged 48, Dunlop had been lapping the 37.73-mile course since the 1970s but, despite all that experience, it had still been a long time since he had won on a big bike.

He had continued to pick up numerous victories in the smaller classes but the superbike win had eluded him.

However, the final flourish that seemed to show the superbike win might finally be back on was a set of new tyres, which Dunlop said had managed to settle the ferocious

Honda down. It allowed an ultra-determined Joey to concentrate entirely on the job at hand.

By the late 1990s, it appeared Joey's and Robert's careers may have been drawing to a close. Joey was now in his late 40s and had been racing on the roads for 30 years.

Robert was eight years younger but badly impaired by his injuries. However, they both returned for the 2000 TT as fellow competitors and brothers working together.

Joey wanted one more good go at the TT and wanted to get back to fitness, while Robert said he would go with him and support him throughout.

Robert turned into Joey's manager for a couple of months and just looked out for his older brother.

It had been ten years since Joey had won a big bike race at the TT and no one thought he had a chance in 2000.

But from the very first lap he just went for it and went on to produce an incredible performance. Everyone in the crowd knew they were witnessing something truly special.

McGuinness was a TT winner in 1999 and, setting off ten seconds behind Joey, he was convinced he was going to beat him. He rode hard but he never saw his hero again as Joey left him for dead.

He was just so relaxed and many people felt this may be his swansong, his final year. The cheers from the crowd were huge, with hardened fans and journalists truly touched by what they had just witnessed.

He had wanted that race so badly and, after ten years of hurt, he got it. He went on to win two more races that week and was even joined on the podium by his brother, Robert, who finished third in the 125cc class.

It seemed it was meant to be because Robert had been such a big part in his older brother's success that famous race week.

For 48-year-old Joey, TT wins 24, 25 and 26 had come 23 years since his first TT win and 30 years since he had first started racing on the roads with his friends and family.

He had added to his record as the most successful TT racer of all time. Back home, he was hailed as the returning hero.

The weather had still looked a little ominous as the riders rolled up to the start line but it was a signal for Dunlop to begin the race as quickly as possible and lay down an early marker. Rutter, however, was having none of it and had managed to stay just 0.2 seconds behind his rival and hero.

Rutter had dropped to fourth by the end of lap two with Jefferies making his move, entering the pits in second place.

Jefferies looked really fired up as he began closing in on the lead, posting the fastest lap of the race on lap four, which saw him edge into the lead.

A fast pit stop saw Dunlop again leading the pack into lap five, and from then on it was neck and neck between the master and the young pretender.

Jefferies had again retaken the lead and it looked as though it could end with a photo finish but, when his Yamaha broke down on lap five because of a gearbox problem, it handed the Formula 1 TT win to Dunlop.

Such was the pace, Dunlop suddenly had a one-minute lead over second-placed Rutter, who was also suffering with his own bike problems, which included a faulty radiator and a loss of handling.

After crossing the finish line, an ecstatic Dunlop proclaimed the Honda to be the best bike he had ever ridden.

And what made the win even more memorable was Joey's win also marked the first time an SP-1 had ever been ridden at the TT.

Most riders had also switched from Dunlops to Pirellis for the race – but Dunlop had not, and he had still won the race, which again left a lot of his fellow racers scratching their heads at his talent once more. Jefferies was understandably gutted to have missed out on another win, but gracious as ever, he was full of praise for Dunlop, while Rutter was also happy to second place, particularly with all the bike problems he had been experiencing.

McGuinness was simply, once again, left gobsmacked and dumbfounded by his hero as he settled for third.

Welshman Ian Lougher, who had also been riding an R1 like Rutter, had come in fourth but not without suffering his own mechanical issues and some serious scares and slides during the race, on the ultra-fast Yamaha. Jim Moodie rounded out the top five.

Senior TT 2000
Jefferies smashes the 125mph lap barrier

If the Formula 1 TT was owned by Joey Dunlop, the Senior was completed dominated by Dave Jefferies who was unstoppable on his 1000 Yamaha as he smashed the lap record once again.

Lapping in 18 minutes, he made even more history by becoming the first rider to break the 125mph – posting a 125.69mph lap to be completely exact.

Early on in the race at Ramsey, Jefferies had pulled out a 38-second lead on his V&M team-mate Michael Rutter, who in turn had a lead of 30 seconds over Joey Dunlop, with the Irishman also enjoying a half a minute lead over Adrian Archibald, meaning the field was very spread out.

McGuinness and Griffiths were in fifth and sixth respectively as they all came in to the pits for their first refuels.

Jefferies continued pushing as hard as only he could and it seemed he was on another very special lap as he took off once again, with Rutter second, Joey third and McGuinness now up to fourth.

DJ had increased his lead further up to 37 seconds and, as he approached the finish line, he had raised the lap record above the 125mph mark en route to yet another stunning big bike win, which meant he joined Joey as yet another rider to scoop a hat-trick of victories in the same week, making the 2000 TT one of the truly special race meetings of any era, past or present.

DJ said after the race that breaking the lap record and winning the Senior TT had made up for losing the other big bike race, the Formula 1 TT, to Joey earlier in the week.

Rutter would make it a one-two for the V&M Yamaha R1 team, with Honda riders Joey and McGuinness in third and fourth respectively.

Rutter said after the race how he had enjoyed riding round with Joey, learning some more of the track in the sections he classed himself as slow and commentated on how fast the pace had been throughout the record-breaking race.

McGuinness had been given the chance to ride with his hero, Joey Dunlop, as his team-mate. He also started riding the bigger four-stroke bikes too, taking on an SP1 Honda.

He also won at Daytona, at the North West and added another TT on a single-cylinder Chrysalis, finishing third in the F1 TT behind Rutter in second and the winner, Dunlop.

Sadly, it would be the final time McGuinness, or indeed any other rider, would be able to lap the TT at the same time as Dunlop as he would lose his life, ironically on the same day McGuinness had wrapped up another 250cc British championship.

It was 2 July 2000. Dunlop had already won the wet 600 and superbike races in Estonia but then died in the 125cc race on the tiny 3.7-mile circuit. A true legend of the road-racing fraternity was gone forever.

McGuinness continued to race and, now a father, he was back running at the sharp end in the British Supersport Championship with the likes of Karl Harris and Kirk McCarthy in 2001.

After winning the Macau GP, he had some good bikes lined up for the TT, but then a foot-and-mouth outbreak would see the entire two weeks of racing on the Isle of Man cancelled.

Formula 1 TT 2002
Jefferies and TAS a match made in heaven

One of the most successful independent teams on the island is TAS, owned and run by father and son Hector and Philip Neill. They have won 18 TTs since 2002.

It all started 60 years ago when Hector was a child. He had a dream, as a schoolboy, he wanted to go to the Isle of Man and win the TT.

Norman Brown was the first to win the TT for Hector and his team when he claimed the 1982 Senior TT on a Suzuki.

Philip joined the team in 2000, following a successful career in motocross racing, and the family formed the TAS Racing team.

They contacted Suzuki who agreed to support the team and they ended up approaching Ian Lougher, who was just getting back into the four-stroke bikes – but then, with everything in place, the foot-and-mouth disease hit and put everything back a year. Suddenly, David Jefferies mentioned he was interested because the Suzukis were the only bikes that passed his Yamaha.

Jefferies had already claimed six TT wins, smashing the lap record on numerous occasions on his V&M Yamaha, becoming the first rider to break the 125mph barrier in the process.

Once Jefferies had teamed up with the superb TAS Suzuki machine it really was an unstoppable match made in heaven.

Come the 2002 TT and Jefferies was on it from the opening flag, leading the field ahead of the likes of Jim Moodie, Adrian Archibald and John McGuinness, posting a 125mph lap from a standing start.

It was clear no one would be able to touch him or the team, and sure enough he crossed the line to win the Senior TT, despite losing nearly 40 seconds due to gearbox problems. He was that far ahead of the field it mattered not.

And then DJ made it a double for the TAS team as he won the Production 1000 TT for good measure too, battling against his team-mate Ian Lougher, which made it a one-two for the TAS team.

But Lougher would taste victory that same week, taking victory in the Production 600 TT and there was also the little matter of the Senior TT still to come.

DJ was always going to be the man to beat and with no faults between man or machine they were always going to be too strong for their rivals.

As Jefferies simply put it, it had been a 'really, really good week', but sadly all that joy would turn to heartbreak a year later.

DAVID JEFFERIES

DJ, AS he was affectionately known, came from a Yorkshire family steeped in Isle of Man history.

However, the future King of the Mountain began his career on the circuits and was one of the rising stars of the British Superbike Championship.

He had a knack even very early in his career of being able to handle, control and get the most out of the bigger bikes.

A natural on two wheels, his passion was always road racing, and when he made his debut at the TT in 1996, aged 24, he immediately showed early signs of what was to come as he claimed the Newcomer's Trophy.

DJ was also an immediate fan's favourite as his easygoing nature and humility, coupled with his exceptional talent, endeared him to all who came across him.

And it was not long before he was ripping apart the record books, which included his famous triple victories in 1999, 2000 and then 2002, firstly on Yamahas and then finally following his switch to Suzukis and the TAS Racing team.

Despite his incredible pace he was also seen as one of the safest riders in the paddock, which was why his tragic accident was even harder to take for so many of his fans and competitors. No one saw it coming when he was killed in a practice accident in 2003. The entire island was left shell-shocked, none more so than his close friend John McGuinness.

During 2002, McGuinness had been given the chance to ride a Motorex Honda CBR600 in the World Supersport championships, which also meant he could ride the North West and TT.

After finishing second to DJ at the TT, his World Superbike campaign went from bad to worse with his bike blowing up everywhere. His bike even let him down at the TT when on the Cronk-y-Voddy straight and he admitted afterwards he had been lucky to survive.

It was a year to forget for the future 23-time winner and he was hoping for better luck and more battles with close friend and rival DJ, but alas it was not to be. After being dropped by Honda, Triumph stepped in and offered McGuinness a contract. And it was a good package too as Anstey would go on to win the Junior 600 on the same bike.

In the superbike race, the Morecambe Missile had agreed to ride Paul Bird's Monster Mob 998 Ducati. However, the entire year would be overshadowed by the death of Jefferies.

Not only was he great friends with the likes McGuinness, he did so much more, including giving Ian Hutchinson, who grew up in the same region, a brand-new Suzuki GSX 1000 he had acquired as a bonus, just to help get him started in road racing. Hutchy would also go on to become one of the most successful TT racers of all time and it was started, in part, thanks to the kind nature of DJ.

He was also one of the very few riders McGuinness admitted was that little bit better than him, even around the TT course. DJ quickly established himself on the big bikes. He just took to them really quickly while others stayed on the 250s, and that was despite missing 1997 due to injury.

He was strong in 2000, missed 2001 like everyone else because of the foot-and-mouth outbreak, dominated 2002 and then died in 2003.

Having already won multiple TTs and a British Superstock Championship, he then won at the North West 200 too, which meant he was heading into the TT full of confidence once more.

After struggling with the Suzuki during practice week, despite having set the new lap record of 127.29mph the year before, he decided to return to his old settings on the new bike, and it worked a treat.

From a standing start, again during practice, he posted a 125mph lap – the fastest of the week.

Then, three miles into his second lap, he died. Adrian Archibald and DJ had gone out first together, with McGuinness and Jim Moodie behind.

McGuinness had been hoping to try and catch his friend, somehow, to pick up a few tips and maybe work out why he was so fast.

Heading through Crosby, he saw yellow flags being waved and he slowed right down. He was one of the first on the scene and it affected him for the rest of his life as, not only had he seen a fellow racer die, he had lost one of his true friends. Again, McGuinness was encouraged to carry on racing, this time by DJ's mother, Pauline, who also told the TAS Racing team to go and win in her son's memory.

DJ never trained, he just had a natural talent for riding motorbikes better than anyone else. Nine TT wins in three years says it all. At the time, McGuinness was finishing second to him, but was finding himself more than a minute behind.

His death also had a huge effect on the TT too for other reasons, because the organisers made major changes to the way the marshalling was carried out while safety was also improved. DJ was never nervous and just naturally pushed the boundaries. Archibald, his team-mate, would eventually go on to win the Formula 1 TT that same year, which was a fitting tribute.

Meanwhile, McGuinness also won his third TT in the Lightweight race, on a Honda, as well as ominously finishing second and third on his superbike.

But the TT would always be remembered for the loss of another true legend of the sport who had done so much TT, raising the bar to unheard-of levels all while keeping a smile on his face.

Formula 1 TT 2003
Archibald does it for Jefferies

TAS had claimed four TT wins in 2002, thanks to the efforts of Jefferies, Lougher and the Suzuki package, and it looked set to be more of the same in 2003 after the team had managed to re-sign both the bikes and the main man, DJ.

However, this time his team-mate would be Adrian Archibald rather than Ian Lougher, but then disaster struck as DJ was tragically killed at Crosby, four miles into the TT course.

It was a huge shock to everyone involved particularly because no one thought DJ could be killed, and the team was ready to pack until his mother came across and demanded the TAS continued racing in her son's memory. And not only did Archibald win TT in Jefferies's memory, he won two.

It was an emotional win to say the least and Archibald admitted after the race it had taken him a few laps to get into his groove but once he had, there was simply no stopping him.

There were muted celebrations on the podium that day but come Senior TT he did it again, bagging two big bike wins and once again he dedicated the win to his team-mate.

Archibald had always been a quiet man, a rider who preferred to keep himself to himself and just let his racing do the talking, which may have helped him find the willpower to win against a backdrop of such tragic circumstances.

He knew he would have to go quick immediately with the likes of John McGuinness hunting him down but once he was in front there was no stopping him.

Again, the celebrations were mooted, but Archibald and the team continued but with a new team-mate, this time in the form of Bruce Anstey.

The team put together a new bike for the New Zealander – and again it was another match made in heaven as Bruce claimed the Production 1000 win 2004.

And then to top the week off for the team, Archibald claimed the Senior TT after McGuinness had broken down, which gave the Northern Irishman his three TT wins.

However, despite all the success, there was more change for TAS Racing as Archibald announced he was leaving the team, but he did return to race alongside Anstey – and when it came to the superstock they were lapping together.

And then Archibald ran out of fuel allowing his team-mate to win the race. Anstey would dominate the superstock class for the next three years, raising TAS's TT win record to 11 in the process.

Another year and this time Archibald really did leave while Anstey remained with the TAS team where he was joined by Aussie Cameron Donald. Once again, it was another match made in heaven.

Donald said it was not so much a question of joining the team, more a privilege, and he was determined to try and win a TT. Sure enough, he would not have to wait long as he claimed the 2008 Superbike TT. Donald said that first TT win had made the pain and sacrifices worthwhile.

So, once the Senior came about, it seemed the Aussie would be the man to beat but a bike problem would pave the way for McGuinness as Donald had to settle for second.

With Bruce also winning a Supersport TT it meant TAS had again won three in a week, but despite that success the team's riders would change again very soon as Guy Martin entered the team but he was unable, personally, to add to TAS's TT success.

The team would have to wait until Ian Hutchinson joined before returning to winning ways at the TT, as well as in the National Superstock 1000 series, as the Bingley Bullet claimed his 15th, drawing him level with Mike Hailwood.

He then added a 16th TT win in the supersport and was going well in the Senior when his poor fortune once again came to the fore when he crashed, again breaking his leg.

Junior TT 2003

Anstey and Triumph back on top

By the 1990s, Triumph was ready to relaunch once again and it unveiled its new motorbikes at the Cologne motorshow. Six new models were ready to go.

The brand-new factory had been built in Hinckley, which would soon see others follow in Thailand and Brazil.

The Bonneville was reborn in 1997; it was ridden by David Beckham on his Brazilian TV adventure, and soon the brand was producing more bikes per year than in its entire history.

All models were being produced down the same production line. Robots are yet to replace the skilled workers, who use top-of-the-range electric tools to put the bikes together.

A lot of money was pumped into the new factory to produce top-of-the-range engines, such as the engine the manufacturer produced to Bruce Anstey in 2003. And he would repay them handsomely by claiming the Junior TT in 2003. It was Triumph's first win on the island for 27 years.

Anstey took the flag followed by two other Triumph riders inside the top ten to mark a watershed for the British manufacturer, thanks to Jim Moodie and John McGuinness.

British motorcycling was back, with Triumph spearheading the charge as a racing force to be reckoned with – with a flying Kiwi piloting their race-winning machine.

Anstey had first begun racing in 1996 having been inspired to take up the sport by returning Mike Hailwood's winning return to the TT in 1978.

Anstey's affiliation with Triumph went a long way back too as he rode one in the Thruxton 200 mile race, eventually rejoining the brand in 2003 when he signed for the Valmoto Triumph Daytona team and claimed the Junior TT win and an eighth-placed finish in the Production 600cc class on a Daytona.

The New Zealander finished more than ten seconds ahead of his nearest rival, finishing in a time of one hour, 15 minutes and 13.98 seconds.

He said winning on a Triumph had made the win extra special, which was saying something as Anstey would go on to claim a total of 11 TT victories.

Meanwhile, Triumph continued going from strength to strength too, making 11,000 bikes at its Hinckley plant every year, with a further 55,000 at its other plants around the world – some are completely new designs, some hark back to the early years, but all are uniquely built.

BRUCE ANSTEY

BRUCE ANSTEY made his competitive debut on Boxing Day, 1990, at the Whanganui Circuit in his native New Zealand, competing on a Suzuki RGV250.

He would switch allegiance to Yamaha between 1996 and 2002, finishing his TT debut 29th place in the Lightweight class before retiring in the Senior TT.

Due to illness, Anstey missed the 1997 TT, returning a year later to compete in Lightweight and Senior races again, taking his Yamaha TZ250 to a 26th-place finish in the Lightweight and 20th in the Senior TT – but he was the third quickest 250cc rider in the Senior, only beaten for pace by Gavin Lee and fellow New Zealander, Shaun Harris.

Anstey's form continued to improve in 1999 as he leapt into the top ten, claiming a seventh in the Lightweight and 24th in the Senior.

By 2000, he was beginning to trouble the podium, finishing second behind Joey Dunlop in his favoured Lightweight TT and was the quickest 250cc rider in the Senior en route to a 14th.

Once racing returned to the island in 2002 following the foot-and-mouth outbreak, he entered five races for the first time enjoying various degrees of success.

He retired in Formula 1 TT, came tenth in the Ultra-Lightweight TT, third in the Production 1000cc class and then secured his maiden victory in the Lightweight TT before ending a successful second half of race week with a hard-fought second in the Production 600cc.

The podiums kept coming thick and fast a year later too. He finished second in the Production 1000cc race, took victory in the Junior TT aboard the Valmoto Triumph Daytona – giving Triumph its first TT win in 27 years – came eighth in the Production 600cc class and seventh in the Senior, having switched to a 1000cc Suzuki for the big race.

His consistently strong performances saw him signed by TAS Suzuki in 2004 and he immediately repaid their faith in him too as he came third place in the Formula 1 and took victory in the 1000cc Production race.

Three second-placed finishes in the Junior 600cc, the Production 600cc and the Senior TT meant he had finished on the podium in every single race he had entered.

The 2005 Isle of Man TT would prove to be a leaner meeting for the Kiwi as bike problems would force him to retire in both big bike races, but he bounced back in true Anstey style by winning the Superstock.

Anstey turned heads as early as practice week in 2006 when he clocked a staggering speed of 206mph in the Sulby Straight – and it proved to be an omen too as he once again took victory in the superstock, came second in the supersport and then claimed the final podium position in the Senior.

A third straight Superstock TT followed in 2007 and then 2008 was a year filled with drama for the popular New Zealander.

After finishing second in the Superbike TT, he claimed what he thought was another win in the opening supersport race, only to be disqualified after an inspection found his exhaust cam did not meet regulations.

However, two days later he swept to victory in the second supersport race following a thrilling battle with Ian Hutchinson that saw him break the lap record after posting a 125.359mph effort.

A solitary second place followed in 2009 and 2010, again producing a mixed bag of results, with his best finish coming in the Senior where he was placed third.

Better fortune followed in 2011 after a switch of team, as he won the supersport race and came third once again in the Senior TT.

The year 2012 would prove to be one of the most fruitful for Anstey who continued to show that age was really no barrier as he took victory in the opening supersport race, also finished third in the Superbike TT, and then a pair of fourths in the Superstock TT and second supersport race.

Three podiums followed in 2013 and another four in 2014, which included his debut in the TT Zero, which was won by John McGuinness who was riding the same Honda Mugen. More trophies followed too as he picked up the John Williams Trophy for the fastest lap in the Superbike TT race and the Jimmy Simpson Trophy for posting quickest lap of the entire race week.

But the highlight of Anstey's race career would come on 7 June 2015, when he claimed the Superbike TT

Anstey rode a Honda RC213V-S at the 2016 TT, specially prepared by the Valvoline Racing by Padgett's Motorcycles team, but his race fortnight began badly as he crashed at Keppel Gate.

Despite his injuries he bravely carried on taking his RC213V-S to a very creditable eighth in the opening Superbike TT, and then won his first TT Zero race despite his injuries to top another successful fortnight for the New Zealander.

Aside from his racing, Anstey has battled against cancer twice. After being diagnosed with testicular cancer in 1995, he was forced to miss the TT two years later as he underwent treatment.

In 2018, it was confirmed cancer had returned, this time with tumours in his lungs and on his spine. It forced him to miss the 2018 and 2019 TT but such is the courage of the racer, he was planning to return as soon as possible. He remains a true legend of the TT and racing in general.

ISLE OF MAN TT MEMORIES

Ian Mills, from Stockton-on-Tees, Teesside, is a road racing photographer who also runs the IOM Road Racing Facebook page with his wife, Sarah:

I was a late starter to the TT, first seeing the races in 2007, although I had ridden bikes since I was 17 years old.

Sarah first went to the TT in 2004, and has ridden since she was 39.

Since 2007, we have always ridden a bike over for the TT from Worcester, where we now live, with that feeling of joining the queue at the ferry – it gets the heart pumping and you know this is where it starts.

The first few years were a bit of a shock to the system, both the racing and riding the actual course, but of course we saw McGuinness pull off that 130mph lap at the centenary.

In 2016 I took the plunge and bought a new camera and in 2018 invested in a second camera for Sarah to use.

From there we have been taking pictures more seriously, getting Southern 100 and Manx GP accreditation last year.

In 2018, we had our logo on a sidecar and in 2019 four teams put it on their machines, Barry Furber being one of them.

We've made so many friends over the years, from other photographers and the teams, to riders and people from around the course who are always willing to chat.

Last year I spent the evening at Crosby Leap chatting to a deaf guy and once practice started I would hold my hand

> up when I could first hear a bike coming so that he could get
> ready with his camera. Obviously when the zeros were due
> out I couldn't help there!

Formula 1 TT 2004

McGuinness breaks lap record en route to a triple

By 2004, John McGuinness had moved to Yamaha and was
paid £20,000 to ride the R1.

He also raced Yamahas in the 600cc TTs, winning at
the North West 200, which had set him up nicely to claim
victory in the Junior TT.

He also finished second in the Production race, but only
after running out of fuel, having broken DJ's old lap record
before his clutch went, which again was a little glimpse of
what was to come.

Another shrewd move was appointing Jim Moodie as his
manager, who helped whip him into shape.

The partnership proved to work wonders as he went on
to win three TTs during 2004.

Such was his speed, skill, discipline and control, he
had been leading every race at one stage or another until
mechanical problems scuppered his chances of winning.

He set the lap record that year on a superbike too – and,
amazingly, he would own the lap record for another ten years
until it was finally broken by Bruce Anstey. It was the F1
TT when McGuinness, on his 1000 Yamaha, lapped in 17
minutes and 43.8 seconds, at a speed of 127.68mph.

There had been plenty of change behind the
scenes too as 2004 was the year ACU signed a 20-year
agreement to hand over control of the TT to the Isle of
Man government.

The Manx Motor Cycle Club, which runs the popular
Manx GP that would later be paired with the Classic TT to

create another two-week festival of motorcycle racing, would also be asked to organise the TT races themselves.

McGuinness set the pace in the opening Duke Formula 1 race, breaking the lap record on the first circuit from a standing start.

He did not look back either as he claimed the win by nearly 20 seconds ahead of TAS Suzuki's Adrian Archibald with his team-mate Bruce Anstey third.

It was a taste of things to come as McGuinness also claimed the Junior TT and Lightweight 400, which meant he joined the likes of Mike Hailwood, his hero Joey Dunlop, Steve Hislop and his good friend David Jefferies in the elite TT hat-trick club.

During the Lightweight 400, McGuinness had stretched a 45-second lead early on to really stamp his authority on the race.

Battling mist on the mountain and bright sunshine on the ground, he averaged 108mph for the third lap, despite his pit stop, as he continued to press on with his advantage and took the win, marking his fifth TT win – with number six to follow soon after.

Anstey did gain some revenge by taking the spoils in the 1000 Production race, breaking the 125mph lap record in the process, ahead of McGuinness and Jason Griffith.

The other winners during the race week was former 125 British champion Chris Palmer, who retained his title in the 125cc TT.

He marked the final time the class was ever raced again on the island in style, breaking the lap record. The 125cc class had been dropped in 1974, reborn 15 years later and finally ended for good in 2004.

The Castletown native averaged 108.93mph for the entire race beating Robert Dunlop and fellow Manxman Nigel

Beattie, who hailed from Laxey. Ian Lougher had looked like challenging Palmer for the win but hit bike problems at Milntown and was forced to retire.

Northern Irishman Ryan Farquhar also made history in the Production 600 race, claiming his first TT while also handing Kawasaki its first win 20 years, after beating the man of the meeting, McGuinness, into third while Anstey was second.

Adrian Archibald cleaned up in the Senior, taking his second successive win in the main race of the TT fortnight ahead of Anstey and Gary Carswell.

Dave Molyneux equalled Rob Fisher's record of 10 TT sidecar victories, when he won the second three-wheeler race.

And such was his pace, he was 0.3 seconds outside of lapping the course in less than 20 minutes.

And Moly would go to complete yet another double with passenger Daniel Sayle beating fellow Manxman and future champions Nick Crowe and Darren Hope, who would soon raise the bar even further in the sidecar class.

He did not have to wait long to rewrite the record books once more as, during the Sidecar B TT of 2005, he became the first to lap under the 20-minute mark.

Indifferent weather greeted the riders as they waited for the track to dry but once the flag dropped Moly got the TT races of 2005 under way as the sidecars were off that year.

His luck was out in the opening race as Nick Crowe and Darren Hope took the spoils – marking Crowe's first of five TT wins – but later that same week he struck back to claim the win, again with Dan Sayle as his passenger.

It was also the year the Superstock TT had been introduced for the first time – and it was won by Anstey, which would be a sign of things to come, with Lougher second and Farquhar third.

There were also notable top-ten finishes for Guy Martin and Ian Hutchinson, who finished fifth and ninth respectively.

McGuinness also enjoyed another successful 2005, once again dominating the superbike classes, winning both races by more than 30 seconds to claim a double win.

Lougher claimed the first Supersport TT, ahead of McGuinness and Jason Griffiths, while Farquhar claimed the second, ahead of the luckless Griffiths with Ireland's Raymond Porter in third.

Sidecar B TT 2006
Crowe claims his first sidecar double

Nick Crowe, a future five-time Isle of Man TT winner and 2008 British F2 Champion, went one better a year later when he claimed a double in the sidecar class.

Having started his career as a passenger, he decided to switch to driving in 2000 and instead was paired with his childhood friend, Darren Hope. Following the foot-and-mouth outbreak, the pair were ready to attack the TT course in 2002 and two years later they bought one of Dave Molyneux's sidecars going on to claim their first win in 2005.

But it took another year for everything to truly click as they claimed both Race A and B in 2006.

It seemed their reign at the top would last for a while and they showed no signs of stopping either as in 2007, with new passenger Daniel Sayle, he broke the lap record.

However, as is so often the case in sidecar races, the machines could not keep up with their blistering pace and they were forced to retire in both TTs that year.

Mark Cox took over as passenger in 2008 and business was resumed as this time Crowe'44s machine did not let him down and he was able to claim both sidecar TTs for yet another double.

The formidable pair qualified on pole for the 2009 TT but suffered mechanical failure while leading race one and then, in race two, they suffered a horrible crash at the 17-mile marker on the opening lap in the most unfortunate of circumstances that once again highlighted the truly unique nature of the TT course.

Both were taken to Noble's Hospital by air with serious fractures following the crash, which had been caused by a hare running on to the course in front of them.

Such was the huge nature of the crash the entire race was cancelled and Crowe was flown to the UK to undergo a series of operations.

The lure of the TT, however, was to prove too strong and he returned once more, only this time it was to run a team.

To this day, he still competes at the TT, and now his sons are also making a name for themselves in the world of sidecar racing.

Ryan and Callum Crowe, aged 23 and 20 in 2019, entered both Sidecar TTs in that same year on a 675cc Triumph.

Finishing fifth and setting the newcomer lap record of 113.53mph, beating the mark set by Tim Reeves, they were awarded the 2019 RST Star of Tomorrow award.

Machine issues forced them to pull out of the second race before the start but it would be fair to say the Crowe name is likely to stay around the TT for many years to come.

Meanwhile, John McGuinness was continuing to push the boundaries in 2006 on the Honda 1000, again breaking the lap record – this time in the 2006 Senior – finishing his lap in 17 minutes and 29.6 seconds, falling just short of the 130mph barrier, clocking 129.451mph instead.

Unsurprisingly, McGuinness was now starting to turn a few heads and it wasn't long before Neil Tuxworth was on the phone to offer him the chance to join the factory Honda team.

The deal was to race for the team at the North West, TT and the British Superbike championships, in the superstock class, joining Karl Harris and Ryuichi Kiyonari at HM Plant Honda, as well as Jonathan Rea and Eugine Laverty, who were in the Red Bull team. It was some line-up that had been put together.

The partnership just felt so right for McGuinness too, so much so he stayed with the same team for the next 11 years.

Between 2006 and 2011, he also had the same mechanics and team around him. The stability made him believe he could beat anyone – and he did, too. In 2006, he won three more TTs – two on a superbike and one in the supersport class – pushing the lap record up to 129.4mph in the process. He also finished in the top ten in the British Superstock series. And yet even bigger things were to follow in 2007.

ISLE OF MAN TT MEMORIES

Richard Beech, from Alveley, Shropshire, watches his son, Harris, race in the British Junior Supersport series, under the Bathams Black Country banner, run by Michael Rutter. Richard also raced at club championship level on two and three wheels:

When John McGuinness did his 130mph lap I was sat in the grandstand with my brothers, James and Ian.

The sun was out and it was just one of those weeks, days and races that I will always remember.

Last year, we had to leave the island before the Senior race for a trip to Scotland that had been planned for a while.

I was hiking in the mountains with a mate but he'd gone off and I was just sat on a bench, on my own, eating some lunch while listening to the race.

Before I knew it, there were seven or eight people round me listening in, and two of them had TT T-shirts on.

I suppose moments like that help you realise how popular the races are and what they mean to people.

Senior TT 2007

McGuinness breaks the 130mph barrier in centenary year

John McGuinness, whose superstitions included having a voodoo doll on his helmet, putting a penny down his leathers and wearing socks with 'daddy' written on them, had been banging in laps around the high 128mphs heading into race week in 2007.

He had told his wife, Becky, prior to the race fortnight, he was ready to push from the 129mph to the Holy Grail, a 130mph lap, which would be the perfect way to mark the TT's centenary.

However, a 130mph lap seemed a long way off at times, especially at the beginning of practice week, when he posted an opening lap of 128.2mph.

But his fans, friends and family need not have worried, because in lap two of the Senior TT he did it – and set another lap record, and this time it was a remarkable average lap speed of 130.304mph.

With the centenary celebrations erupting all around him, it helped to bring out the best in McGuinness as he remained the only rider to post a 130mph throughout the race week, which made the achievement even more special.

He would go on to win the Senior TT by more than 30 seconds as he set the race alight.

Not only did he lead from start to finish, he also became the first man to break the magical 130mph barrier. It sent the HM Plant Honda rider into the record books once more as he claimed his 13th victory during the final race of the week.

In a repeat of the Monday's Superbike race, it was Guy Martin and Ian Hutchinson who again took second and third positions.

McGuinness had made his usual fast start to break the outright lap record from a standing start, but Martin was pushing him hard and there was only seconds in it during the first 24 miles.

However, McGuinness's mastery of the mountain section was again evident, and by the time the riders had completed their first lap, he was almost ten seconds clear.

Martin matched him over the first part of the second lap and, although he was also inside the old lap record, with a speed of 129.816mph, McGuinness's scintillating lap of more than 130mph sent him clear.

Martin himself had pulled clear of Hutchinson, while another pre-race favourite, Bruce Anstey, was out early on.

Irish hopes were also dashed with Martin Finnegan and Ryan Farquhar both being early retirements.

With yet another superb pit stop, McGuinness's lead was extended further, while Martin had caught Hutchinson on the roads.

Ian Lougher was in a secure fourth, but fifth place was anything but, with Adrian Archibald and Conor Cummins disputing the position. At the head of the field, McGuinness's lead was up to 23 seconds and, although Martin chipped away at his disadvantage, the Morecambe Missile had everything under control and pulled away on the final two laps.

His final winning margin was more than 32 seconds, although his cause was aided slightly when Martin ran into trouble at two-thirds race distance, when the chain began jumping off its sprocket from the fourth lap onwards.

A change of wheel at his second pit stop did not help so he nursed the machine home to take another second place, his third podium of the week.

Hutchinson's excellent week continued with third place although he later admitted to having a somewhat lonely race, being 20 seconds behind Martin and 20 seconds ahead of Lougher, who salvaged his week with a solid fourth.

Archibald got the better of Cummins to give TAS Suzuki a decent result and young Cummins also secured his fourth top-10 finish of the week – reclaiming the title of the fastest Manxman at the TT for good measure too with a second lap speed of 126.466mph.

Steve Plater's brilliant debut week continued with a seventh place and a lap of 125.808mph, which had cemented his place as the fastest-ever newcomer in the history of TT at the time.

Michael Rutter came home in eighth while Ian Armstrong, who was again the first of the privateers was in ninth, and James McBride rounding out the top ten.

The final day, however, was marred by an incident at the 26th Milestone.

Marc Ramsbotham, 34, from Norfolk, was declared dead at the scene from injuries sustained in the Senior race.

To make matters worse, one spectator was also confirmed dead at the scene and another died after admission at Noble's Hospital. Two further spectators were also involved but, thankfully, only sustained injuries.

A year later, however, the racing world would once again be shaken to the core following the death of five-time TT winner Robert Dunlop at the North West 200.

Just six weeks after his brother Joey had died, Robert was back racing again. He had suffered a great loss but he wanted to race on.

And, by 2004, two of his three children had also become road racers – but Robert still wanted to continue too.

He was 47 by the start of the 2008 season and it seemed his sons' careers were taking over. He was more interested in how they were going.

But he still entered the North West 200 and, during the final practice day, disaster struck.

Riding a slightly bigger bike than normal at that stage of his career, a 250cc, he set off with the rest of the riders. William and Michael were also on the start line with them.

There was white smoke coming out of Robert's bike, which William could see when he passed him, but he could not catch him to tell him something looked wrong.

His engine had seized, which locked up the back wheel. He was thrown from his machine while travelling at 150mph. Michael got down beside him and held his hands as the doctor arrived on the scene, praying he would be okay.

The doctors and medical staff did everything they could but they could not save him. It was a racing crash that had tragic consequences.

The day after the fatal accident, Robert's body was back at the family home, just a few miles from the circuit where the accident happened.

Michael, it appeared, had no intention of riding, but William was seen working on his bikes, ready to race on the Saturday.

No one really believed he would race but William just wanted to be on his own, working on his bikes, to try and take his mind off everything – and sure enough something special was about to happen.

William and Michael both made their ways to the circuit, just two days after their father had died; however, the race organisers were not convinced they should compete.

Both brothers were adamant they wanted to race. They had been banned but they stormed on to the start line anyway, placing the organisers in a very surreal situation.

With the boys on the grid, there was little anyone could do to stop them from racing. There was no option but to let them race.

For William, however, mechanical problems stopped him from even starting the race, meaning everything was resting on a young Michael Dunlop's shoulders.

Michael, only 19 at the time, was on the charge from the opening lap and battled with Christian Elkin and John McGuinness, seemingly prepared to ride through them if needs be – and, sure enough, he was leading the race and eventually took the chequered flag.

The pain of loss was temporarily relieved with the joy of one of the greatest wins in the history of road racing.

Tragedy may be inevitable in the sport but it also breeds true heroes, such as Michael Dunlop on that day, who would go on to achieve so much in such a short space of time.

He continues to win to this day, despite the loss of his older brother, William, who died while racing at Skerries in Northern Ireland in 2018. The sons remained so proud of their father and uncle. They became two of the respected riders in the paddock, carrying the Dunlop name as both of their careers blossomed over the years.

Michael's affiliation with the Isle of Man TT would continue to grow as he became unstoppable in almost any class, on any bike and with any team.

Taking his first TT win just a year later, in the 2009 supersport race, by 2019 he had claimed 19 TTs to sit third on the all-time leaders list, behind McGuinness and his uncle Joey.

Senior TT 2008
McGuinness equals Hailwood's 14 TT wins following three-way battle

As well as equalling Mike Hailwood's number of TT wins, the year 2008 also marked John McGuinness's fourth Senior victory on the bounce.

The win, however, had been far from easy as he was unable to build up his usual early advantage thanks to a resurgent Cameron Donald, who had been on fire all week.

Armed with a new Fireblade, courtesy of Padgetts Honda, McGuinness had been forced to battle throughout with Donald as well as Kiwi Bruce Anstey during the entire race.

It was the year when Australian Donald had been on absolute fire, claiming two TT wins in a week, and the talents of all three shone through as the lead changed seven or eight times during the Senior.

The Aussie was hungry for more heading into the Senior and was determined to add the Blue Ribbon race to his collection.

McGuinness, however, was in no mood to give up his crown – and so ensued one of the closest-ever Senior TT battles.

Somewhat bizarrely, the lap record was never broken, but not for one second did that detract from what was a truly spectacular race.

McGuinness had not enjoyed much luck during race week, having broken down in the superbike race and second supersport race, as well as finishing second in the superstock and first supersport race.

But come Senior race day, pretty much everything fell into place – and with Donald also in such fine form, it set up a superb spectacle, with the pair barely separated by a second for the majority of the race.

It took Donald suffering a bike problem with his TAS Suzuki on the sixth and final lap for McGuinness to make his break for the finish line on his Padgetts Honda.

The issue meant McGuinness would eventually take the chequered flag with a lead of more than a minute but the final result certainly did not tell the full story of what had been a thrillingly close race.

The win, however, brought McGuinness level with another great in Hailwood, as he equalled his 14 TT victories. At the time, it pulled him to equal second in the all-time winners list, behind his hero, Joey Dunlop.

His 14 victories had also come in just 12 years of racing on the island.

The result could have been ever so different as Bruce Anstey had set the early pace, leading by the end of the second lap, only to be forced to retire after entering the pits.

His retirement had turned the three-rider battle into a two-rider contest, McGuinness and Donald swapping the lead on no fewer than seven occasions.

McGuinness had to use all his 12 years of experience to win the Senior that year, which included a big scare when Conor Cummins's bike blew up in front of him.

But after settling down again, he used laps three and four to really put the strain on Donald. Such was the battle, the island was still buzzing for hours after the race had finished because the crowd knew they had truly witnessed one of the most memorable TTs.

Despite his pace, McGuinness was just not able to break Donald, like he had to so many riders in past – and would continue to do to so many more in the future – and even Anstey's breakdown had played in his favour.

Yet his fighting spirit continued to shine through because, every time Donald took the lead, McGuinness would bite straight back and retake first place.

Despite being seven seconds down by lap five at Ramsey, he had edged out a two-second lead by the start of the sixth, such was his determination on the day.

And when Donald hit bike problems, he was able to cruise home for the win. It was a fitting way to end yet another memorable TT, with Donald also claiming two wins, Anstey one and Steve Plater also picked up his first win on the island.

In 2009, we were also introduced to Gary Johnson and Keith Amor coming on to the scene, while the pace of a young Guy Martin suggested that his first TT win would be just around the corner.

ISLE OF MAN TT MEMORIES
Kelly Driver-Fisher, from Hatfield Peverell, in Essex:

I love the TT because of the way it brings the whole island community together and you always get to meet interesting people.

Due to our friend, John Cleator, who lives in Laxey, we see some amazing sights – both on and off the race track – that are off the main tourist areas. And, while I like the bikes, it's more the atmosphere and fun for me.

Each year is different and there is never any trouble, everyone is just happy to be there, even if the weather's bad, and everyone has a common interest – the bikes!

The best moment, however, was watching my husband, James [author's note: I completely deny all knowledge of this!] run and jump over the wall when Anstey broke down at the 33rd Milestone.

Because he was zoomed while filming the action, he thought Anstey's bike, which was on fire, was coming straight at him.

It still makes me laugh because John and me did not have a clue what he had seen until he was over the wall.

By that point all we could see was a little smoke coming from his bike.

Anstey had to pull up and spent the whole of the day with us at the 33rd, while John's dad, who was chief marshal, offered him queenies and drinks. He was such a nice bloke too.

Senior TT 2009

Plater's sector time lasts for nine years

Steve Plater won the Blue Riband Senior TT on his HM Plant Honda taking the victory by 20 seconds from Conor Cummins, with Gary Johnson and Adrian Archibald in third and fourth.

John McGuinness had led for the first three laps and looked set on adding another fifth straight Senior TT win when he raised the lap record to 131.58mph.

But after being forced to retire with a broken chain at Cruickshanks on lap four, it completely opened the field – and that was where Plater pounced, setting a best sector lap time between the Ramsey and the Bungalow, which amazingly stayed in place until 2018 when it was finally beaten by Peter Hickman during the Superstock TT.

Plater and Cummins also smashed the 130mph lap barrier but it was not such great news for Guy Martin as he was forced to retire on lap four while in third.

Bruce Anstey, Ryan Farquhar and Michael Dunlop also retired while Ian Hutchinson came off without injury at Quarter bridge.

Plater's victory also meant he had won the inaugural TT Championship Series, collecting the Joey Dunlop Memorial Trophy and an additional £10,000.

It marked a second TT success for the Lincolnshire rider who had won a Supersport race the year before.

However, the Senior was the pinnacle of a great career for the ultra-competitive rider-turned-commentator, team manager and race liaison officer, who was sadly forced to retire following a crash.

His career had really kicked off when he won the British Powerbike Championship in 1998 and finished third a year later at Bol d'Or on a Kawasaki.

After missing most of 2001 through injury, he still claimed three podiums and then enjoyed a superb season in 2002 before turning his attention to road racing.

After claiming both Superbike races at the North West 200 in 2007, he was voted Best Newcomer at the 2007 Isle of Man TT on Yamahas, having been mentored by former racer Mick Grant

After winning the Supersport TT race in 2008, after Bruce Anstey had been disqualified, he beat Billy McConnell to the British Supersport crown in 2009, the same year he claimed the Senior TT while setting a new race record in the process.

A year later, he crashed badly at the North West 200, breaking his arm and his neck, and decided to retire from racing.

But he would always be fondly remembered by Honda as his Senior win came during the manufacturer's 50th anniversary of racing at the TT.

Race week had begun business as usual for the Japanese, only it had been through the tried and tested Honda-McGuinness partnership as he notched his 15th win, setting a new lap record along the way in the opening Superbike TT.

Honda made it a clean sweep on the podium too as McGuinness was flanked by Steve Plater and Guy Martin, who were with the same manufacturer.

In fact, Honda claimed the top five finishers with Ian Hutchinson and Gary Johnson rounding off a superb race for the Japanese team.

And even when McGuinness's chain snapped in the Senior he still went on to finish third in the British Superstock championship for Honda while Plater claimed a TT win.

TT 2010 – THE RECORD-BREAKING YEAR

IT MAY have been the extra coverage, the growing popularity of the race, the introduction of the ITV4 covering the race highlights or the superb launch of the film, *Closer to the Edge*.

Either way, there was something about the 2010 TT that was extra special, aside from the fact Ian Hutchinson did what no one believed was possible and won five solo races in a single week.

He needed a bit of luck, bundles of talent, a great package and team, single-minded determination and, most importantly, the skill to ride motorbikes across three different classes better than anyone else, to claim an unprecedented clean sweep.

Accompanied by the wonderful film, which focusses a lot on Guy Martin, who exclaimed road racers as 'a bit mad, tile short of a roof, lights are in but no one's home', McGuinness also revealed one of his early childhood heroes was Evil Knievil and he even wrote to *Jim'll Fix It* to meet him one day.

'I have never been interested in anything else, it's just been bikes my whole life. I'm still a little boy at heart,' he said.

After winning his first 250cc race in 1999, he admitted it had just made the bug get that much bigger at the time.

By 2010, he already had 15 wins to his name but he still felt nervous and was constantly thinking about the race all the time. Martin's father also revealed how, during his first TT in 1974, he thought he was going to be a TT superstar.

But after coming into Glen Helen, he went straight over the bank and broke his back but still returned the following year.

Guy then went into detail about how despite a 120mph crash at the North West 200, the buzz still made him come back for more, despite the knowledge that if he went just an inch wrong in certain sections, he could be dead. Three or four of his biggest 'moments' at that time had come at the TT but he explained how it was such moments that kept him coming back for more.

Martin put it quite bluntly, recalling how he had been at fellow road racing star Martin Finnegan's wedding in 2007 and then his funeral in 2008.

Martin's feelings were simple: when your time's up, your time's up in their line of work and if success in the TT was easy, every man and his dog would be after it.

McGuinness explained how a rider could never get complacent with the TT because, 'If you get overconfident it will bite you. Going down there 200mph plus.'

Donald described how being on the race line, he had never experienced anything like it, with absolutely no room for error.

Amor says you have to beat the track not the other racer, while Cummins simply described the race on the island where he was born as 'the most powerful race you'll ever do in your life, and it's legal'.

Jenny Tinmouth, the fastest woman around the course, put it another way, saying, 'You do feel like you shouldn't be doing it. You feel a bit cheeky and a bit naughty.'

Sidecar star Nick Crowe discusses how, in 2009, while leading the race, a hare ran on to the track and caused him to crash at 160mph.

It damaged the front part of his fairing and then hit him in the face – and that was it. He went straight into the trees and suffered severe injuries but, as he puts it, he 'was lucky to get away with that one'.

And then there was Michael Dunlop who, while still classed very much as newcomer, had this message for his rivals, 'I will push any rider until the bitter end.' He was, and always will be, such a hard racer to beat.

But if you want real passion, you can look no further than TT winner Milky Quayle, who explained what it was like being forced to retire from racing following his horror crash on the island in 2003.

'I can't get my buzz, cannot get it out of my system. I keep myself busy taking riders round, meeting dignitaries and looking after newcomers,' he explained.

As he continues, it's clear to even a native Manxman who is so passionate about the TT it can take many years to learn the course.

'Ballagarey, most important corner on the circuit but also the most scary. You cannot see your entry point.

'Still on the gas, at the 30mph signs, come off the gas, change down a gear, get your head out the bubble and your head's getting ripped off your shoulders.

'Still looking for the peel in point but still cannot see. As soon as I see the kerb on the side I just lie the bike on its side and drive it. Fly through. So, so fast. Guthrie's, third-most important corner on the circuit. Approaching three left-hand bends but it's very steep.

'Get the first one right, back into number two and three, on the brakes hard, back on the power, drive it through.'

*Guy Martin in Parc Ferme, dressed in his new Honda livery. [**Ellan Vannin Images**]*

*Guy Martin at Ballacrye Leap during practice in 2017. [**Ellan Vannin Images**]*

*Guy Martin in action during the 2017 Superbike TT race at Signpost Corner. [**Ellan Vannin Images**]*

*Rutter exits Parliament Square, Ramsey, on his way to victory in the 2017 Lightweight TT. [**Ellan Vannin Images**]*

Norton rider David Johnson on the start line for the 2017 Senior TT. [**Ellan Vannin Images**]

Michael Dunlop celebrates his 2017 Senior TT, with Peter Hickman, left, and Dean Harrison.
[**Ellan Vannin Images**]

Waiting to set off during the opening Saturday practice session, which had been delayed due to a person on the track being arrested at Crosby Leap in 2018, are, from left, James Hillier, Michael Rutter and Ian Hutchison. [**Ellan Vannin Images**]

Jamie Coward prior to Senior TT gathers his thoughts on the Glencrutchery Road in 2018. [**Ellan Vannin Images**]

Dan Kneen during the 2018 TT Tuesday practice evening at Union Mills. [**Ellan Vannin Images**]

Dan Kneen with his girlfriend, Leanne, during the Saturday of practice week in 2018. [**Ellan Vannin Images**]

Senior TT winners Steve Plater and Hicky have a quick chat before the Saturday practice session in 2018. [**Ellan Vannin Images**]

Harrison gets some air at Ballacrye during the 2018 Senior TT practice on Wednesday race day. [**Ellan Vannin Images**]

Hutchy prepares to launch his TT fortnight in 2018. [**Ellan Vannin Images**]

Conor Cummins in action during the Superbike TT, at Parliament Square Ramsey, in 2018. [**Ellan Vannin Images**]

Rutter during 2018 Lightweight TT race at Sarah's Cottage. [**Ellan Vannin Images**]

Dave Madsen-Mygdal during 2018 Superstock TT at Sarah's Cottage.
[Ellan Vannin Images]

Harrison is all focus on the grid for the start of the 2018 Senior TT.
[Ellan Vannin Images]

Hicky heads through St Ninian's during the record-breaking Senior TT in 2018.
*[**Ellan Vannin Images**]*

The 2018 Senior TT winner, with Dean Harrison, left, and Conor Cummins.
*[**Ellan Vannin Images**]*

Champagne time.
*[**Ellan Vannin Images**]*

Harrison press conference following the 2018 Senior TT. [**Ellan Vannin Images**]

Harrison in action during evening practice at the Gooseneck in 2019. [**ottpix@btinternet.com**]

*McGuinness in action during evening practice at the Gooseneck in 2019. [**ottpix@btinternet.com**]*

*John McGuinness at the Gooseneck in 2019. [**ottpix@btinternet.com**]*

*Riders line up for the Senior practice session. [**ottpix@btinternet.com**]*

*Hickman at Crosby Leap in 2019. [**ottpix@btinternet.com**]*

Davey Todd, a rising star of the future, at Crosby Leap in 2019.
[ottpix@btinternet.com]

Barry Furber on his superbike at the Creg in 2019.
[ottpix@ btinternet.com]

The Morgan brothers prepare for their first-ever TT.
[*ottpix@btinternet.com*]

Michal Dokoupil on the grid in 2019.
[*ottpix@btinternet.com*]

Josh Daley and his father, Andy, on the grid in 2019.
[*ottpix@btinternet.com*]

Maria Costello during the Lightweight TT at Bungalow in 2019.
[*ottpix@btinternet.com*]

*Maria Costello and
Julie Canipa at Signpost
Corner during Sidecar 2
TT in 2019.*
[ottpix@btinternet.com]

*Michael Dunlop, the
Lightweight TT winner,
at Quarry Bends in 2019.
**[ottpix@btinternet.
com]***

*Dunlop at Signpost Corner during the
first Supersport TT in 2019.
[ottpix@btinternet.com]*

*Lee Johnston en route to his maiden
win during the Supersport TT in
2019.* **[ottpix@btinternet.com]**

Tim Reeves and passenger Mark Wilkes at Signpost Corner during the second sidecar race in 2019. [*ottpix@btinternet.com*]

Hutchy during the 2019 Senior race at Union Mills. [*ottpix@btinternet.com*]

Deano – Senior TT race winner Dean Harrison at Union Mills in 2019.
[ottpix@ btinternet.com]

Legends: Tony Rutter, Phil Read and Giacomo Agostini.

Legends: Stuart Graham, Tony Rutter, Jim Redman, John Surtees and Giacomo Agostini.

That was just a very small section of the course he was describing but even just with those few sentences it immediately gave a feel – and only a feel – of what it must be like to race round a course that was as equally feared as it was loved.

Meanwhile, in the background, there was a lad called Ian Hutchinson, who had already won three TTs heading into 2010 and was really beginning to make a name for himself.

If anyone was the polar opposite of Guy Martin and, to some degree, John McGuinness, it was Hutchy.

A bike fanatic from birth, it was his parents who had bought him his first trials bike and then, by 17, he owned a race bike.

With little or no money, he took the bikes in a van all round the country, had a few beers and a barbecue during the evenings, and then he would go racing.

His dedication to fitness – or at least his regular trips to the gym – made him at odds with McGuinness, who has always preferred enduro bikes and laps around circuits to weights and running, while his quiet and introverted nature was at completely the other end of the spectrum to Martin.

But whichever route they had all decided to go down, their personalities, race craft and desire to win – along with the likes of Adrian Archibald, Bruce Anstey, Cameron Donald, Michael Rutter, Ryan Farquhar and Ian Lougher, as well as rising stars Conor Cummins, Keith Amor and brothers Michael and William Dunlop – all helped ensure that 2010 was indeed a truly golden year for racing.

Superbike TT 2010

Hutchy wins as Cummins and McGuinness drop out

Guy Martin had been working with Craig Wilson prior to the 2010 TT as he wanted to go back to racing with a smaller team.

However, his TT preparations had not gone well as, like Cummins, he had crashed at the North West 200 a few weeks before, hitting the kerb and ending up in the grass, but thankfully both were unhurt.

Martin over-revved the bike and blew up his engine but Wilson remained calmed and said it was a learning curve – and Martin knew he would be going to the TT with two brand-new engines.

Practice arrived and suddenly all the riders who had previously rolled their bikes into the garage knew that within two miles of the circuit they would soon be pushing 200mph.

As they got smoother and more confident with the 37.73-mile circuit, going faster and faster each time, everything would start to slow down as they began thinking four or five corners ahead, keeping the rhythm up.

Wilson was quietly confident his rider could do it and believed if he won the first race, he would win some more.

First out the traps was John McGuinness who led on the roads ahead of Bruce Anstey.

McGuinness had enjoyed an amazing start but was only 0.08 seconds ahead of Conor Cummins with the Manxman taking the lead.

It was change near the top soon after as first McGuinness broke and Martin was nearly taken out by Michael Dunlop.

Once things had settled down, it was Cummins who still led, this time ahead of Ian Hutchinson who in turn had a one-second lead on Martin.

By lap two, Hutchy was leading on the road after posting a lap of 130.496mph of while slowing for the pits.

Meanwhile, Cummins raised the bar with a 131.511mph lap while Cameron Donald made a mistake and overshot at Signpost.

As Martin entered the pits, Cummins stalled and lost a lot of time. There was a big shake of his head as his lead was reduced to just four seconds.

There was all to the play heading into the final two laps with Cummins, Hutchy, Martin and Dunlop rounding out the top four. And then there was real drama as Cummins was reported missing at Glen Helen while Martin came charging through instead. It was later confirmed that Cummins had retired with mechanical failure at Laurel Bank.

It meant Hutchy was now leading with Martin in second place. That was until the new pit lane timing system gave the latter a 30-second penalty, which moved him down from second place into fourth.

It meant Hutchy was now a clear leader with Dunlop second place and Donald, who was finishing very strongly, looking for the final podium.

And that was how it ended, with Hutch taking the win on the Padgetts Honda. Martin, feeling very aggrieved, jumped off his bike and went straight into his van. Having just done 224 miles, he was bitterly disappointed to be given a 30-second penalty for going 0.1 seconds over in the pit lane. Team boss Craig Wilson also said it was harsh.

But there was no time for Martin to dwell on it as he was soon back in action, taking an early lead in the first supersport race of the week ahead of Hutchy and Dan Kneen in third.

He looked determined but Hutch had soon halved the gap and then led at the end of the first lap.

The pair kept swapping places and, when they pitted, Martin had etched out a 3.3-second lead with Dunlop slotting into third.

A slower pit stop meant that, by Ballaugh, Martin had reduced the time to less than three seconds having given up the lead, but that was how it stayed for the rest of the race with Hutchy taking his second win of the week with Dunlop third following a final lap of 126.587mph.

Martin, still feeling aggrieved following his penalty in the superbike race, did not come into the winner's enclosure and decided to go straight on.

After some thought, he came back but did not hide how livid he had been about the superbike race and did not hang around on the podium for any of the celebrations.

Superstock TT 2010
Hutchinson beats Ryan Farquhar by 1.32 seconds

The superstock race of the 2010 TT festival was always going to be Ryan Farquhar's best chance of another TT win and he signalled his intentions from the off.

With good conditions all round, Farquhar took an early lead at Glen Helen ahead of Michael Dunlop, Conor Cummins and Ian Hutchinson.

By Ramsey, the Dungannon rider had opened up a slight gap over the chasing pack led by Dunlop with Cummins close behind battling for second place.

Farquhar's opening lap had given him a 6.78-second lead over Dunlop on his KMR Kawasaki superstock, and his lead was up to more than four seconds early into lap two, but Hutchy was beginning to make his move, clawing back time on third-placed Cummins and second-placed Dunlop.

As is so often the way at the TT, pit stops played a crucial role in proceedings as Dunlop dropped back to fourth and Hutchy had jumped ahead of Cummins at the start of lap three.

Farquhar, who had set a new lap record of 129.816mph on the second lap, was still leading by more than five seconds over CBR1000 Honda Fireblade superstock bike of Hutchy.

Cummins, on a McAdoo Racing Kawasaki, held third place while John McGuinness had moved into fourth in front of Guy Martin, Keith Amor, Ian Lougher and Dunlop, who had dropped all the way back to eighth.

As the fourth circulation began, Farquhar's lead had ominously been reduced to four seconds while Hutchy had stretched his gap to 20 seconds over Cummins, which meant it was a straight final-lap battle between the top two.

It was clear that Hutchinson was on a charge and as each sector passed he was reducing the lead bit by bit, setting up a grandstand finish.

Farquhar gave it his all and he was forced to endure a terrible, agonising wait after he had crossed to see if he had done enough to win the Superstock TT.

However, Hutchy was just too hot to beat and put in a phenomenal lap of 130.741mph, the first ever 130mph-plus lap by a superstock machine.

And, having hit the front for the first time on the final run over the mountain, he grabbed the win by a slender 1.32 seconds.

Cummins claimed third and was followed home by McGuinness, Martin, Keith Amor, Ian Lougher, Dunlop, Michael Rutter and Adrian Archibald, who rounded out the top ten.

It meant Hutchy had now three in a week and fans were wondering if four, or five, was now on.

Supersport B TT 2010
Hutchinson beats Dunlop by 1.45 seconds to equal McCallen's record

By the Wednesday, the weather had taken a turn for the worse, so instead the second supersport race was moved to the Thursday.

It was almost a carbon copy of the first, such were the tiny margins, but this time Hutchinson was embroiled in a ferocious dice with another Ulsterman – Michael Dunlop.

Guy Martin had begun the race in fourth but once again it was Hutchy who appeared to be in unstoppable form, trailing Dunlop by 1.82 seconds but continuously closing the gap, with Keith Amor in third.

The gap between Dunlop and Hutchy continued to shorten and widen every lap, with the Ulsterman closing in on the run to Ramsey only for the Bingley Bullet to pull away over the mountain.

Going into the final lap, Hutchinson had stretched his lead to 3.19 seconds but that was like a red rag to a bull for Dunlop as amazingly he edged ahead for the first at Ballaugh Bridge.

The gap had increased to almost two seconds at Ramsey but Hutchy knew, if he kept Dunlop within a certain distance, he could pull the gap on the mountain section.

And sure enough, he crossed the line and claimed his fourth win in four races by 1.45 seconds, with Keith Amor coming home in third.

Both riders had smashed the lap record but overall it meant Hutchy had matched Philip McCallen's four wins in a week.

He had become the new King of the Mountain but, sadly, the race ultimately had a tragic end as New Zealander Paul Dobbs lost his life.

Paul Owen had been coming up behind him at the time, saw the yellow flags come out and just knew something had gone wrong.

He just ran into the track with a flag himself to slow all the other riders down but sadly Dobbs had lost his life to the sport that he loved.

The bravery of his wife was unbelievable following the accident, as she explained that her husband's death had made her and her family appreciate what they had got, to make sure they had a good time and also to ensure they all got the most fun out of life possible.

She said she still loved the TT and the island because it was impossible to love the thrill without knowing how dangerous it was.

Her words and bravery touched every fan, rider and team who has ever been in, involved with, or eagerly watched, the TT.

ISLE OF MAN TT MEMORIES

Barry Furber, from Bishop's Castle, in Shropshire, is a current TT racer who has a highest-placed finish of 11th in the Supertwin class. Barry is a top competitor who has also raced at the Manx GP, Ulster GP, North West 200 and Southern 100 races:

Hutchy's five in a row in 2010 is an obvious standout year. So many things had to come together at the right time for him to have all five wins.

With that in mind, and with all the injury issues Hutchy suffered after 2010, the 2017 Senior TT is particularly memorable for me.

Dunlop was on the all-new Suzuki, Anstey on the RCV and Brooks on the Norton.

There was also Hillier's massive moment on the opening lap at Ballagarey and then Hutchy crashed on the mountain while leading, breaking the same leg again.

I remember being sat in Ramsey after it was red-flagged and there was a very sombre atmosphere when we found out it was Hutchy who had gone down.

We had a short break before restarting and then it was all put behind us – and off we went again.

Senior TT 2010

Hutchy claims an incredible fifth TT in a single week

This race doesn't really need an introduction. It was simply the day when the impossible dream was achieved.

Hutchy would go on to win all five races and, as it was before the TT Zero had been added and the Lightweight had been reintroduced, it meant he won every solo race possible.

Philip McCallen's long-standing record of four in a week had seemed impressive enough – especially as he still remains the only racer to have won five North West 200s in the same week too – but to win five TTs? Words could not really explain how impressive a feat that would be.

It had been such an eventful race week too, with Conor Cummins and Guy Martin suffering two huge crashes.

But the Padgetts Honda remained strong, steady and reliable throughout, which in turn helped make Hutchy unbeatable.

He had come into 2010 in good form, having won the supersport and superstock races on the same day the year before, as well as finishing fourth and second in the two superbike races.

But Hutchy's winning mentality was such that he headed into the 2010 Senior TT feeling that if he *just* won four TTs the feat would not be remembered. He simply did not want to be beaten.

Hutchy had sailed to the island with the intention of winning every race – and now he managed to do it.

There had been an element of fortune – Martin's horror crash bringing out the red flag and leading to a shortened race, John McGuinness setting a furious pace and breaking down, and Cummins, who had been on a flier – in both of the superbike races – broke down in the first and then suffered his own huge crash once the Senior had restarted.

Cummins had been leading on time before the crash and the breakdown, so those unfortunate incidents may have had a bearing on the outcome, but, nonetheless, Hutchy more than deserved his place in the history books.

Martin had headed into the final race of the week having finished fourth, second and fifth, and admitted he had not had the greatest of weeks.

Hutchy knew everyone had been gunning after him all week and the Senior now marked their last chance to win a TT in 2010.

When the flag dropped, it was Martin who led the race early on by less than a second from Conor Cummins, who in turn was less than a second ahead of third-placed Hutchy.

McGuinness was also breathing down their necks meaning there was only one-and-a-half seconds covering the entire top four.

Martin's opening lap of 131.08mph was his fastest ever around the TT course. However, Cummins then swung into the lead but had just a 0.58-second advantage over Martin, who responded to reduce the gap to 0.1 seconds as they entered the pits.

Martin posted a 130.642mph while Cummins pitted with a 130.278mph. Both got away cleanly as they were both pushing to absolute limits; the commentary team suddenly revealed the news there was a huge gap between Dunlop, Hutch and Keith Amor, with no sign of Martin.

The road went quiet as everyone waited for machine number eight to come through, but instead it was the McAdoo Kawasaki of Cummins who appeared instead.

Disaster had struck as the red flags came out and the fire engines were sent to Ballagarey – and that was because Martin had suffered a 170mph crash on lap three. It had turned his Wilson Craig machine into a fireball.

When Martin had not appeared at Glen Helen, it was clear something was wrong and then the red flags came out too because his bike had set fire to a nearby field.

Nobody knew what was going on but they did know a hedge had caught fire. It could be seen a mile away and up close it was clear his bike was in a yard. Martin had come to a stop a quarter of a mile away from the crash site.

Wilson later said that if a rider is forced to jump off a bike at 170mph, the team has to worry.

Gary Johnson, who was close behind, believed it may have been a rider error with Martin hitting the wall. Either way, it looked like a bomb had exploded and it had left a horrendous mess.

But the show had to go on, there was another four laps to go and, as Johnson pointed out, they would not be going any slower second time round.

It left the majority of the fans willing Manxman Cummins to take his first win, and he was looking good too for the first couple of laps.

However, Hutchy was the early pace setter after the restart, leading McGuinness by just 0.61 seconds.

Donald had been forced to retire at Joey's and, soon after, McGuinness's week to forget continued as he too was forced to retire once again.

It meant Hutchy now led Cummins by 3.24 seconds but then there would be another horror crash, this time involving the local rider.

As he lost control at the Verandah, he was thrown off his bike, down the mountain and into the air, cartwheeling all the way until he came to a sickening stop.

As fans waited eagerly for Cummins at the Bungalow after Hutchy had gone through safely, it became clear all was not well for the local hero as he failed to appear.

Ultimately, what it all meant, was Hutchy had done the unthinkable. Aged just 30, he had rewritten the history books by claiming his fifth TT win of the week.

Martin had time to reflect on his crash from his hospital bed once the dust had settled.

Leaving the pits and battling for the lead, he thought he had got it going through Ballagarey and had the grip, but with a full tank of petrol he lost the front end at one of the fastest corners of the track – and he jumped ship.

After suffering singed eyebrows and eyelashes, being knocked unconscious, suffering a few broken ribs, a punctured lung, four chipped vertebrae and two cracked vertebrae, in typically biker fashion he declared things could have been worse.

Unfortunately, the same could not be said about Cummins who had suffered even more.

After returning to the scene of the crash months later, Cummins could still see bits of his bike and leathers on the road where he had come off.

His main injury was to his back, which he had broken in five places, as well as his arm in four places and also caused some slight nerve damage.

His knee was dislocated and he had fractured his pelvis, as well as his shoulder blade and even bruised his lung.

Getting his head round it was the biggest challenge but he was determined not to give up and wanted to return to racing as soon as possible, such was his love for the sport and particularly his love for the TT.

McGuinness, who had returned every year since 1997 with a podium, admitted it felt weird not getting a cheer or a clap during 2010.

Leading the first race and then suffering a kill switch failure in the Senior, he still realised things could have been a lot worse after what had happened to Dobbs, Martin and Cummins that week.

Meanwhile, Hutchy had left the island on a crest of a wave, only to suffer arguably the most career-threatening injury of them all when he crashed at the second-to-last British Superbike meeting of the year weeks after the TT had ended.

The medic discussed amputating his leg but he refused because he could not imagine never riding his motorbike again.

He wanted a foot that was capable of winning races. Of course, it was a long road to recovery but, after some unbelievable sacrifices, he was able to do it.

Sidecar B TT 2010

Klaffi pips Holden to claim a double win

Unlike the world and British championships, where 1000cc machines are used, the TT only allows 600cc machines, which means that many of the top racers have to adjust their styles.

Klaus Klaffenbock admitted, during his first lap of the TT, riding an F2 chassis, he felt like pulling in but the world champion decided against it, and the rest, as they say, is history.

After being passed on the road early in the race during his debut in 2004, he was a huge five minutes down on the likes of Moly per lap, but then he began enjoying it as he finished 19th. Fast-forward six years and he was TT winner.

He continued to improve from 2004 onwards but struggled with mechanical problems picking up an eighth in 2005 and a fifth in 2008.

However, once he was paired with Manxman Dan Sayle in 2010, he took both sidecar victories and set the fastest lap in the second race.

Having claimed the opening sidecar race, he was pushed to his absolute limits by TT legend John Holden, pipping him to the win by just 1.12 seconds.

The opening sidecar race had been a close affair but the second was even more dramatic, especially when Dave Molyneux and Patrick Farrance, along with Simon Neary and Paul Knapton, were both forced to retire.

Holden and his passenger Andy Winkle led Klaffenbock and Sayle by eight seconds after the first circuit, lapping at a blistering 113.569mph.

On the final lap of three, the lead had been stretched to ten seconds but then Klaffenbock and Sayle really got the hammer down.

The gap continued to decrease throughout lap three and by the Nook, Klaffi had managed to get his nose in front and held on to the lead to claim win number two of the week crossing the line just over one second ahead of Holden and Winkle.

Klaffi and Sayle were back for more in 2011 and won the opening sidecar race. However, they were unable to claim another double after their sidecar developed problems during the second race forcing them to nurse it home sixth, despite having led for the first two laps.

ELECTRIC RUTTER

THERE HAS been a mixed response to the introduction of the TT Zero to the two-week motorbike festival on the Isle of Man.

Some fans will never accept them, others feel a one-lap race is not worthy of a Silver Lady and then there are those who feel the fact that the number who actually finish the race numbers in single figures means it's not a real contest.

The inaugural electric bike was launched in 2009 as TTXGP franchise and it was won by Rob Barber riding a Team AGNI motor-cycle, in 25 minutes and 53.5 seconds, at an average race speed of 87.434mph.

The race was relaunched as the TT Zero a year later and American Mark Miller, riding a MotoCzysz E1pc, claimed victory with a lap of 96.82mph.

It was a huge jump in speed and, once the bigger manufacturers and more established names began to get involved, the escalation in speeds and quality was stratospheric.

Any rider who wins a TT deserves their place in history, so the likes of Barber and Miller deserve their place in TT history. But one name that will forever be linked with the TT Zero is Michael Rutter.

The veteran and road-racing legend first tried his hand at the TT Zero in 2011 and joined the MotoCzysz team, which had become the first American manufacturer to win an Isle of Man TT race since Oliver Godfrey in the 1911 Senior TT with an Indian V-Twin, when Miller claimed the win in 2010.

He would soon raise the bar to unprecedented levels and, as of 2019, he remained undefeated in the class, winning five TTs in five races.

He became the first rider in TT history to lap at more than 100mph on an electric bike and, since then, he has raised the speeds to above 120mph – and that included 2019 when the weather meant most lap records remained intact.

Weighing around 40 to 60 kilograms more than a petrol engine bike, as well as containing all of the top-of-the-range technology – and complete lack of noise – they have to be ridden in a completely different style.

It takes sublime skill and knowledge to be able to ride one of those machines at such high speeds and it's no surprise Rutter has been at the forefront of its development as a rider.

TT Zero 2011

Rutter wins but just falls short of the 100mph lap

Michael Rutter's focus turned, for the first time in his illustrious career, to racing an electric bike around the world-famous Isle of Man circuit in 2011.

It had all gone well at the beginning, with Rutter setting a leading lap of 92mph average – some 10mph quicker than his closest rivals – during practice week.

Speaking to the *Bridgnorth Journal* newspaper, he explained how it had all come together and revealed his first thoughts about racing an electric bike: 'It all came together when I started speaking to the two sponsors – Segway and MotoCzysz – so in the end, we decided to enter a bike in the TT Zero races.

'On the electric bike we're hoping to get 100mph out of it.

'Going through the Sulby Straight you can still get 150-160mph out of them – so they're pretty fast.

'The only problem is, at the moment, you can't keep a constant speed going. The top speeds are only hit twice during a lap.

'The bike power delivery is really good though. To be honest I wasn't too impressed with them when they first came out, but they are very fast.

'On the electric bikes we'll be looking to break 100mph average – there's a ten grand prize for the first person to do that.

'All of the lads came over from the BSB race, but the mechanic team didn't arrive until Tuesday so it's been a bit hectic, but they're a specialised team who we've flown over specifically for this.'

The race saw 2010 race winner Mark Miller off in the number one position, followed by team-mate Rutter, who had passed him on the road by the first checkpoint at Glen Helen, with John Burrrows, riding for Lightning Motorcycles, running in third.

Rutter topped the speed trap times at Sulby, posting an impressive 149.5mph, and he later revealed he thought the bike could have gone even quicker, having held back to conserve power, despite lapping in 22 minutes and 43.68 seconds.

After hearing of his near 100mph average lap, Rutter said, 'No way! I tried to conserve battery life and stay smooth but we won the race and that's the main thing. It's a totally different way of riding but I really enjoyed it.

'We only saw the bike on Wednesday, so I think if we had more time there would be more to come set-up wise. We'll be back next year to try again.'

In the end, it was a case of so close, yet so far for Rutter as he claimed the win but just missed out on the £10,000 prize, lapping in 99.604mph on his MotoCzysz, followed closely behind by his new team-mate, American Mark Miller, with an average lap speed of 98.288mph while Scotland's George Spence put in an 88.435mph effort en route to third.

Rutter, however, would again raise the bar a year later and smashed through that 100mph barrier along with his team-mate.

ISLE OF MAN TT MEMORIES

James Driver-Fisher, from Dudley, West Midlands:

I wasn't sure whether to add my own memories to this book but, in the end, I felt I had to.

I was a bit of a late bloomer when it came to loving bikes and the TT. Passing my CBT aged 24, I got my licence two years later.

It was only then I really started taking a serious interest in motorbikes.

I immediately began to love the MotoGO, BSB and World Superbikes, but when I discovered road racing I was changed for life.

My good friend John Cleator, who luckily for me lives in Laxey on the Isle of Man, introduced me to my first TT in 2009.

He sat us at Lezayre. He had told me the bike would be travelling at around 180-190mph but, having never seen a bike go that fast, let alone on a country lane, I didn't really take it in.

Come the first race, the Superbike TT, I could hear them approaching. I didn't really grasp the timings either but John was there counting down the minutes, knowing exactly when they would be flying past.

'Here they come, fella,' he says as he taps me on shoulder and then, when that first bike flew past, I had never experienced anything like it.

I could not get my head around what I was witnessing and then another came past at the same speed, and then another.

From that point on I was hooked, not only on the races but the history, culture and everything to do with the Isle of Man TT. And I have to thank John, along with his mother Helen and her partner, Dicky, for taking me to the best spots and introducing me to the greatest sporting spectacle in the world.

Two years later I was sat on the Cronk-y-Voddy straight. The Senior TT had been delayed for about four hours. It was one of those days where we were sat in glorious sunshine while other parts of the island were experiencing rain and even hailstones.

It's fair to say most people were well lubricated when the race eventually got underway but I class myself so lucky to have been sat on that bank for the first time when it did get going.

Lezayre was great but this was something special as I felt the wind from the bikes brush against my legs, as they slightly tipped in while keeping it pinned, nailing it down straight.

Words cannot express what the TT means to me but I'd just like to thank all the riders for doing what they do. No one comes close to them in any sport. They are heroes, they are gladiators and they will always have my ultimate respect, and that's from first place to last.

Senior TT 2011

McGuinness beats Martin in epic battle

It seemed this might be Guy Martin's best chance of winning a TT. He had been in good form leading up to the race and seemed determined not to let John McGuinness make his early break.

The only problem is, when McGuinness is on it, no one can stay with him so despite Martin setting the early pace he just could not keep up with him over the course of six laps.

It was such a valiant effort, particularly as he was still recovering from his horror crash just a year before, but with McGuinness breaking the lap record there was nothing he could do.

McGuinness eventually secured his 17th TT by seven seconds having reeled in Martin early with Bruce Anstey a further eight seconds behind in third.

The race winner set the fastest lap of the race at 131.25mph on his fourth circuit and also set a new race record.

The race had been delayed by five hours because of wet roads on the north of the island but once the flag dropped Martin had stormed into an early 4.5-second lead over Bruce Anstey at the end of lap one, with McGuinness in third.

Martin led Padgetts Honda rider Anstey by four seconds after lap two but McGuinness was already closing the gap to second place from 2.5 seconds to one.

It was not long until he had taken the lead, pulling a 2.5-second gap on Martin by the end of lap three.

The fourth lap turned out to be McGuinness's fastest of the race as he lengthened the lead to 12 seconds.

Martin trailed by a further second by the fifth and despite trying everything to close the gap, he was forced to settle for second place, with Anstey in third, Cameron Donald fourth, Keith Amor fifth and Michael Dunlop in sixth.

Simon Andrews confirmed his status as the best newcomer by taking 11th place, including a lap at more than 125mph.

McGuinness's win made it another big bike double, having already claimed Superbike TT earlier in the week,

He also finished second in the superstock race and in one of the supersport races, which meant after 50 TTs he had been on the podium 32 times.

Dunlop had been riding a Kawasaki for Paul Bird, who had built bikes for Tom Sykes in the World Superbike Championship, as well as Chris Vermeulen and Stuart Easton in the British Superbike series.

Dunlop ran a Kawasaki in the superbike class and another in the superstock, which he ran himself, during the 2011 TT.

Starting on pole, he had eventually finished fourth in the superbike class at the North West 200 but bad weather and even a bomb scare had ended the meeting prematurely.

Moving on to the TT, he finished fifth in the superbike race and then, riding a Yamaha R6 in the first supersport race, he broke down again.

In the superstock race, he enjoyed a close battle with Martin, eventually breaking him on the final lap to give him his first ever win on a big bike.

Dunlop also broke down in the second supersport race, while leading, and then finished sixth in the Senior TT, as the fastest Kawasaki.

He followed that sixth place with three wins at the Southern 100, including the coveted championship race, again after another great race with Martin.

At the Ulster, he took two supersport wins, battling against his brother, and one superstock win. It was a sign of the dominations that were about to come.

ISLE OF MAN TT MEMORIES

Ben Plant, from Wem, Shropshire, has raced at the Manx GP, Tandragee 100, Cookstown 100, Skerries 100 and Southern 100:

The calibre of the road racers is superb and I cannot be anything other than amazed at seeing what they can do and the speeds they now hit.

Having ridden around the course myself it puts it into perspective even more. I'm going as fast as I possibly can but then you see the bar raised to 135mph, which is just incredible to see.

My first ever experience was the superbike race in 2012 and that race was the reason I started road racing myself.

When I started road racing, I knew that was it – it was everything I thought it would be. Now I've got near the top

I've got even more respect for the riders. Racing on the roads is a completely different style.

We went to the TT for the first time in 2012 as a group of mates, just watching the races. From then, I just developed such a huge passion to start racing properly – I wanted to be an Isle of Man TT racer.

I started doing a few track days and then went for my ACU licence. The whole reason behind everything I'm doing is to race the TT.

Supersport TT 2012

Anstey wins by less than a second in memorable week for Honda

The 2012 TT was completely dominated by Hondas as the manufacturer to make a clean sweep in the opening superbike and supersport TTs.

In total, Honda claimed three victories and 11 podiums during race week – and that despite the Senior being cancelled that year.

John McGuinness, riding for the Honda Legend TT team, took victory in the superbike race, and then Bruce Anstey on a Honda CBR600RR claimed the second-closest TT win in history, edging the supersport race by just 0.77 seconds.

The New Zealander repeated his 2011 success by winning the 600cc race but he was unfortunate not to make it a supersport double as, while leading, he was forced to retire.

Michael Dunlop was winner of the race, which had been delayed by weather – something that would play havoc with the remainder of the week.

Dunlop had planned to go back to Honda for the superbike race but, due to various problems, he opted to run his Kawasaki again at the TT and came home in tenth.

Another breakdown followed in the first supersport race but he managed to take a podium in the superstock before claiming his third TT win in the second supersport race and finishing 15th in the Lightweight class.

A clean sweep followed at the Southern 100 with five wins and then he won the two superbike races at the Ulster and superstock meetings for good measure, to once again really show his potential.

Having won the opening superbike race, McGuinness made more history by winning the Superstock TT for the first time, raising his tally of victories to 19. The triumphs had increased Honda's number of TT successes to 163 – a truly staggering achievement.

Honda also claimed 11 out of 15 podium spots in the petrol-powered solo races.

The only downside for the team was a crash by Honda TT Legends rider Simon Andrews at Grahams during the superbike race.

He was taken to hospital to receive treatment for his injuries but made a full recovery.

Dave Molyneux had also returned to the Isle of Man TT, following a self-imposed year-long hiatus, in stunning fashion, by claiming both Sidecar TT wins.

Everything pointed towards the Senior TT following in another glorious week of racing but, after the race had been delayed for a day due to heavy rain and low cloud, it was rescheduled and then cancelled for the first time in its history due to persistently bad weather.

It meant the final race of 2012 was the Lightweight TT, which was making its return to the race programme. The class had been pioneered and championed by Ryan Farquhar, who went on to win the inaugural 650cc race.

TT Zero 2012

Rutter makes history as three riders break the 100mph barrier

Michael Rutter turned back the clock and put in one of the rides of his life to win his fifth TT at the Isle of Man, smashing the race record in the process during the 2012 TT Zero.

The speed set by Rutter and the Team Segway Racing MotoCzysz team was seen as one of the most significant landmarks in the history of the TT – and it bagged Rutter the £10,000 prize from the Isle of Man government for good measure too, although he did share it with his team-mate, Mark Miller, who came third.

One of the main reasons the race was so memorable, however, was the battle that raged between Rutter and John McGuinness, who was just beginning his own journey on the electric bike with Honda's Team Mugen Shinden.

The battle was a sign of things to come for the next few years although both riders would dip in and out of the class, with Rutter eventually joining McGuinness at Honda Mugen, which would later be renamed Bathams Honda Mugen as Rutter's long-term sponsors decided to get involved.

Rutter's MotoCzysz team-mate Mark Miller took the final podium slot, with all three breaking the prestigious 100mph mark, which was first achieved by a conventional bike by Scotsman Bob McIntyre in 1957. After a series of weather delays and revisions to the running order, ten riders lined up for the race. And they were nervous too as damp patches had been reported around the course.

Either way, Rutter led them off and established a lead of more than half a minute by Glen Helen from McGuinness, with Miller a further three seconds back in third.

Yoshinari Matsushita, racing for the Japanese team Komatti-Mirai Racing, was in fourth with former winner Rob Barber fifth.

Matsushita had dropped before Ballaugh but at the front Rutter continued to set the pace with an average speed of, at the time, 118.730mph and a lead of almost a minute from McGuinness.

Miller was quickest through the speed trap at 132.6mph, which was well down on the 152mph Rutter had set in qualifying, but even still he remained on track for the golden 100mph lap.

The undefeated TT Zero star eventually crossed the line with a 104.056mph lap, writing both his and the MotoCzysz names in the record books.

By the end of the race, three riders had broken the 100mph barrier as McGuinness crossed the line second with a lap of 102.215mph with Miller not far behind, lapping at 101.065mph, to come third.

Team owner Michael Czysz could not hide his delight after the race as he knew his team had made history and would be synonymous with the Isle of Man TT races for the rest of his life.

Rutter had lapped in 21 minutes and 45.33 seconds to win the race and book his place in the record books, finishing ahead of then 19-time TT winner McGuinness and MotoCzysz team-mate Miller, to claim his second successive SES TT Zero race victory.

He had gone into the race as favourite to break the record on an electric bike after posting a lap of 102.508mph in Monday's practice session. But his attempt to make it official was hampered by poor weather which led to continuous delays to the day's race schedule. However, when the action finally got under way, Rutter did not disappoint.

It was his second win in a row and more success was to follow.

TT Zero 2013

Rutter beats McGuinness by 1.6 seconds in epic battle

Perhaps Michael Rutter's greatest win on an electric bike was his success ahead of his fierce rival and good friend John McGuinness, mainly because no one, including Rutter himself, had backed him to win it.

Honda Mugen had really raised the bar in the electric bike class, ploughing millions into the bike and technology, so when Rutter turned up with his tried and tested MotoCzysz not many had given him much of a chance of winning.

The TT can throw up some wonderful surprises and one such shock occurred in 2013 when Rutter and McGuinness went toe-to-toe.

McGuinness led the field with his Mugen Shinden Ni and few believed MotoCzysz could make it four in a row at the 2013 Isle of Man TT – and a hat-trick of wins for Rutter too.

McGuinness took an early lead headed through Glen Helen and held a nine-second lead on Rutter, who in turn was ten seconds ahead of Miller.

Suddenly, Rutter went on the charge and began reeling in the Mugen, closing the gap more and more as each sector passed.

He was quickest through the Sulby Straight speed trap, with a speed of 142.2mph, while McGuinness was down on 131.8mph. Barber, who again was back competing on an electric bike, also posted an impressive 122.7mph.

By Cronk-ny-Mona, Rutter had closed the gap to less than a second. Rutter crossed the line first on the roads and then had an agonising wait for McGuinness to appear, to see if he had claimed a hat-trick of wins. McGuinness arrived 21.672 seconds later, clocking a speed of 109.523 mph, but having started 20 seconds later on the roads, it meant Rutter had won the race by 1.671 seconds.

Rutter had also recorded a new lap record of 109.675mph, just short of the 110mph barrier, but that record would be smashed soon after.

Meanwhile, Miller had been forced to retire at Ballaugh Bridge, which meant he was unable to add to his own impressive tally of TT Zero podiums, which promoted inaugural winner Rob Barber, riding for the Ohio State University student team, into third with a lap of 90.4mph.

Senior TT 2013

McGuinness wins as Dunlop misses out on fifth TT

Heading into the Senior of 2013, Michael Dunlop had won all four TTs on the bounce. His dominance was such that his supersport lap record would last for years while he also pushed the superstock lap record up to a 131mph average speed.

During that particular year, John McGuinness and Dunlop had been on identical machinery, which had also been prepared in the same way, on the bigger bikes.

And yet Dunlop had simply looked unstoppable. His Honda TT Legends team-mates, McGuinness and Michael Rutter, had been quick all week too but no one had been able to keep up with the pace of the young protégé.

But cometh the hour, cometh the man. McGuinness did not just show everyone he was still capable of winning at the TT, he blew his competitors out of the water by setting lap records for fun and showing one and all that when it came to riding a superbike fast around the 37.73-mile course, he was still well and truly the master.

Having already broken the lap record in the first superbike race, setting a 131.671mph lap – while wearing the colours of Joey Dunlop as a tribute to the late, great star – he then broke it again in the Senior. It was one of those race weeks where the pace remained ridiculously fast throughout, from start to finish, in every single race.

When you have sat at the top of the mountain for so long, there will always be young, hungry riders behind gunning for your crown, status and title.

Dunlop had certainly shown he was the new kid on the block in 2013, having already bagged four wins and looking dead set to match Hutchy's historic five wins in a week.

But McGuinness had been lying in wait the entire week, ready to pounce when it mattered most.

Having set a new lap record six days earlier, McGuinness had the pace to win but he just needed to find a way to put it all together again.

A nasty crash at Bray Hill delayed the race for some considerable time and when the Senior eventually restarted it had been reduced to four laps.

Whether that played into McGuinness's hands or not, we will never know, but when they all set off once again at 4.30pm it was Dunlop who set the early pace, leading his team-mate by 1.3 seconds.

And for the remainder of the race, the warhorses went toe-to-toe producing one of the most thrilling TTs ever seen.

By the end of lap one, Dunlop had increased his lead to 1.387 seconds, having posted a lap of 130.985mph from a standing start, with McGuinness close behind with a 130.790mph.

At Ramsey on lap two, McGuinness had finally got his nose in front, by just 0.2 seconds, a lead he maintained after breaking the 131mph barrier, while Dunlop stayed in the high 130s.

Despite the battle being one of the island's closest contested races ever, McGuinness sensed that once he had edged in front there were very few capable of passing him back again.

Dunlop looked to be clawing some time back during lap three, setting a 124.486mph lap out of the pits, but smooth pit stops have always played a big role in the most keenly contested TTs, including McGuinness's previous wins, and the 2013 Senior was no different.

Following the first pit stop, McGuinness had extended his lead to 9.801 seconds.

Dunlop again fought back on lap four, breaking the 131mph for the first time but McGuinness was also on a flyer, setting a 131.165mph lap to increase his lead to more than ten seconds.

Again Dunlop went quicker but, pulling out the pits to start lap five, McGuinness had opened up an unassailable six-second advantage.

As Dunlop's challenge gradually faded, McGuinness was able to cross the finish line with relative ease having opened up a lead of ten seconds, having again broken the race record.

But when McGuinness ended the race victorious, Dunlop – just like Guy Martin in 2011 – had been the first person to shake his hand and praise him for a job well done.

McGuinness, by his own admission, had won numerous TTs during his career by quietly pushing harder than anyone else at the start of the race, which meant no one could catch him come the closing stages.

However, now the other riders, particularly the younger ones, were beginning to follow suit.

An equally close and intriguing battle had also been raging behind the front two during the 2013 Senior.

Dunlop had passed Bruce Anstey during the race but the nine-time TT winner – as he was at the time – refused to give up on third and re-passed the Northern Irishman on the mountain during the sixth and final lap. He not only bagged third place with his late charge, he also set the fastest lap of the race with a stunning 131.531mph effort, which pushed James Hillier back into fourth by just 0.9 seconds.

Guy Martin finished in fifth and Rutter took sixth to ensure the Honda TT Legends team would take three of the top six places.

Behind them there were plenty of retirements and breakdowns including Josh Brookes, who only managed a single lap, while his Australian compatriot Cameron Donald joined Gary Johnson in calling it a day with mechanical problems following the second lap.

Conor Cummins was forced to park up his Milwaukee Yamaha midway through the final lap but good weather on the island tends to produce blisteringly fast times and the 2013 Senior was no different as 14 riders posted a lap of at least 130mph or more, with eight breaking the 131mph barrier.

Most importantly, however, the win gave McGuinness time to reflect on another Senior triumph.

He had gone faster than ever before during the race week but had still failed to win a race, which left some, including himself, fearing the worst.

But deep down he knew he was more than capable of winning and had given everything in the superstock and supersport races, which were classes he never felt confident of winning in. Having started the superbike race slowly, by his own high standards, and then receiving a 60-second penalty for speeding in the pit lane, he knew quite early on he was not going to win that particular race.

Yet he, and every other racer on the start line, knew that come the Senior TT, he would be at the front again.

The race week had also included a very surprising defeat for McGuinness in the TT Zero.

Gunning for his 20th TT win on the much-favoured Honda Mugen, he had been shocked by his team-mate Rutter, who rode an incredible race to claim the win.

The Mugen had looked unbeatable but Rutter rode one of the laps of his life to steal a third victory for the MotoCzysz team, which also marked his own third TT Zero win.

McGuinness, however, was soon back in the groove, grabbing the final podium spot in the second supersport race, which had set him up nicely for his assault on the Senior.

And the tears of despair that had greeted him in the Honda garage after his second-place finish in the TT Zero were soon changed to tears of joy when he finally notched his 20th TT win in the best way possible, claiming yet another Senior win.

McGuinness knew the crowd were behind him all the way too. He had, and always would be, a huge fan favourite on the island, which was plain to see during the final race of the memorable 2013 TT.

Aged 41, the win also saw him equal Mike Hailwood's record of seven Senior TT wins, which he admitted put the victory right up there with his best.

Having recovered from a very rare superbike defeat on the Saturday, a class he had been pretty untouchable in for nearly a decade, he had stormed back to reclaim his King of the Mountain crown.

It also signalled that McGuinness had no plans to retire, because he knew he had more race wins left in him.

Dunlop's TT had also been truly memorable. With financial problems looming over him and his mother back home in Northern Ireland, he had eventually agreed to become a factory Honda rider, signing up for a three-rider Honda TT Legends team that included fellow road racing greats McGuinness and Rutter.

After winning on his own 600cc machine once more at the North West 200, he had put the Honda on pole for the superbike race only for the race to be called off.

The meeting also marked the first time Dunlop had ever agreed to have any team-mates. And, come the TT, his Fireblade just would not go, while McGuinness and Rutter were bombing around the circuit during practice week.

Come race day for the opening Superbike TT, McGuinness had been selected by Honda to wear livery in tribute to his hero, Joey Dunlop.

Michael Dunlop admitted later to being slightly confused by the whole situation as he felt that, as a Dunlop, he should have been the one asked to pay homage to his uncle Joey.

But, leaving the start line as number six, he never looked back and won the race.

It marked his fourth TT victory at the time and what made it even sweeter was that Dunlop now had the full set of race wins – supersport, superstock and, finally, superbike.

Next up was the supersport race, and he not only won it but he broke the lap record. Then, trailing Gary Johnson's Kawasaki ZX10R in the superstock race, he once again broke the lap record on the final lap to claim his third win of the week.

Trading places with Anstey in the second supersport race, he took the win by just two seconds – again, breaking his own lap record.

Conditions took a turn for the worse for the Senior TT and it was restarted following an incident involving Jonathan Howarth. The race was rescheduled when 11 spectators were taken to hospital after a crash on the opening lap.

When it did restart, McGuinness produced a stunning ride to win the Blue Riband Senior TT and claim his 20th success at the famous Isle of Man road races.

The Morecambe man's victory denied Dunlop a record-equalling fifth win of the week. Ian Hutchinson's record from 2010 would remain intact for a while longer yet.

McGuinness saw off Dunlop by ten seconds to set a new race record, with New Zealander Bruce Anstey in third.

However, the Honda-Dunlop partnership would not last much longer as the Northern Irishman refused to re-sign with the team after learning his team-mate, McGuinness, would still be earning more than him despite his four wins a week.

Not only that, Dunlop even made the decision at the end of the 2013 campaign to retire from road racing entirely as it was the same year bailiffs finally came knocking and threw both him and his mother out of the family home, as he revealed in his autobiography, *Road Racer*.

Dunlop admitted he had been in denial about the whole financial situation and how everything had been too much to take on following his father's death. Thankfully for the entire racing fraternity, he would be back for more in 2014.

ISLE OF MAN TT MEMORIES
Paul Myler, from Telford, Shropshire, is a 12-time club racing champion:

My most vivid memory of watching races at the TT came during the 2014 Superstock race. Guy Martin, who was racing number four with Tyco Suzuki, went past and we saved his life. We got him stopped when his front wheel nut fell off by us at Cronk-y-Voddy. The marshals stopped him at Ramsey. We even got a photo of the nut coming off too.

Superbike TT 2014
Dunlop wins BMW's first TT in 75 years

The year 2014 looked like it might be a bleak one for Michael Dunlop, with all his bikes either locked away or sold.

But then, from nowhere, Stuart Hicken of Hawk Racing got in touch. Making contact immediately meant something to Dunlop because Hicken had worked with his father, Robert, in the past, including when he had suffered his serious accident at the TT in 1994.

However, at first, the younger Dunlop had been reluctant to take their initial conversations much further but Hicken kept phoning.

Despite numerous knock-backs, Dunlop finally agreed to meet him in Belfast. A BMW representative accompanied Hicken to the meeting and, with more negotiating taking place, Dunlop finally agreed to ride the bike just days before the North West 200.

Things had begun to look rosier at home for Dunlop too because, despite the house being up for auction, it was not sold, meaning he had been able to buy it back.

Dunlop would later credit Hicken with saving his career but what was to follow was just the beginning of another truly incredible campaign.

During the North West 200 superbike race, Dunlop had once again become involved in a mighty tussle with his brother, William, who pipped him into second.

But he was able to win the superstock and then, in the Blue Ribbon superbike finale, he broke the lap record twice which set up his trip to the TT perfectly.

The North West 200 victories also meant Dunlop had now won international road races on Yamahas, Kawasakis, Hondas and BMWs.

The BMW superbike was full of power but incredibly difficult to handle.

Dunlop, in the only way he knew how, simply gave his all as he always did. Despite poor forecasts, the sun was shining come race morning of the Superbike TT.

Covered in blisters, Dunlop set a new lap record of 131.730mph in the race and then broke the record again on his way to victory.

It was an emotional victory for the German team too as, after a 75-year lapse from racing at the Isle of Man, a BMW had finally won a TT race after all those absent years.

Eventually, victory would prove to be rather easy as Dunlop secured his eighth success by 20.5 seconds from Suzuki's Guy Martin, with Manxman Conor Cummins a further three seconds behind.

James Hillier was the early leader but Dunlop quickly assumed control, breaking the absolute lap record on his first circuit. He upped the record to 131.89mph on his second lap but, once again, it was Kiwi Bruce Anstey who was lapping quicker than anyone else towards the end of the race, as he clocked an average lap speed of 132.30mph on the final lap to again claim the record.

Dunlop had decided to go flat out from the start and then nurse the BMW home towards the end after building up a good lead over Martin.

He crossed the line with a final lap of 129mph, 20.570 seconds ahead of Martin who in turn stretched his lead on Conor Cummins towards the end of the lap.

With backing from the BMW factory in Germany and the Buildbase British Superbike team, his lead during the race had improved from 9.5 seconds after lap one to 16.5 seconds by the end of the second circulation.

The lead was up to 20 seconds after three laps, 25 seconds after lap four and, only when he eased off the gas a little did the gap stopping growing, as he smartly began to control the race from the front.

Behind the top four of Dunlop, Martin, Cummins and Anstey was Michael Rutter and William Dunlop, who rounded out the top six. Seventh place eventually went to McGuinness but there had been a good reason why the Honda star had not been competing at the front end as usual.

Eleven weeks before the start of the 2014 TT, he had crashed his enduro bike. McGuinness ended up with a broken wrist, broke a few ribs and basically knocked himself about pretty badly.

It meant he got nowhere near the podium during the TT and was even forced to tell Clive Padgett he would not be racing in the second supersport or the Senior, such were his injuries.

The injuries suffered by McGuinness, however, all paled into insignificance as his team-mate and good friend, Simon Andrews, would be killed at the North West 200 in 2014.

Riding in the Honda TT Legends team, his tragic crash had rocked the biking community really hard once again.

More bad news was to follow too as three-time British Supersport champion Karl Harris was killed during the Superstock race on the Tuesday afternoon.

The 34-year-old from Sheffield crashed at Joey's Corner, during the second lap. Harris was the second rider to die in as many days during race week following the death of Bob Price in the opening Supersport TT race.

Harris had made his debut at the Isle of Man in 2012, finishing 21st in the superbike race and 28th in the superstock race, lapping at more than 121mph.

During the rest of the 2014 TT race week, Dunlop would also come away with a third and first in the two supersport races while riding a Honda and even took the superstock win on his own Kawasaki for good measure.

And then he made it four wins in a week for the second straight year with victory in the Senior. McGuinness was able to add to his own haul of TTs by claiming victory in the electric bike class while Dean Harrison took his first win on the island in the Lightweight TT.

But the year once again belonged to Dunlop who, after the TT, went to Frohburg after signing with Rico Penzkofer, who ran the Penz13.com team, and won the Joey Dunlop race while breaking the lap record.

Everything appeared to be looking rosy until Hicken suddenly announced he had lost the BMW contract. Out of respect for his friend, Dunlop decided not to rejoin the team and instead began looking elsewhere once again.

Supersport TT 2014
Johnson beats Anstey by 1.4 seconds to claim second TT

Gary Johnson not only pipped Bruce Anstey to the win, he did it with one of the closest winning margins in TT history to claim his second Silver Lady.

Mounted on a Triumph Street Triple, it marked the first win for the British manufacturer since 2003.

And what made the win even more remarkable was that 2014 also marked the first time Smiths Triumph had ever entered a team into the TT.

Johnson ended up circulating with Michael Dunlop, who had already won the Superbike TT and eventually completed the rostrum in third.

By that stage Johnson knew he had sewn up the win because, when a rider catches Dunlop on the road, it is usually a good sign they have won the race.

Victory, however, did not come easily for Johnson – who had claimed his first TT win back in 2011 – as he endured a race-long battle with Anstey who, at the time, was the lap record holder.

Anstey had been on fire during race week, having posted a stunning lap of more than 132mph in the opening

Superbike TT, and he had moved into the lead during the first supersport race by lap two.

But when the weather conditions changed for the worse, Anstey decided to ease off a little, which gave Johnson the chance to claim the win by just 1.448 seconds.

The win also ended Triumph's 11-year wait for a TT win and helped the British manufacturer break the Honda, Yamaha and Suzuki stranglehold on the island.

Having faced a few teething problems with the bike in 2013, which was also entered in the British Superbike Championship, the team had won two British Supersport races at Oulton Park before heading to the Isle of Man, which had given them confidence a victory could be on the cards.

The team was also full of praise for Johnson's team-mate Michael Rutter, who had helped Triumph to develop a race-winning bike. Rutter eventually finished ninth.

Sidecar 1 TT 2014

Conrad Harrison claims emotional first Sidecar TT

There was another emotional victory during 2014 too as Conrad Harrison claimed his first TT during the opening sidecar race.

While his son would follow him on to the top during the same week, the first sidecar race belonged to Conrad who made the most of a few retirements and some superb weather to take victory.

Alongside passenger Mike Aylott, the 50-year-old finished 17 seconds ahead of John Holden and Andrew Winkle and immediately exploded with delight exclaiming his dream had finally come true.

Brothers Ben and Tom Birchall had been the early leaders but the Mansfield pair crashed out at the Black Dub on lap two, sustaining minor injuries.

Manxman Dave Molyneux, partnered by Patrick Farrance, then took the lead and had maintained a good lead.

Sidecars, however, can be notoriously unreliable machines and so it proved as the second set of race leaders were forced out of the race, this time with Moly and Farrance suffering a breakdown.

The Birchalls had been leading themselves early on in the race, pushing on to take four seconds from Molyneux and Farrance, with Holden and Winkle in third.

Once the Birchalls had crashed, Moly took control and set the fastest lap of the race on his second circuit before being forced to retire with mechanical problems.

Harrison and Aylott, who started at number five for the 2014 races, moved into the lead and after keeping Holden and Winkle at bay took their debut win.

Having claimed six podiums in their last seven races, the pair had shown brilliant consistency while being unable to match the pace of the front runners.

It meant the victory had been long overdue for the Bradford driver but once the pair embraced on the finish line they knew they had finally been confirmed as TT winners.

In the second and third positions were Holden and Winkle, followed by multiple world champion Tim Reeves and Gregory Cluze

Ian Bell, from Bedlington, finished fourth on his return to the TT following a lengthy absence, with son Carl in the chair.

Moly and Farrance would gain revenge in the second Sidecar TT marking yet another win for the Manxman, with Harrison and Aylott in second, with Holden and Winkle taking the final podium spots.

Superbike TT 2015

Anstey finally grabs first superbike win

Bruce Anstey knew he had a potentially race-winning package before the contest had even started.

Despite running standard pistons, valves and a generator, the Kiwi felt it still had the raw power to win – and he was right too as he gave Clive Padgett his first big bike win since Hutchy had rewritten the record books with five wins during 2010. It had always been Anstey's dream to win a TT on a big bike because it was the class victory that had so far eluded him during his already stellar career.

But aged 45, he managed to keep Kawasaki-mounted Ian Hutchinson and John McGuinness at bay.

With breakdowns having scuppered his earlier chances of winning on a superbike, this victory was even more sweet.

Trailing Hutchy by 1.2 seconds after the first lap, the early omens were looking too good, as Anstey was renowned for peaking towards the end of most races.

Hutchy had extended his lead to more than four seconds by the end of lap two but Anstey, having pushed too hard on the opening laps, settled into his usual, smooth rhythm to close his rival down.

By the second pit stop, Anstey had the lead but then Michael Dunlop flew past him, which disrupted his rhythm.

It was because the Northern Irishman was on his own mini mission, determined to grab the final podium spot, having been let down by a slow pit stop.

Anstey used Dunlop's flying lap to his advantage and responded in the best possible way, posting a 131.797mph lap – the fastest of the entire race.

And things again turned sour for Dunlop as he ended up crashing following a coming-together with Scott Wilson, who had already crashed his own bike.

The race was red-flagged early and Anstey, who had already crossed the finish line, was announced as the winner.

Such was the Kiwi's pace he had recorded a new race record speed of 128.749mph over the six laps.

Anstey, who had started road racing along with the likes of John McGuinness and Dave Jefferies, had won his first TT in 2002, on a 250cc. He had patiently waited another 13 years before claiming his first big bike victory and it was a win the Isle of Man public were delighted to see.

Supersport TT 2015

Hutchy finally back on the top step after horrific injury

Following his horror crash in 2010, Ian Hutchinson resumed his career in 2012, amazingly just two years after his horrific injury during a British Supersport championship race which almost led to him losing his leg.

Having missed all of the 2011 TT, the man who had won five TTs in a single week was back on two wheels in 2012 but had been left fighting a deadly infection, which not only threatened to take his leg again but also his life.

The bone in his lower leg had refused to knit, but rather than resting up and recovering, he instead built his own carbon fibre cast to go over his leg.

The only luck Hutchy had come across during the entire ordeal was the fact he had come across doctors and surgeons who agreed the challenge of trying to save his leg was one worth taking up.

Despite 19 operations in 2011 alone, he somehow still managed to register a podium at the Macau GP on his R1 that very same year, finishing behind winner Michael Rutter and Martin Jessopp.

But just as he was beginning to feel competitive again, he picked up the infection – and then, to make matters even worse, Hutchy re-broke his leg at the Motorcycle News Live show.

It meant a return to the leg fixator, a bone transportation operation and no racing for another year – or at least that would have been the case for most ordinary human beings.

Hutchy asked the doctors and surgeons to postpone his operation so he could go racing at the TT. After some persuasion they agreed and even allowed him to remove the fixator too. Packing his leg with antibiotic pellets, he was sent on his way to go racing.

Hutchy felt the best he could do was get the Yamaha ready for a proper attempt in 2013. So he headed to the North West 2000 with no data while his team were still completely in the dark about his infection and how dangerous it could be. Only his father knew what was really going on behind the scenes.

Despite everything that was working against him, Hutchy managed to secure an 11th-placed finish in a superstock race and a stunning sixth in one of the supersport races on the Isle of Man.

With the TT now over, it was time to focus on saving his leg again, which meant going through more operations before eventually trying to get back to full fitness. By April 2013, doctors said the transportation operation and surgery had worked well. And the rest, as they say, is history.

After claiming a stunning victory at the Macau GP, it was a sign of things to come as once more he was truly ready to return to TT, ready to try and get back on the podium. What followed a year later, in 2015, however, was truly magical.

Five years after breaking his leg, Hutchy finally managed to climb back on to the top on the Isle of Man.

Now aged 38, and having battled through more than 30 operations, he teamed up with Prodigy's Keith Flint – a fellow bike nut – to win the 2015 supersport race on a Team Traction Control Yamaha.

With tears in his eyes, Hutchy realised his comeback was finally complete. He had nearly claimed his elusive win earlier that week too, coming second in the Superbike TT behind Bruce Anstey, who himself was overjoyed to have claimed his first superbike win on the island.

In the opening supersport race, Hutchy had taken the lead over Gary Johnson but less than a second separated the pair, with Anstey also circulating close behind in third.

Michael Dunlop had broken down and Guy Martin had been docked 60 seconds for speeding in the pits, which had removed two of the fastest riders from the equation early on.

Hutchy smelled blood and put in two laps of 126mph plus, to take a 2.5 second lead over Anstey, who had knocked Johnson back into third place.

Hutchy kept his lead, despite a charge from the Kiwi, to ensure three Yamahas took the top three positions on the podium.

Senior TT 2015

Never write McGuinness off at the Isle of Man

During 2015 the pace had once again increased with several riders looking capable of breaking records in all the classes throughout race week.

McGuinness had already claimed victory in the TT Zero on the Honda Mugen and even felt by 2015 the electric bikes were beginning to get too quick to race after just two practice laps.

Most riders lining up for the TT Zero are usually handed a brand-new bike, which has to be ridden completely differently to any other petrol-powered machine. They are also constantly being upgraded and updated. The Mugen had given McGuinness another, albeit nervy, win on the island but when it came to Senior race day he knew the competition would be ferocious.

McGuinness, however, remained his normal self and went through his usual pre-race routine, which was always the same.

He scrubbed his tyres before the big bike races down at Douglas Head, running it up and down a private road a few times and then went to bed, thinking about how it felt during the build-up to race day.

Michael Dunlop had been in impressive form despite suffering a nasty spill in the opening Superbike TT and having switched bikes midway through practice week.

And with Ian Hutchison's comeback now complete and Bruce Anstey finally winning a superbike race, the competition was as fierce as ever.

McGuinness himself was only just coming back for another injury, which had ruined his 2014 effort, but he returned with a bang during the 2015 Senior TT breaking his own lap record and also matching Mike Hailwood's record of seven Senior victories, collecting his 23rd Silver Lady along the way.

Having finished fourth in the superbike race, few had tipped him to win the Senior but deep down he knew he could win it – and, ultimately, that was all the motivation he needed.

Perhaps not having the attention on him before the race helped? Who knows, but whatever it was it worked, because on Senior race day McGuinness went off number one and simply never looked back.

Unfortunately, Jamie Hamilton's crash on the Cronk-y-Voddy straight, which would eventually force him to retire from road racing, played its part in the win too.

Before the race had been restarted, just three seconds had separated McGuinness, Hutchinson and Dunlop.

The restart, however, meant the race would be reduced from the normal six laps to four.

James Hillier was the early pace setter once the race restarted, with McGuinness and Hutchinson slotting into second and third respectively. Now, just one second separated the top three.

But a record-breaking lap from a standing start of 131.850mph would see McGuinness eventually open up a 1.2-second lead on Hillier.

Despite slowing down for a pit stop on the second lap, the Morecombe Missile then clocked another lap record of 132.70mph on his Honda Fireblade, much to the delight of the Isle of Man crowd.

McGuinness said the fans' reactions at the time had matched the emotions he felt when he set the first 130mph lap back in 2007, but he knew he still had a job to do.

A mistake by Hutchinson as he pulled into the pits meant he now enjoyed a 12-second lead over second place.

McGuinness was even able to slightly ease off and take in some of the atmosphere while drama unfolded behind him as Hillier's stunning 132.414mph final lap moved him ahead of Hutchinson into second.

Guy Martin also broke the 132mph barrier for good measure, while Dunlop was not going to miss out entirely on the party and became the second fastest rider in the history of the TT with a lap of 132.515mph on his Buildbase BMW.

McGuinness credited changing the rear tyre compound, which was slightly harder, as one of the reasons for his impressive win as it had given him extra confidence making a big difference on the day to his feeling on the bike.

Having been given odds of 16/1 to win the Senior before McGuinness had even twisted the throttle in anger, it had proved to be the fire he needed to push himself harder than ever before and make yet another statement, showing why he remained King of the Mountain.

With an earlier victory in the TT Zero on his Honda Mugen earlier, he ended the week as a 23-time TT winner. He admitted at the time that equalling Joey Dunlop's record of 26 successes and then hanging up his boots would be the perfect way to sign off on his stunning career.

The Senior in 2015, however, remains his last TT triumph but, if that race taught the world anything, it was to never bet against McGuinness winning again.

The 2015 race week had been a year for new records too as McGuinness, Dunlop, Hillier, Martin and Anstey all entered the 132mph club.

There were also early signs of what was to lie ahead as Peter Hickman posted a time of 131.622mph on his superstock BMW machine in the Senior.

Two years later, however, McGuinness's career would be left hanging in the balance following a high-speed crash at the North West 200, which would leave him badly injured and unsure of his future as one of the finest road racers to have ever graced the Isle of Man.

The year 2015 had been another strange one for Dunlop too as he had started it with Milwaukee Yamaha after the team had come in with a deal.

He had won on Yamahas before too and felt the package looked like a good prospect to win again.

Dunlop used the North West 200 as the litmus test but immediately felt things were just not right.

Then, during the first and second TT practices, nothing had changed in his head so he made the hugely bold decision to just walk away from the team altogether. After phoning Steve Hicken, son of Stuart Hicken – who had helped him to win four TTs during the 2014 campaign – he managed to find a replacement: a Buildbase BMW he thought he had an outside chance of winning on.

During the opening superbike race, he had worked his way up to third and was pushing for a win – as well as a 132mph lap – when back-marker Scott Wilson came off his bike in front of him at The Nook, a blind right-hander. His bike ended up bouncing back into the middle of the road.

Dunlop was on his final lap and was just one mile from home when suddenly he was sliding down the road at 100mph.

Wilson was okay but Dunlop had lost a possible win, a possible 133mph lap and also potentially £12,000 in prize money.

He broke his wrist, damaged his leg and wrecked his shoulder for good measure too but he did not reveal the extent of his injuries because he wanted to keep on racing that week.

Bravely riding on, he managed to finish second in the superstock race and fifth in the Senior, alongside two more DNFs, but all in all it was a week to forget for Dunlop.

ISLE OF MAN TT MEMORIES

Josh Langman, from Aldridge, Walsall, currently competes in the Thundersport GB club racing championship:

I went in 2016 when Michael Dunlop and Hutchy were going tooth and nail for the wins – and Dunlop set his first 133mph lap, which nearly hit 134mph.

Bruce Anstey took the RCV213 for the first time and the two-stroke Suter was also there and I just loved the smell of it. Mark Higgins was blazing around the course in his Subaru.

> But predominately I remember that week for the weather, as it was two weeks of wall-to-wall sunshine – I couldn't believe I ended up with terrible sunburn! All of my other TT memories are on telly that year and that battle between Hutchy and Dunlop really sticks out.

Senior TT 2016

Dunlop completes big bike double in record-breaking style

Despite again attracting more interest from the bigger teams, Dunlop decided to return to Stuart Hicken and they set about building a BMW for the 2016 campaign.

Hicken spent £12,000 buying a new bike and then five times that amount on turning it into a race winner under the Hawk Racing banner.

Over at Tyco, William had been replaced by Ian Hutchinson and was now partners with Guy Martin.

When the North West 200 rolled around once more, Michael won the opening superbike race by eight seconds to lay down a real marker for the TT having beaten the likes of Hutchy, William, John McGuinness, Bruce Anstey, Ryan Farquhar, Conor Cummins, Michael Rutter, Peter Hickman and James Hillier.

Michael Dunlop was simply too strong, posting the fastest-ever lap of 123.207mph in the process.

The positive omens continued at the TT too as, during practice, he broke the lap record. It was clear that without any technical hitches, the race would be between him and Hutchy during the opening Superbike TT.

Dunlop got the hammer down from the beginning and posted a 133.369mph lap from a standing start. It meant he was also the first rider to break the 17-minute lap.

Lap two was even quicker at 133.393mph and, at one point, Dunlop had found himself leading on the road as well as on time, until Hutchy came back right at the end to claim second spot ahead of McGuinness in third.

Dunlop also came second in the first supersport race behind Hutchy but was later disqualified for accidentally fitting an illegal cam bucket, having changed the engine at the last minute.

Another second followed in the second supersport race but there was yet more controversy when Tyco were reported for using overlong pistons. Hutchy's second supersport win, however, would stand while he also claimed the Superstock TT on a BMW 1000RR too.

It meant everything had built up towards the Senior but if there was ever any doubt over who would win the final race of the week, Dunlop soon showed what he was truly capable of.

After breaking his own lap record with an average speed of 133.962mph, he would go on to win by more than 20 seconds – this time leading on the road, too.

The race had started three hours later than scheduled due to mist but once they got going it was Dunlop and Hutchinson who set the pace.

Dunlop established a 2.8-second lead over his rival at the end of the opening lap thanks to a speed of 133.256mph and then set the Mountain Course lap record to extend his advantage to 9.3 seconds.

After coasting his bike home to victory having broken his rivals early on in the race, Dunlop would later call it one of his finest achievements because, having felt undervalued by Honda and then BMW in previous years, he had claimed both superbike races in 2016. He was a start-to-finish winner in the Senior too, beating Hutchinson by 31 seconds. The win moved him one behind Hutchinson and Mike Hailwood, who both sat on 14 victories.

John McGuinness took the final podium spot, 33 seconds behind Hutchinson, who had already clinched a hat-trick of wins for the second year in a row.

McGuinness, modest as ever, said it was a pleasure to be on the podium with two such excellent young riders while behind him Dean Harrison was starting to turn a few heads with his fourth-placed finish, with Bruce Anstey in fifth and Conor Cummins sixth.

Among the high-profile retirements were Norton rider David Johnson, Gary Johnson and Peter Hickman, who had held third place at the end of lap one.

However, it was Dunlop who everyone on the island was talking about at the end of another truly memorable week.

But he was determined to go faster and try harder despite, at the time, being the fastest road racer of all time and having 13 TT wins to his name at the tender age of 27.

ISLE OF MAN TT MEMORIES

Mike Cookson, from Welshpool, in Shropshire, is a sidecar racer who has competed at the TT for more than 30 years and has a highest finish of sixth:

There was a French team in front of me during the first 2016 sidecar race. They passed us twice and we passed them back again.

Our bike was not performing properly so I backed off a bit. Then he crashed right in front of us at Quarry Bends, and I thought that was that.

My life flashed in front of my eyes. It was the last lap and I thought that was me finished.

I thought about packing it all in after that but as it was someone else's fault I decided to carry on. The place is as dangerous as you want to make it.

Overtaking can be a dangerous manoeuvre pretty much anywhere on the course and I won't overtake unless I am absolutely sure the person in front has seen me.

If they don't see you they can wipe you out. You're doing about 140mph in some places around that course and things can go wrong very quickly.

That near miss is just one of many I have experienced during all those years of racing at the TT but every single race has been so memorable – and I'm as keen as to race there as I've ever been.

Sidecar 1 TT 2016

Holden wins action-packed opening sidecar race

In 2016, three-time TT winner Klaus 'Klaffi' Klaffenböck, who by now was a team owner, announced he had received the backing of Honda and would be teaming up with 17-time TT winner Dave Molyneux.

Focussed, dedicated and a brilliant engineer to boot, Manxman Moly had already become a TT legend and enjoyed success on the national and world stage.

Building his own chassis, the engine was then tuned by Klaffi. It appeared a dream team had been formed.

And if that team did not seem strong enough, Molyneux was also paired with passenger Dan Sayle, a former Manx GP winner in the solo class who had also made the successful switch to three wheels instead of two. He too knew all about his machines.

But with just two weeks to go before the start of the TT, Moly and Klaffi parted ways. Moly cited a difference of opinion and did not want to use the Honda engines Klaffi had brought in so they both agreed to go in separate directions.

Klaffi instead decided to switch riders and instead teamed up with Tim Reeves and passenger Patrick Farrance.

Reeves had already won five world titles, two world cups, five British championships and three Southern 100 championships, as well as claiming a TT win and six podiums on the island, so his pedigree was there for all to see.

As with all sidecar teams on the island, none of them had enough funds to pay for full-time staff – the teams were all there, first and foremost, because of their love for the motorsport, even the bigger set-ups. And all the riders and passengers knew their machines inside out – they have to be racers, engineers and mechanics all rolled into one.

During the opening practice session, Moly had retired at Ramsey, following an overheating problem.

Klaffi himself had previously been on a six-year journey to get to the top step at the TT and was not going to give up before he had conquered the mountain.

Despite all his previous victories, he admitted the feeling of winning at TT was better than them all. All he had experienced up to that point, seeing people dying in front of him, the trouble he had mastering the course, had all come to the forefront – and he felt invincible.

He promised his family he would be on the podium once but he needed to come back again. And when he won again in 2011 he decided to quit while he was ahead.

Klaffi instead moved into team management but still felt the same fear as when he raced, only now it was concern for the welfare of his team riders, because he knew as well as anyone how dangerous competing at the TT was.

During sidecar races, the passenger helps determine how well the machine handles. Even Klaffi thought riding around the TT at 150mph holding on to just two handles was nuts and it was not something he would have ever tried himself. He was the driver, and that was that.

Passengers decide how much front-end and rear-end grip the drivers get. It makes it a massive team effort where two people have each other's lives in their own hands. During practice week in 2016, Reeves and Farrance were also a retirement – with the passenger having to receive treatment.

Reeves had tipped his bike into Laurel Bank but Farrance had hit the wall, which had left him winded and meant they too would not be able to carry on for the rest of the practice session. Farrance spent all day in physiotherapy to make sure he was fit enough for the following night's practice session, such was his commitment.

Moly soon followed with another mechanical problem. He had managed a 112mph lap from a standing start but even that time had not been good enough to qualify outright.

The Manxman, who had broken so many records during his illustrious career, was left sweating along with the likes of Conrad Harrison as neither had managed to get in the three practice laps needed to qualify for the actual TT, so by Wednesday the pressure was starting to build on two of the favourites for the win.

Moly's bike was still overheating but he was allowed to enter the final practice session, much to the relief of his small team.

There were a lot of potential winners for the 2016 title too, with John Holden and Andy Winkle, Ian Bell and his son, Carl, as well as the Birchall brothers who had already claimed three TT wins by this stage but would go on to raise the bar and set new records in years to come.

The Birchalls had been supported by Klaffi, who had told them his TT secrets, as early as 2012. Despite crashing a few times, they began to build up their skills, craft, speed and would end up dominating the class.

For now though, Klaffi was busy passing on his experience and skills to Reeves and Farrance.

The final practice session lived up to expectations as the sidecar heavyweights went toe-to-toe. Moly posted a 114mph lap, but Reeves was going even faster – reaching his own personal best around the 37.73-mile track.

Most importantly, they had also all qualified to set up a thrilling race. However, real drama was soon to follow as Moly announced he had decided against racing altogether at the TT following a poor practice week and the realisation he would not be competitive.

The team had been left distraught but they realised after discovering an electrical fault, which could very easily have ended in a terrible accident had it made the bike cut out while it was out on the track, they had put safety first.

It had not been an easy decision but it meant the race was now even more wide open for the rest of the field.

So the remaining racers, with that sick feeling in the pit of their stomachs, rolled their sidecars to the start line ready for battle to commence. The Birchalls were first off, following Moly's decision not to race, followed by Holden and Winkle, Reeves and Farrance, and Ian and Carl Bell.

Immediately, Holden had a six-second lead over the Birchall brothers, with Reeves – who had been just half a second down earlier in the race – now eight seconds behind second place to sit in third.

With his bike misfiring, Reeves was soon 39 seconds behind the leaders but then the red flag came out following an incident at Rhencullen. It soon transpired there had been a tragic accident, where Australian racer Dwight Beare had crashed and succumbed to his injuries.

His passenger Benjamin Binns survived but it had brought a black cloud over the entire paddock. Binns almost lost his leg too but it was eventually saved despite being severely broken. Even still, he remained as keen as ever to get back out racing at the TT as soon as possible.

The accident also meant the full sidecar race would be restarted which, under terrible circumstances, had given the other crews a chance to iron out some minor problems.

It was the Birchalls who again set the early pace, leading on the road and in the race, followed by Holden and Reeves.

Unfortunately for Reeves and Farrance, the misfiring issue had not been sorted; however, when Ian and Carl Bell were forced to retire, it moved them back into third.

The Birchalls were on fire, breaking the lap record – previously held by the absent Molyneux – with a 116.798mph.

Meanwhile, Reeves was still struggling while Holden was now ten seconds behind the leaders. And then more drama struck as the Birchalls were forced to retire at Sulby crossroads, which meant Holden and Winkle were now the race leaders and, miraculously, Reeves was back in third.

But, eventually, the tough TT course proved too much for the Klaffi-backed machine as Reeves and Farrance were agonisingly forced to pull in at Glen Duff on the final lap, despite being second fastest in practice. It transpired a broken terminal on the quickshifter had been the cause of all their problems. At the end of a truly eventful race, Holden became a two-time TT winner, five years after his first victory, with Peter Founds and Jevan Walmsely second, followed by Alan Founds and Aki Aalto in third.

Sidecar 2 TT 2016

The Birchalls' domination begins with hard-fought win

Come Senior race day, mist and fog had drifted in meaning all the riders were faced with some nerve-wracking delays.

Finally, the weather began to clear with Moly and eight-time TT winner Sayle back on the start line while Reeves and the Birchalls were hopeful they had both managed to sort out their own mechanical problems.

Moly was on the pace immediately and was just 0.1 seconds down on Holden, with the Birchalls in third and Reeves fourth.

They were soon all dicing and swapping position, as Moly took a slender lead, with the Birchalls now second and Holden third at the end of the first lap.

With mist lurking around the mountain section, the Birchalls had made up time and taken the lead, passing Moly on the roads.

And things would soon get even worse for the Manxman as smoke began bellowing out of his sidecar, forcing him to retire. It meant Holden was now in second and Reeves, who was on a bit of a charge, had moved into third.

And that was how they remained across the finish line. It marked a fourth TT win – and another lap record – for the Birchalls, as well as another podium for Holden and Winkle, while Reeves and Farrance, who were fastest through the speed traps, had also salvaged a podium finish in the final sidecar race of the week.

Klaffi was also pleased with the podium, following all the disruption that had come before it, but out front it was the Birchalls.

Little did the rest of their rivals realise that, by 2019, the brothers would still remain undefeated, shattering race and lap records in the process. They would become simply unstoppable.

Lightweight TT 2017
Rutter's second petrol-powered win comes 19 years
after his first

Michael Rutter turned back the clock and put in one of the rides of his life to win his fifth TT at the Isle of Man – smashing the race record in the process.

Then aged 45, he had used all his years of skill and knowledge of the TT course to react better than the rest of his rivals to the damp conditions on the island.

Rutter would go on to claim victory in the Lightweight class, finishing the four-lapper seven seconds faster than anyone before.

Rutter, starting number four on the road, soon started reeling everyone in and was left to battle it out with Martin Jessopp for top spot.

But his Paton had the pace to keep edging further and further ahead around the 37.73-mile course and he took the chequered flag 8.8 seconds ahead of Jessop, with Peter Hickman in third, during the afternoon race.

Rutter, who claimed his first victory on the island in the Junior TT back in 1998, had also claimed three TT Zeros wins by this stage of his career in between electric bikes.

However, he explained during an article in the *Express & Star* newspaper, 'It's brilliant to win another TT race, especially as I'm getting on a bit now!

'I got my head down on the first lap but lost a bit of time at the pit stops so I had to dig deep to pull Martin back and once I'd caught him, we had a lot of fun.'

He had shown once again in 2017 that his road racing skills were still up there with the best and how he had really got to grips with the 650cc lightweight machines.

He had ridden a KMR Kawasaki to a 14th win during the North West 200 the month before switching to a Paton for the TT, which proved to be a fruitful decision.

Rutter had ridden his Bathams/SMT Superstock machine to a strong fourth-placed finish during the morning's Superstock TT and had also finished fifth in the opening Superbike TT, showing he could continue to keep up with the best on pretty much any bike.

The year 2017 would also prove to be a great year for Peter Hickman too who would finish on the podium in every race he entered, while Ian Hutchinson also claimed another two victories – in the Superbike TT and Superstock TT – while Michael Dunlop took the opening supersport and Senior TT wins. Bruce Anstey claimed the TT Zero while the Birchalls cleaned up both Sidecar TTs.

Hickman had finished second in the Superbike TT, third in the first Supersport TT, second in the Superstock TT, third in the Lightweight TT and second in the Senior TT. However, he would not have to wait long before securing his first win on the island.

ISLE OF MAN TT MEMORIES

Sarah Mills, from Whitley Bay, is a TT road racing photographer who also runs the IOM Road Racing Facebook page with her husband, Ian:

The first memorable race that springs to mind is 2018, which was billed 'H-Bomb'. Both Peter Hickman and Dean Harrison went head-to-head for the Senior.

We were up at Keppel with the radio on full blast, listening to the commentary as the race ebbed and flowed.

We've always been big fans of John McGuinness too and were at Glen Helen for the first 130mph lap.

The year 2016 was my first time on the start line, the second supersport race.

To be up close with all the riders and feel the emotion pre-race, capturing John with his son, Ewan, at the side of his bike on the grid, was a very special moment.

RECORD-BREAKING 2018

THE 2018 TT may never be bettered in terms of the number of lap and race records that were broken in a single week as the Isle of Man was bathed in golden sunshine for the entire fortnight.

Superbike TT: It began as Michael Dunlop secured his 16th Isle of Man TT win by taking an emotional victory in the opening Superbike TT.

The 29-year-old's success came just three days after the death of his Tyco BMW team-mate Dan Kneen in a practice crash on the island.

Dunlop finished 51 seconds ahead of Conor Cummins with James Hillier third. Dean Harrison had set an astonishing lap record on lap one but then retired on the fourth circuit.

The speeds were a sign of things to come as, in every class and in every race, records were destroyed as the stars were able to raise speeds to new, unheard-of heights once more.

Harrison had built up an 18-second lead over his rivals after lapping his Kawasaki at new absolute lap record speeds of 134.432mph.

The Yorkshireman's advantage was reduced by the end of lap two and his retirement on the fourth lap left Dunlop with a comfortable lead as he took his fourth

Superbike TT win of his career, adding to his wins in 2013, 2014 and 2016.

It meant he had won six of the last nine 'big bike' races around the Mountain Course, adding his six superbike wins to his three Senior TT triumphs. Six of those victories had come on BMW machinery too.

Harrison had taken an 11.5-second lead over Dunlop early on but, once Harrison retired, Dunlop would go on to win in race record speeds

Manxman Conor Cummins came second with a personal best lap of 132.589mph ahead of third-placed James Hillier.

Michael Rutter rounded out the top five with Lee Johnston sixth while Peter Hickman, another of the pre-race favourites, was forced to retire at the end of lap one.

Supersport 1 TT: Dunlop then smashed the lap record on his way to record victory in the opening supersport race.

Harrison had made the early running on lap one but Dunlop was just 0.2 seconds behind at Ballaugh.

The Northern Irishman had taken the lead by Ramsey with James Hillier in third, himself just 0.2 seconds ahead of Peter Hickman.

Dunlop posted a lap of 128.265mph to lead Harrison by 1.74 seconds with Hickman slotting into third.

As pit stops loomed, Dunlop began his charge and found another few seconds to lead at Ramsey by 4.6 seconds en route to a lap of 129.533mph.

Dunlop's lead by lap three was nine seconds, while Hillier's quick pit stop had pulled him right back into podium contention as he made up almost four seconds on Hickman.

With Dunlop and Harrison circulating on the road together as lap four began, Hickman, on the Trooper

Triumph, made a charge from Ballaugh and moved back into third place ahead of Hillier.

Dunlop crossed the line to take his 17th TT victory – and his second of the week – ahead of Harrison in second place and Hickman in third, Hillier fourth, Cummins fifth, Josh Brookes sixth, Gary Johnson seventh, Lee Johnston eighth, James Cowton ninth and Ivan Lintin tenth.

Superstock TT: Hickman clinched his first TT win by taking victory in a sensational record-breaking four-lap event, setting a new class lap record at 134.403mph on his final circuit to win by 4.5 seconds from Dunlop, with Harrison third.

Hickman also demolished the race record by almost a minute on his BMW. Having finished on the podium six times, he finally claimed his first win, lapping in under 17 minutes having nearly thrown the race away on the opening lap

Hicky had found himself in tenth position after overshooting at Braddan but had somehow battled back to third by the end of that same lap.

Harrison had an early 4.5-second advantage over Dunlop but as Hicky's charge continued he had stolen a 1.2-second lead. Just three seconds separated the top two.

After the top three continued to swap positions, Hicky put in a lap of 134.403mph on his final circulation, just outside Harrison's outright lap record in the Superbike TT, to claim the win. Dunlop was 4.4 seconds back in second with Harrison in third. Australian David Johnson, James Hillier and Michael Rutter completed the top six.

Victory meant Hicky could now add his TT triumph to his four Ulster Grand Prix wins, two Macau Grand Prix victories, a British Superbike race win and a fourth place overall finish in last year's BSB series. A year later he would claim further victories at all the international road races, including the North West 200.

Supersport 2 TT: Harrison took his second TT win in more perfect conditions during the second supersport race, having renewed his rivalry with Dunlop.

After making another quick start, he opened a 1.8-second lead over Dunlop with Hillier in third and Hickman fourth.

Harrison increased his gap to 2.7 seconds following the Sulby Straight while Hicky was busy hunting down Hillier for the final podium spot.

Harrison's opening lap of 128.188mph was a sign of things to come as he increased his lead to 5.5 seconds over Dunlop by the second circuit, while behind them Hicky and Hillier were having a great ding-dong.

Crossing the line at the end of lap two, Harrison's time of 129.099mph – and Dunlop receiving a 30-second penalty for speeding in the pit lane – suddenly gave him a huge advantage.

With a 21-second lead over Hickman, who in turn was 5.7 seconds ahead of Hillier, as they went over the mountain, Harrison maintained his lead to take a second TT win, with Hickman second and Hillier third.

Lightweight TT: Dunlop, however, would complete yet another hat-trick of TT soon after by claiming the Lightweight TT – once again in record-breaking time.

His record final lap of 122.750mph saw off the challenge of Derek McGee by 14.6 seconds. It was his 18th TT win and he was only 29 years old, having already claimed the Superbike TT and opening supersport race. The triumph also meant he had won all petrol categories as he added the Lightweight TT to his previous superbike, superstock and supersport wins, all while riding for six different manufacturers. He had now won TTs on a BMW, Kawasaki, Suzuki, Honda, Yamaha and Paton.

It may have been different had Ivan Lintin not been forced to retire leading after two laps at Bedstead Corner.

Either way, Paton-mounted Dunlop soon had a four-second lead on KMR Kawasaki's McGee at the end of lap two but the gap was down to 1.6 seconds.

However, Dunlop really pulled the plug on the final lap shattering records along the way to take the win from McGee.

With Rutter taking third, followed by Stefano Bonetti and Joey Thompson, it meant Paton machines had taken five of the top six places.

TT Zero: Rutter claimed a superb Isle of Man TT victory, the sixth of his career in the competition, with a win in the TT Zero event.

It was a superb day for the 46-year-old who followed up the success with third place in the supertwins series.

Rutter received his first place rosette from the Duke of Cambridge Prince William, who was present at the electric bike event.

Team Mugen rider Rutter set a new lap record for electric bikes in claiming victory in the TT Zero race.

The 46-year-old became the first rider to complete the one-lap sprint of the 37-mile (60km) course at an average speed of more than 120mph.

He said, 'To do a lap of 121.824mph on an electric bike is amazing.'

It was yet another record-breaking win at the 2018 TT and it paved the way for one of the island's most memorable Seniors as Hicky and Harrison again went toe-to-toe.

Senior TT 2018

Hickman wins thrilling race with stunning last-lap dash

Peter Hickman entered the race confident he could win, especially having collected five podiums in five races the year before, as well as claiming his first TT victory in the superstock class earlier that same week.

After setting out his goals in 2017, based around what he thought he was capable of achieving with Smiths BMW, they came to the TT that same year and came second in all three big bike races.

In the second year, with the same bike and the same people around him, Hicky, as he learned more and understood more about the BMW, arrived with pretty much the same machine, which also helped boost his confidence.

One of his biggest rivals, Dean Harrison, was also back with Silicone Racing Kawasaki and had been given a superbike specifically built for the TT.

And in 2018, his renewed confidence, faith in his machine and team, and having had another year to learn the track, all shone through as he posted a lap of 133.4mph during practice week.

Meanwhile, Hicky was steady as ever, pushing 132mph but knowing he had more left in the tank. One of his biggest concerns was how much his BMW was moving about around the circuit but after having a conversation with Dunlop tyres they came up with a plan to improve the stability – and it worked.

After the opening superbike race, Harrison had posted the first 134mph lap, from a standing start, but broke down on lap four.

He came back to win the second supersport race, while Hicky put in an amazing performance in the superstock race to claim his maiden TT victory.

In the background, Michael Dunlop had been busy collecting a further three TTs, in the superbike, supersport and supertwin classes, meaning all three were looking good and super-fast heading into the Senior.

Harrison, heading into Glen Helen on lap one, did exactly the same as he had in the superbike race and set the early pace, although it was a lot closer on this occasion, with just 1.228 seconds separating him from Hicky.

And then the race almost went so wrong for several of the riders when James Hillier's Kawasaki spurted out oil. Michael Rutter, who was just behind on the road, was first on the scene of the engine failure and hit the oil while travelling at huge speed and nearly ended up being thrown through a fence at Barregarrow.

Thankfully, such was his pace the bike had managed to sort itself out and he stayed on, albeit with his heart beating a lot faster.

By the time the likes of Harrison and Hicky had arrived on the scene, they were able to see the line of oil and the flags were out warning the riders, so it did not affect their times too badly.

Michael Dunlop had dropped to fourth, with Conor Cummins into third, while Hicky was by now five seconds down on Harrison.

Hicky had also decided to space his timing boards out around the track, whereby his board at Sulby Bridge would be his Ballaugh time, the board at the Bungalow was a Ramsey time, and then his final board was at the Creg, which showed his position at the Bungalow.

His reasoning was that, because he knew Harrison was faster than him in the early sectors of the race, they were evenly matched in the third but then he was so much stronger in the final sectors, so he decided to play to his main strengths, which was his unbelievable speed over the mountain.

As they pitted for the first time, Cummins was third, Hicky second and Harrison was leading by just 1.4 seconds. And the pits would play quite an important role too, as every time they came in to refuel Harrison was always out faster than his main rival, which would give him an extra few seconds' advantage each time.

Harrison by now was 4.8 seconds ahead once again and was determined to try and break Hicky, who in turn had realised it was time to respond himself. For the rest of the race the pair just kept pushing each other more and more, which ultimately led to the records tumbling once more.

And once Harrison had established a lead of eight seconds, Hicky knew it was time to respond or the race could be lost there and then. The lead was soon cut to 6.2 seconds and by the end of lap three it was down to 5.8 seconds. The race was well and truly on.

Harrison was five seconds inside the lap record at Glen Helen and Hicky was six, which was down to two seconds for both riders later in the lap as they both encountered back-markers.

Ultimately, by the end of lap four, as they came in to pit for the second and final time, Hicky had broken the lap record with a 134.45mph, to once again close the gap, only for another slower pit stop to give Harrison yet another boost of four to five seconds as they began lap five. The actual timings saw the 1.4-second gap rise to 6.2 seconds, such was the difference in the pits.

The deficit was down to five seconds at Ballaugh and Hicky knew he had the pace to win the race over the mountain if he kept it that sort of difference or even reduced it further.

His reasoning was simply because, from Ramsey to the Grandstand, he had been just under a second faster on lap one, 3.2 seconds on the second, 2.4 on lap three and crucially 5.5 seconds on the fourth lap, which was when he had really decided to start putting the hammer down.

And sure enough, by the end of lap five, the gap was now down to just 1.9 seconds as Hicky his final 37.73-mile circulation.

As the final lap started, traffic once again began to take its toll on the rider, with Hicky estimating that he had had to get past nine back-markers on lap six.

The difference was soon back up to 3.7 seconds and Hicky was losing speed from Braddan Bridge up to Union Mills because of back-markers, while Harrison was having to drop down from sixth to fifth gear to make sure he could stay safe and, ultimately, get passed.

Harrison would lose four seconds in his quickest sector while Hicky was also negotiating slower riders on a regular basis, but neither complained as they knew it was just part and parcel of racing at the TT.

Either way, Hicky arrived at Ballaugh with a deficit of around five seconds, which meant he knew he had a really good chance of winning the race, especially as he had only lost three seconds amongst all the traffic, which was down to just two seconds as he rounded Ramsey Hairpin.

And sure enough, he was soon 0.8-seconds ahead of Harrison, taking over the lead halfway around the final lap, while being five seconds under his own lap record – having been held up by traffic.

Hicky, getting positive pit boards towards the end of the sixth lap, knew he just had to keep it together. He did hit yet another back-marker at Governor's Dip but, after taking a wider line, which he had been able to do courtesy of the superb weather, he managed to keep his speed up to cross the line with an average lap speed of 135.4mph to take one of the most memorable wins in recent times.

At the end of a truly memorable fortnight, it was Michael Dunlop who claimed the Joey Dunlop Championship by finishing the week with three victories and a tally of 94 points ahead of Hickman in second place and Harrison in third.

In the privateer stakes it was newcomer Davey Todd who picked up the award ahead of Sam West in second and Philip Crowe in third.

Hickman's brace of wins helped secure the team award for Smiths Racing. Silicone Racing and Padgett's Racing finished second and third respectively, with Dunlop's MD Racing team fourth.

Kawasaki ended the TT as the top manufacturer while Todd also picked up the newcomer award and the inaugural RST Star of Tomorrow prize.

However, 2018 was also filled with tragic deaths on the island. Adam Lyon, 26, who was making his debut, died near the 28th mile of the Mountain Course during the Supersport 1 race.

Manxman Dan Kneen, 30, sustained fatal injuries at the Churchtown section during a superbike qualifying session.

Kneen, from Onchan, was riding for the Northern Ireland-based Tyco BMW in the superbike and superstock classes that year and had set his personal fastest lap of the TT Mountain Course the night before, setting a 132.258mph.

Kneen was also crowned Irish Superbike champion in 2014 but his best TT finish was a third place in the 2017 superstock race.

Tyco BMW team manager Philip Neill said all involved with the team had been numb following the death.

Kneen's crash also had a knock-on effect as it led to rider Steve Mercer fighting for his life. He had been instructed to ride back along the course to the paddock following Kneen's fatal accident and was making his way back when he collided with the car near Ballacrye.

Mercer recovered but was left with terrible injuries. TT organisers said the car's driver was not injured and announced changes to the event's red-flag rules to begin with immediate effect.

ISLE OF MAN TT MEMORIES

Andy Hayes, from Aldridge, Walsall, West Midlands, has regularly lapped the TT course at more than 100mph as a passenger after making his debut in 2018:

The 2018 TT was the first time I had ever raced as a side-car passenger.

It had been a dream of mine for nearly 30 years and I managed to achieve it.

We didn't just make the numbers up either.

Within the whole field you could just feel the respect for each other, from the fastest racers all the way down to the newcomers. There was no hierarchy.

We got to know so many people while we were there and managed to even get behind the scenes for the Senior TT.

I was stood under the scoreboard when Peter Hickman flew past and set that incredible lap record.

I was standing right on the edge of the track, by the start-finish line when he went flying past.

During the presentation and prizegiving and I also standing right next to Hickman when he was being handed his trophy and awards, so that is a memory I will treasure forever, along with being part of the record-breaking sidecar races that year too.

BIRCHALL BROTHERS

THE MANSFIELD natives may have attempted the TT for the first time in 2009, but their affinity for racing on the island goes back much further than that.

The Isle of Man TT was always the Birchalls' annual family holiday. Watching the bikes and sidecars coming flying through Barregarrow was when the seed was first planted that the brothers might want to try it themselves some day.

By 1998, Ben had begun his racing career, as a passenger rather than a driver, but half a decade later he had decided to switch roles, while Tom, who is ten years his junior, was also beginning his own racing career.

The siblings were soon paired up and began racing together, always with the ultimate goal of one day taking on the TT.

On the circuits, they contested their first world championship in 2006 and two years later they had decided, with a little encouragement from some of their fellow pros, to chuck their entry. Supported by the likes of Nick Crowe and John Holden, they were circulating the 37.73-mile course with Ben concentrating on remembering the corners rather than focusing on speed.

After a frustrating 2008, they lapped at more than 110mph a year later and then went even faster in 2010, taking fifth and seventh place in the two Sidecar TTs.

And the first podiums began to flow as they took second and third in 2012.

A year later, the Birchalls' domination really began to kick in as they claimed their first TT win.

However, a crash in 2014 temporarily put the brakes on their rapid progress. A spill at Black Dub left Ben with a smashed right hand, which required five operations to fix.

They were soon back to winning in 2015 and remained unbeaten through to 2019, taking five wins in five races ever since. The brothers would also continue to keep raising the lap record every year too.

Crowe, whose 116.667mph lap record stood for eight years, may have reached their heights earlier had he not crashed and suffered severe injuries, but the fact remains the Birchalls have simply been unstoppable in recent years.

Preparation is the key to their success, whether it is working on personal fitness, working and building their race-winning machines, or trying to learn about the TT course.

It is a routine that has seen them start 18 races, finish 14 and win 12, as of 2019, as well as claiming ten silver replicas.

If their record had not been great before, their performances during the truly magical 2018 fortnight saw them really leave their mark.

Not only did they lap at more than 119mph, they also became the first sidecar outfit to finish a circuit in under 19 minutes. And in 2019, Tom became the most successful passenger in the history of the TT, claiming his tenth win in the second sidecar race.

The worrying thing for the rest of the field is that no other outfit has really come near to stopping them. It is because, back in the garage, the brothers are constantly battling to get the balance between speed, safety and reliability when building the perfect sidecar.

The position and ease of movement for the passenger also weighs heavily in their designs.

When first starting out, the brothers received a lot of help, advice and support from three-times winner and fellow multiple world champion Klaus Klaffenbock, between 2012 and 2015.

They then decided to go it alone before teaming up with Louis Christian who, after reading the brothers were capable of making their own machines, encouraged them to start making more.

By 2019, a dozen of racers in the same field as the Birchalls were competing on their sidecars, including the likes of Dave Molyneux and John Holden. But still there was no stopping them as they completed another clean sweep taking both sidecar TTs.

Sidecar 2 TT 2018

Birchalls continue to take sidecars into unchartered territory

Ben and Tom Birchall began their campaign in stunning style in 2018, the year when records continued to tumble throughout.

Not content with breaking their rivals and then bringing their machines home steadily for the win, the brothers went out and broke their own lap record on every one of their three circuits to win their fourth consecutive TT.

It was victory of pure domination as they led from start to finish, eventually winning by almost a minute over regular bridesmaids and serious competitors, John Holden and Lee Cain, with former TT winner Tim Reeves and new passenger Mark Wilkes taking the final podium spot.

The brothers had put in yet another faultless performance, smashing lap and race records after the race had been restarted following a red-flag incident on the first lap involving Tony

Baker and Fiona Baker-Holden, the wife of the second-placed finisher, Holden.

The pair were taken to Noble's Hospital by helicopter with Baker reported to have suffered a broken leg and Baker-Holden soft tissue injuries.

Despite the obvious worry running through his mind, Holden did tremendously well to bring his machine home in second and, despite being unable to catch the front runners, it did give fans some hope the second Sidecar TT may be that little bit closer.

Holden and Cain had given the Birchalls some food for thought early in the second race as they were the leading outfit at Glen Helen on lap one but it was short-lived as Ben and Tom soon found their rhythm, edging in front by the Bungalow.

From that point on they never looked back as they broke new ground, setting more lap records while also becoming the first sidecar pairing to lap the course in under 19 minutes.

It was on lap two when they circulated in 18 minutes and 59.018 seconds, averaging 119.250mph, on their way to a fifth straight victory.

They were simply too hot to handle. Holden and Cain did all they could, setting their own fastest-ever lap of 117.878mph while Tim and Wilkes, who again finished third, joined the 117mph club with a 117.729mph effort.

McGUINNESS RETURNS

A YEAR later, John McGuinness was back – and he was ready to attack the Isle of Man TT circuit, following two years out.

His fairytale return was made even more eye-catching as he had agreed to ride for Norton – not just in the superbike class, but also the Lightweight TT.

Norton had never run a supertwin in the new format but for 2019 they had gone all out, not only signing up McGuinness but also the man of the moment, Peter Hickman, and a rising star, the super-fast Davey Todd.

Norton was hoping their new-look bikes and line-up could propel them back to their rotary engine days, which had been discontinued back in 2000 because, despite being race-winning packages, they were no good for everyday use.

The decision had again sent the company into downfall and it almost became virtually defunct once more.

The brand name was taken over numerous times in future years but no one had been able to make a real go for it.

American dealer Kenny Dreer announced ambitious plans to revive the Commando but ran out of money.

Norton was again put up for sale and that was when successful British entrepreneur and Norton fan Stuart Garner stepped in, in 2008. After taking on Donington Hall, he vowed to rebuild the brand and bring back the Norton name.

Simon Skinner was called in as designer with the mission to produce Dreer's prototype. It was a starting point and the new version of the Commando was released in 2010. The new Dominator soon followed in 2015 following a complete redesign.

Even today, there is no automated production line at Norton's factory, with everything put together by hand. The brand produces around 1,000 bikes a year but their racing heritage remains in the background. Enter John McGuinness.

With 94 wins, 322 podiums and scooping the first TT win in 1907, stepping into the shoes of Norton is no mean feat – even if you are McGuinness.

With the Australian duo of Josh Brookes and David Johnson doing great work in the previous few years helping with the bike's development, the mantle was passed to the TT master.

But it soon became clear a lot of work remained before the manufacturer would be able to return to the top step for the first time since Steve Hislop rode the bike to that famous win in 1992.

The speed appeared to be there early on but reliability remained an issue and stopped Norton achieving much during the early years of its return to the TT, much the same as 2019.

After being taken on by Gardner, he came in with a masterplan all aimed at returning the famous brand back to the top step.

With TT winners Mick Grant and Steve Plater busily working behind the scenes, the bike is now at least in a position to challenge for race wins.

The marriage of McGuinness and Norton could have conceivably been a match made in heaven, with two of the biggest names in TT history joining forces with equal determination to win races. It had already been a long road back to contention following the bike's reintroduction back in 2009.

It was Michael Dunlop who first took the plunge and agreed to sign for the manufacturer – but after failing to complete a single race during the entire race fortnight, it did not even make the start line.

Ian Mackman was the first rider to really do anything of significant note on the new Norton, riding it to 16th in the 2012 Superbike TT, lapping at 122mph, but he failed to improve the following year, finishing 18th in the Superbike TT and 24th in the Senior TT.

The late Dan Hegarty also signed for the brand in 2013, making it a two-rider team, coming 36th in the Senior on the SG2.

Cameron Donald was the first in a line of Australian stars to ride for the manufacturer and he increased the lap times to 124mph on the SG3.

Development was really ranked up a notch in 2015 as fellow Aussie Davey Johnson became the first Norton rider to break the 130mph barrier. His official time was 130.872mph on his way to an impressive seventh-place finish in the Senior TT.

Josh Brookes, another Australian, went even faster on the SG6, posting a 130.883mph lap, finishing sixth in the 2017 Senior TT, just 2.6 seconds ahead of his team-mate, Johnson.

Brookes had first raced the TT in 2014 and immediately became the fastest-ever newcomer to lap the TT – before Peter Hickman burst on to the scene.

He then took a two-year hiatus to concentrate on winning the British Superbike Championship, which he duly did in 2015, before turning his attention to World Superbikes a year later.

On his return to TT action, he believed he was capable of getting on the podium but admitted, following a two-year break away from the 37.73-mile course, he had not quite been able to push hard enough.

Norton again worked hard to develop the bike in time for 2018, adapting the aerodynamics and improving the bodywork. And he returned their faith in a fifth-placed finish in the Senior that same year.

The team was determined to give McGuinness the best possible bike in time for the 2018 TT but he was sadly forced to sit the meeting out due to injury.

* * *

A year later, however, he was finally ready to make his return to the island following a two-year hiatus, as this article in the *Express & Star* revealed:

The undisputed modern-day King of the Mountain has returned to do what he does best, riding fast and winning races.

Following a horror crash at the North West 200 in 2017, which caused a broken back, injured knee, dislocated thumb and severely damaged leg, the 46-year-old was forced to miss the last two TT fortnights.

But following 'a dark 12 months', the 23-times TT winner bounced back in the only way he knows how, with a win at the Classic TT in August and victory at Goodwood. He also took the Norton out for a spin at Darley Moor.

A tenth-place finish at the Macau GP, in November, really blew the cobwebs off as it marked the first time he had ridden a superbike in anger in serious competition since his crash.

'After all the bumps and scrapes it was great to make my 20th visit to Macau,' said McGuinness, during a talk held at the Cleveland Arms, in Wolverhampton. First time I went was in 1998 on a two-stroke and then I won it in 2001. I've been on the rostrum many times since.

'I was given the option to ride for Paul Bird again on his Ducati, so I just thought "let's do this".

'I needed to go and ride. The Ducati is quite a strange thing to ride because it has no frame but I qualified eighth and finished tenth.

'It meant a lot to me just to get back on a superbike again because although I'd won at the Classic TT and Goodwood, these bikes have 230bhp.

'It was nerve-wracking, despite all the miles I'd done on a bike over the years. It marked a big step for me.

'I'd not ridden a superbike properly for a long time but I hoped to be there or thereabouts and was pleased with a top ten, especially as the bike is so different to the Norton.'

McGuinness was in a completely different place this time last year and, while lying on a golf course in Northern Ireland, with his leg 'pretty much hanging on with a bit of skin', he had wondered even then if a comeback would ever be possible.

Then followed the gruelling recovery. With 26 pins in his leg, he had to lengthen his bone by 50mm, to help it grow back, turning a screw a quarter of a millimetre every six hours for months on end.

'There were days during that when I did not know if I'd be back on a bike again,' he said. 'I was a right grumpy bugger at times at home and I'd have a pop at the kids but it was my family and friends who kept me going.

'I had 26 pins in my leg and it was a bit of a weird injury. It still swells up now and I've had a special boot made for it.

'It was such a difficult injury to go through but at least the circulation in my foot is okay now.

'After Macau, everything was hurting but a couple of days later I felt good.

'It made me feel like I could do this again and now I just need to get in some more training and time on the bike.

'I mean, racing is just a drug that keeps you coming back for more.'

McGuinness had already made a comeback, of sorts, securing an emotional win at the Classic TT, riding the Paton, with his mother and father waiting in the winner's enclosure for him.

He is now embarking on a two-year contract with Norton, to race at the North West 200 in Northern Ireland – the scene of his injury – and the TT.

It marked the end of a long affiliation with the Honda factory team that had brought both parties tremendous success.

But McGuinness remains angry with how he was treated after his crash and is in no doubt how the accident happened.

'It was an auto blipper problem,' he said. 'When changing down from fourth to third gear, doing about 120mph, the throttle remained open by about 42 per cent.

'It meant I'd lost control and I just went down to get off the bike. I was bouncing down the road, which is something I wasn't used to because I like to keep safe and ride neatly.

'I've done 49,000 miles around the TT, which is twice round the world, with not many crashes.

'Eventually, I went through a fence and ended up on a golf field, and the worst part was I f***ing hate golf.

'Honda were not there for me really. I'd been with the factory team since 2006 and it took the management three months to come out and see me.

'It was tough times. I was feeling a little bit down. I could have gone through a lot of stuff but it wasn't going to fix my leg. So I just took it on the chin but it was a very frustrating time. The bike had a lot of issues and it's still not competitive now. My input was not making any sense with them.

'I'm not the most educated person in the world but I know the Fireblades inside out.

'I knew I should not have taken that bike any further before the crash. When I was bouncing down that road I was so mad with myself. But I don't want to hold a massive grudge.'

Having finally been able to start putting his injuries behind him, McGuinness is still keen to win races and, for good reason, believes he can still win at the TT.

The logic is there too, and not only because he sits second on the all-time winners list, behind Joey Dunlop on 26.

Josh Brookes and Dave Johnson have put in near 132mph laps – average lap speed around the 37.73-mile TT circuit – on the Norton, and McGuinness is quicker than both.

Although Dean Harrison, Michael Dunlop and Peter Hickman raised the bar in 2018 posting 134mph and 135mph laps, the TT was blessed with two weeks of beautiful sunshine.

It's unlikely that will happen again so add a few seconds to Harrison's and Hickman's times, and scrub off a few with McGuinness on the Norton, and it's clearly achievable.

'I have to think I can win and I need that direction. I've got 17 seconds to find per lap but the Norton is capable of doing a 134mph. I'm going to attack it,' said McGuinness.

'With the right package around me it's possible. Norton has also produced this new 650cc supertwin for the lightweight race and I'll be back on the Honda Mugen in the electric bike race.

'I really didn't want to end my racing career in the middle of a golf course but I also can't go on forever. I just hope I do eventually retire on my own terms.

'I did say I was done in private to the missus a few times but then I started feeling better and decided I was going to return. It's tough sometimes and that's when the real people come out of the woodwork.

'Ian Hutchinson was going through a similar injury at the time so we'd just be talking about rubbish on WhatsApp but I think we helped each other get through it. It's been hard work but I am back now.'

Regardless of what the future holds, McGuinness has enjoyed one of racing's finest-ever careers – and to top it all off, he's still the same working-class brickie from Morecambe who had a dream of winning one TT and one British Championship all those years ago.

'It's been an amazing career. I never thought I would have won 23 TTs, raced in world championships and won multiple British titles,' he said.

'I'll definitely be doing some domestic championships next year because everyone at the sharp end of the TT is doing BSB. I might try and do a few Ducati Cup rounds with Paul Bird.

'Harrison turned from an amateur club racer into a world-class TT star. He just hit the ground running this year.

'Hickman is a natural racer, a bit like Dave Jefferies was, and looks race fit too, which is what I need to focus on now. The BMW is also a stronger bike but we'll just have to see how far we can take the Norton.'

* * *

Sadly, there was to be no happy ending with Norton for McGuinness on his return to action, as a series of mechanical failures and breakdowns meant he would fail to finish a single race on a Norton, after breaking down in the Superbike TT, Lightweight TT and Senior TT.

He had managed to secure his 47th career podium on his Honda Mugen in the electric bike class, but was lucky to leave the island without any injuries in the end.

An engine bolt broke in the Senior race, which almost forced him to crash, but with hardly any practice sessions and a few run outs in the supersport class, following a last minute deal with Clive Padgett, he was at least happy to have returned safely in one piece.

Supersport TT 2019

Johnston claims first TT win

Lee Johnston had endured a few quiet years on the racing scene, by his own, usually very high, standards.

Having signed up for what he believed to be golden opportunities, which included racing for the factory Honda team, it looked like more wins on the roads would be just around the corner.

However, the dream turned into a mini nightmare as his performances went downhill and his podiums dried up.

The Northern Irishman decided he was better suited as a privateer and returned for the 2019 campaign with a new team, surrounded by people he knew and trusted.

After claiming victory in the supersport race at the North West 200, he arrived on the Isle of Man as one of the favourites to win the 600cc class once more.

He admitted to feeling much more comfortable in his new surroundings, and his return to form, which included impressive rides during the 2019 British Supersport Championship, saw him finally claim his maiden TT victory.

As expected, the first Supersport TT had been another close affair, with Johnston taking victory in the two-lap race by 3.6 seconds from James Hillier and Peter Hickman in third.

Johnston, running his own operation, had designed and built the bike from scratch, making the win even more special and emotional.

Hillier had set the initial pace and led Johnston at Glen Helen by just over a second, with Gary Johnson in third, a further 1.2 seconds behind.

Hillier still led by Ballaugh and had slightly increased his lead and he continued pressing on but Johnston was soon on the charge and had cut the gap to just 0.6 seconds by Ramsey Hairpin.

Less than five seconds covered the entire top six as they started the mountain climb and then, with an opening lap of 126.03mph, he had taken the lead with Hickman now in third, Johnson in fourth, Dean Harrison fifth and Michael Dunlop sixth.

Johnston continued to set the pace and was nearly four seconds up on Hillier, who in turn was being closed down by Hickman.

It was then Hillier's turn to respond and he had clawed back nearly three and a half seconds at Ballaugh with the top two matching each other's pace as the gap stayed more or less the same.

However, just when the fans had settled in for another close four-lap battle, rain began to fall, which forced the officials to end the race after just two.

As the chequered flag came out at the end of lap two, Johnston had claimed his maiden TT win by 3.6 seconds from Hillier, with Hickman third.

Harrison, Dunlop and Conor Cummins took fourth to sixth place positions as Johnson, Coward – the first of the privateers to finish – Davey Todd and Ian Hutchinson completed the top ten. Two records were also broken during the weather-hit fortnight, with Ben Birchall and Tom

Birchall setting a race record of 57 minutes and 24.005 seconds, averaging 118.317mph, in the opening sidecar race.

Mounted on a Honda Bathams Mugen, Michael Rutter also set a new fastest lap of 121.91mph en route to his fifth victory in five races in the TT Zero class.

He was pushed hard by his team-mate and good friend, 23-time TT winner John McGuinness, who trailed him by 8.5 seconds over the finish line.

Rutter's seventh victory meant he equalled his father Tony's tally of seven wins on the Mountain Course, as well as maintaining his record of having never been beaten in the TT Zero class.

'Honestly, I rode so hard from the very start,' he said. 'I knew I'd have to put everything into that single lap in order to beat John. You can't make a single mistake when you're racing him. The rear was spinning in places and I lost the front coming into Kirk Michael.

'Genuinely, I don't think I could have gone any faster. Obviously I'm thrilled to add another TT win, and to beat someone as good as John, but equalling Dad's record of wins feels especially good.'

The one-lap electric bike race was also one of just two TTs to run over the full distance, with the other being the six-lap Senior, which was won by Harrison.

The fortnight, however, will also be remembered for the death of Daley Mathison, who died during the opening Superbike TT, aged 27.

Lightweight TT 2019

Dunlop wins 19th TT as Costello breaks yet more barriers
It is very rare that Michael Dunlop leaves the Isle of Man without a win – and 2019 proved no different as he claimed his 19th TT in the Lightweight class.

There was so much that made the victory a special one. Having only decided to return to racing a month previously, following the tragic death of his brother William in 2018, he had failed to trouble the podium positions in the superbike, supersport or superstock races.

It had been a very tough year for the Ballymoney man so to come back and win the Lightweight TT on a Paton, ahead of Kawasaki's Jamie Coward, who was just 1.2 seconds behind, and Lee Johnston, was a truly stunning performance.

Dunlop admitted himself that his win had been unexpected following his early struggles, and he had also sat out the second half of the 2018 season due to William's tragic accident at Skerries in Northern Ireland on 7 July.

He had already lost his uncle Joey, in 2000, and his father Robert, in 2008, to the motorsport but decided to carry on.

But not only did he return, his Lightweight win was also the 50th for the Dunlop family, adding to Robert's five triumphs and Joey's record of 26.

Maria Costello also made TT history in the same race by becoming the first female competitor to compete in both sidecar and solo classes at the same meeting.

Having competed on two wheels at the Isle of Man for more than 20 years – with a best result of a podium during the Classic TT in 2016, also on a Paton – she turned her attention to three wheels and went on to lap at more than 100mph despite the entire fortnight being plagued with bad weather.

Both the Lightweight TT and second Sidecar TT took place on the same day too, instead of Wednesday and Friday as originally planned, which made her record-breaking feat even more impressive.

The all-female crew of Costello and her sidecar passenger Julie Canipa finished 21st in the opening race but then improved to 17th in the second, with a fastest lap speed of 102.671mph.

Later that same day, Costello was back on two wheels to compete in the Lightweight TT, finishing with another solid 24th place.

The race had also been built up as a battle between manufacturers Paton and Norton – the latter entering the modern lightweight class for the first time, with John McGuinness, Peter Hickman and Davey Todd forming what seemed a formidable three-rider line-up.

However, Hickman was the only one to finish as Todd and McGuinness broke down on the first lap.

It was a different story for Paton, as the Italian brand claimed its third straight Lightweight TT win, following Rutter's victory in 2017, and Dunlop's in 2018 and 2019.

The 2019 TT lightweight class had pitted Norton against Paton again for the first time in 50 years.

Half a century ago marked the last time a Norton had made the top step in a GP of any description too, which came in Yugoslavia.

In second place during that same race was a Paton. It was part of a successful era for the brand thanks to the genius of Giuseppe Pattoni, who built the bikes in Milan.

Hailwood competed in his first TT on a Paton in 1958, bringing the bike home in seventh place, and the brand would continue to compete at GP standard until 2001, two years after Pattoni died.

The brand was taken on by his son, Roberto, who continued to build race-winning machines that now dominate the Lightweight TT as well as the Classic TT races.

Recent victories include John McGuinness's emotional comeback win during the 2018 Classic TT, while Rutter also notched his second petrol-powered TT win in 2017, some 19 years after his first.

Dunlop has since dominated the last two Lightweight TTs, on a Paton. His 2018 victory was particularly special as it marked the manufacturer's 60th anniversary.

Dunlop was also followed home that year by five more Patons, which had taken all but one of the top six places.

Only second-placed Derek McGee, on a Kawasaki, had been able to keep up on a different manufacturer during 2018.

Another standout Paton win came at the North West 200 in 2019 when Stefano Bonetti became the first Italian winner of the road race in Northern Ireland, when he claimed victory in the Lightweight class.

Paton was taken over by the SC-Project in 2016, which also coincided with the brand's rapid rise back to the top.

THANKS TO YOU ALL

THIS BOOK has been a real labour of love. I knew how historic the Isle of Man TT was – otherwise I would never have started writing about it – but it was only when I started researching the races in depth that I truly began to realise how special the fortnight really was.

It is impossible to cover all the memorable races, as each race means something different to the millions of fans around the world, for so many reasons.

The idea was to pick a few, from 1907 until 2019, when the book was published, and try to include as many as possible that stood out.

Whether it was lap records, first-time winners, closely fought battles, special victories on iconic machines, comebacks or complete domination, all the races in the book were chosen to try and give a feel of the last 100-plus years of racing on the island.

Scattered throughout were memories from fans, TT racers – past and present – road racers, club racers and photographers.

It was to give the book another dimension, to show how important the TT races are to so many people, across all different age categories.

Some have grown up with the TT in the backyard, so to speak, others have made the pilgrimage from childhood into their senior years, while some are relative newcomers – myself included – but all have been bitten by the bug and all agree there is nothing quite like the Isle of Man TT.

On that note I'd like to thank all those who have contributed their memories. John Dickenson, whom I have simply known as 'Dicky' for the last two decades, put my wife and I up in his house, along with his partner, Helen, when I first caught the TT bug back in 2009.

Chris Lewis, whom I had been covering on the club racing scene for three years until he announced his retirement in 2018, has always been so generous with his time, as has fellow veteran racer Paul Biddulph, who still competes to this day.

Photographer Tony Else does so much to promote racing, on the circuits and the roads. He particularly champions young racers and the smaller Irish road races and has always helped me out at the newspaper.

Then there are fans and racers like Richard Beech and Paul Myler. Their passion for motorbikes is so appealing and it is always great to chat to them. Thanks also to Josh Langman.

The road racers, those who eat, sleep and drink the motorsport we all know and love, come next. So down to earth, always on the end of the phone and constantly playing down their heroic efforts.

It is just in their nature and it has been a privilege to follow their careers. So thank you Kevin Morgan, Barry Furber, Ben Plant, Wayne Martin, Mike Cookson, Andy Davies and Andy Hayes.

The book would not have been possible without the photographers, who not only supplied some superb images but also helped me out with the captions – names, places, classes, etc. – sometimes at the 11th hour. The help was massively appreciated from Ian and Sarah Mills, of the IOM Road Racing Facebook page, and Jim Gibson, of Ellan Vannin Images.

A massive thank you to my employer, the Midland News Association, for the use of its archive photos and reports, as well as the Wolverhampton Archives, which supplied the AJS photos from the early 1900s.

Thanks also go to my good friends, John Cleator and Belinda Barnfather. It was John who first introduced me to the TT, took me to all the best spots, took me on board the 'Happy Bus' during its annual trip to Glen Helen for the Superbike TT and just generally encouraged my obsession with the TT to grow.

My wife Kelly has put up with a lot during the writing of this book and has got through countless box sets sitting alone in the front room while I'm staring at a laptop, but she never complained. I love you.

The final thanks goes to Michael Rutter and his family. It was my old editor, John Griffiths, a huge bike enthusiast himself, who first told me that a certain Mr Rutter had moved to Shropshire and it might be worth introducing myself.

That was more than ten years ago and it has been an absolute privilege to follow his career on the roads and circuits closely for various newspapers ever since.

He has allowed me to interview him in between races, on the road, while spannering in the garage and even while on the Isle of Man.

He took me for a lap of Brands Hatch on the back of his Ducati once too – although I'm not sure whether I should be grateful for that one. He did not go slow.

I even hosted an evening with Rutter and Peter Hickman a few years back. Luckily for me they both chatted happily away for two hours about their careers in front of a packed crowd at The Royal Oak, in Alveley, Shropshire, because I did not have a clue what I was doing.

Nothing is ever too much trouble for Rutter, and even for this book he agreed to write the foreword and lent me some of his family's precious photos – mainly of his father, Tony, and other legends of motorbike racing – to include.

Again, without his input – as well as some help from his new PR rep, John McAvoy – I could not have finished this book. Thank you all who contributed and here's to another 100 years of racing on the Isle of Man.

Also available at all good book stores

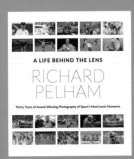

9781785315466

9781785313929

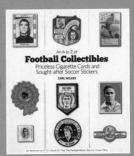

9781785315602

9781785315381

9781785315220

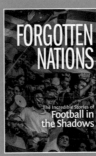

9781785314568

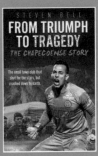

9781785315237

9781785315060

9781785315015

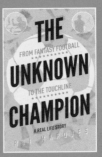

9781785315046